HERDING GEESE

THE STORY OF THE INFORMATION SUPPLY CHAIN

BY STEVE KEIFER

ISBN-10: 0615582567
ISBN-13: 978-0-615-58256-6

Acknowledgements vii
Preface ix
Section 1—Introduction 1
    Chapter 1—The Information Supply Chain 3
Section 2—The Manufacturing Supply Chain 15
    Chapter 2—B2B e-Marketplaces 17
    Chapter 3—The Automotive Supply Chain 29
    Chapter 4—E-Procurement 37
    Chapter 5—Private Marketplaces 49
Section 3—The Retail Supply Chain 57
    Chapter 6—VANs and Internet EDI 59
    Chapter 7—XML and B2B Standards 77
    Chapter 8—Data Synchronization 87
    Chapter 9—Product Information 99
    Chapter 10—RFID 109
    Chapter 11—Barcodes 119
Section 4—Health Care 127
    Chapter 12—Electronic Health Networks 129
    Chapter 13—Health Care Claims & Payments 141
    Chapter 14—Pandemics and Medicare Fraud 155
Section 5—Financial Services 165
    Chapter 15—SWIFT and Bank Communications 167
    Chapter 16—SEPA and Electronic Payments 177
    Chapter 17—Securities Trading and FIX Networks 187
    Chapter 18—STP and Securities Clearing 197
Section 6—Government 211
    Chapter 19—International Trade Gateways 213
    Chapter 20—Supply Chain Security 223
    Chapter 21—Electronic Invoicing 231
    Chapter 22—PEPPOL and E-Procurement 245
Section 7—Closing 253
    Chapter 23—Carp EDI em 255
Epilogue 271
References 273

HERDING GEESE

For my daughter Jane—who loves to chase geese.

Acknowledgements

I would like to especially thank many of my co-workers such as Alex Schumacher, Scott Molitor, Dave Kraemer, Nick Marchetti, Rory O'Neill, Anthony Payne, Melanie Nuce, Pradheep Sampath, Bryan Larkin and Ted Stanley who invested the time to educate me on the nuances of the B2B market during my time at GXS. Sadly, most of these individuals have left the e-commerce sector becoming disappointed during the period I refer to as the "Lost decade of B2B." Hopefully the ideas in this book will encourage them to reconsider a career in the B2B e-commerce sector.

Additionally, I would like to thank the outstanding journalists at the various publications that I cited throughout the book, including but not limited to: *The Wall Street Journal, The New York Times, Business Week, The Miami Herald, BBC, Fortune, Time, Information Week* and *Finextra*. The historical references in these publications enabled me to provide additional business context for the importance of B2B.

I would also like to thank Bobby Patrick who encouraged me to take the time to write this book. Finally, I would like to thank Karin McNair for devoting countless hours (outside of her usual job) to edit and supervise the production of this work.

Preface

This is a book about how businesses exchange information with one another electronically. In the technology industry we refer to this capability as Business-to-Business (B2B) e-commerce or B2B integration. I know what you are thinking. Ugh! What could possibly be more boring? However, if you invest a few minutes to better understand this sector, then I think you will come to share the opinion that I have formed. B2B e-commerce technologies provide a critical foundation necessary to overcome some of the most challenging issues facing both the public sector and private sector today.

Wider adoption of B2B e-commerce technologies such as Electronic Health Records and Medicare Fraud Monitoring are critical to unlocking $75 billion of inefficiencies in the US health care system. And B2B is playing an important role in the harmonization of the European Union's financial system by knocking down barriers to cross-border trade. Furthermore, the use of B2B technology can enable faster growth in emerging markets from Southeast Asia to Latin America by accelerating exports and reducing tax evasion.

Government agencies around the world use B2B technologies for homeland security. Not a ship, truck, train or plane enters the US without the Department of Homeland Security screening an electronic manifest of the cargo and passengers. Retailers use B2B e-commerce to send purchase orders to their suppliers for the goods they want to have delivered to their stores. Mutual funds and hedge fund managers use B2B technologies to send trading instructions to their brokers.

Most people have never heard of B2B e-commerce even though it plays such a critical role in supporting the activities performed in their daily lives. Even the CIOs of major corporations often under appreciate the value of B2B, that is, until it stops working. When B2B e-commerce platforms go down, as all technologies do from time to time, the economic impacts can be quite significant. Supply chains are interrupted—which can mean there may be no milk in the store. Funds transfers between banks are cut off—which can mean you may not get your paycheck.

I became fascinated with these technologies about 10 years ago when I first learned about them. So I left my role at a web hosting firm and joined a little known company named Global eXchange Services (GXS). When I joined in 2004, GXS had just been spun-off from GE. During the Jack Welch era, GXS was one of the nine divisions of GE. However, GE never really understood the IT business, so it made sense for GXS to become an independent company. Today, GXS is one of the leading technology vendors in the B2B e-commerce market with almost $500 million in annual revenues.

Throughout most of my time at GXS I have been charged with leading the company's strategy to target different vertical industries. As a result, I have had the opportunity to explore how B2B technologies are used in vertical industries, ranging from government and health care to manufacturing and financial services. The more I learned, the more it became obvious to me that there were a number of great stories about the B2B e-commerce sector that needed to be told. These were not only stories about how B2B can save the world, but also about some of the bizarre market dynamics that occur between the technology vendors, industry standards organizations and venture capitalists in the space.

In 2007, I started to write a blog, entitled EDInomics, available at (http://www.gxsblogs.com/keifers). The letters EDI refer to Electronic Data Interchange, one of the most widely used B2B e-commerce technologies. The goal of my blog (and this book) was not to target the community of technology vendors and corporate end-users in the B2B sector. Most people using these technologies are already familiar with both how interesting and challenging B2B e-commerce can be. Instead, my goal was to educate and influence opinion leaders outside of the B2B sector about the potential benefits to be gained from a more extensive use of these technologies.

Unfortunately, the B2B e-commerce sector has struggled with a lost decade from 2001-2011, during which many of the investments made by venture capitalists, large corporations and government entities failed to achieve the desired return on investment. I am hoping to generate a groundswell of support for another wave of investment in B2B e-commerce technologies that I believe will not only improve the competitiveness of individual corporations, but also help to solve some of the world's toughest economic challenges.

HERDING GEESE

SECTION 1
Introduction

HERDING GEESE

Chapter 1
The Information Supply Chain

If you were to open up an iPad, iPhone or iPod you might be surprised to learn that many of the components inside of these magical and revolutionary devices are actually not made by Apple. While Apple enjoys most of the credit for its blockbuster products, a great deal of the innovation occurs in other parts of the supply chain. Consider the iPad2. Within the tablet there is an A5 microprocessor that is designed by Apple, but manufactured on its behalf by Samsung. The 16GB or 32GB of memory available with the device is also supplied by Samsung. Apple's dependency on Samsung is interesting given that it is one of the key competitors in the tablet market. Another chip, manufactured by Broadcom, provides the Wi-Fi, Bluetooth and FM tuner functions. The controller for the touchscreen display is also supplied by Broadcom. STMicroelectronics provides gizmos such as the accelerometer and gyroscopes that enable you to control the machine by tilting it in different directions.[1]

Apple is not the only company to source components from outside suppliers. If you review a teardown of a Nikon digital camera, a Barnes & Noble e-book reader, a RIM Blackberry or a Sony HDTV you would find that most of the components are sourced from third parties as well.

Not only do high tech manufacturers source the component parts for devices from third parties, but they are increasingly dependent upon outside companies to design, build, ship, sell and service their products. The term Original Equipment Manufacturer (OEM) is utilized to describe companies, such as Dell, IBM, HP, Apple, Motorola, RIM, Nintendo, Sony, Microsoft, Cisco and Alcatel Lucent, whose brand names are on high tech products. However, in today's high tech supply chain some of these OEMs never touch the products sold under their brand name. There are specialized service providers that will design, manufacture, transport, distribute and service products on an outsourced basis.

The high tech industry was not always so fragmented. When the first mainframes were introduced back in the 1960s a single company performed all the manufacturing and servicing of the computers. High tech manufacturers, such as IBM, GE and Honeywell, not only assembled the mainframe, but designed the memory, storage (DASD) and processors inside. The operating system, database and even some applications were developed by the same vendor who manufactured the hardware. Maintenance and repair activities were typically performed by the manufacturer as well. If the mainframe broke or needed an upgrade, the original hardware manufacturer provided the repair and service.

Contrast the mainframe model to the complex, multi-tiered value chain in today's computer industry. I am writing this book on an "IBM Think-Pad." However, while the logo on my laptop says IBM, the manufacturer of the machine is actually a Chinese company—Lenovo—which only contributes a small percentage of the parts in my laptop. The components inside the laptop are sourced from third-party suppliers. Kingston supplies the memory. Seagate manufactured the hard drive. Intel designed the microprocessor. Also noteworthy is the fact that Lenovo does not typically sell the machine directly to its customers. My laptop was purchased through our company's preferred distributor—CDW. The software on the machine is made by another group of specialized companies. Microsoft publishes the Windows operating system and Office application suite. Other software vendors, such as Adobe, Symantec and Apple, provide additional applications for document viewing, desktop security and digital music. And when my laptop breaks, who do I call? Not Lenovo, but a third party, such as a high tech distributor, for warranty support and repair.

My point is that the computer industry has migrated from a vertically integrated model to a highly specialized, heavily outsourced model. Orchestrating today's highly outsourced, globally distributed high tech supply chains can be extremely complex. The activities of designers (ODMs), contract manufacturers, 3PLs, distributors and aftermarket service providers must all be synchronized to ensure the right products are in the right places at the right times.

A critical factor for success is the ability to exchange real-time information with a community of business partners in the supply chain.

OEMs, such as Apple, Nikon and Lenovo, need visibility into the available supply of parts, such as processors, memory and storage as well as the raw materials used to make these components, such as silicon, tin and tungsten. Is there a shortage of supply expected in the near future? If so, then the OEM may not be able to manufacture its products in sufficient quantities to meet customer demand.

Specialized "contract manufacturers" will buy the parts, assemble the devices and perform quality testing on behalf of an OEM. Contract manufacturers act effectively as an outsourced factory. Examples of contract manufacturers include Foxconn (Hon Hai), Flextronics and Celestica. OEMs also need visibility into the "work in progress" activities of contract manufacturers. How many units of each SKU are being produced? When will these products be assembled and shipped? Are there any expected delays arising due to problems with workers or the supply of parts?

Specialized and Outsourced

This type of highly outsourced model, in which OEMs outsource much of the components to suppliers, is growing more common in all discrete manufacturing sectors. Boeing outsourced 65% of the design and manufacturing for the recently released 787 Dreamliner. Boeing enlisted the support of 100 different subcontractors and parts suppliers to build the plane. Rolls Royce and GE Aircraft designed the engines. Honeywell and Rockwell Collins provided flight guidance and control. There were suppliers located in Korea and Japan; Russia and India; France, Germany, Italy, UK and Australia.

The manufacturing industry is not the only sector that has become highly specialized with extensive outsourcing. The structure of the health care industry has developed in a similar manner. Doctors, for example, have always been specialized. If you are diagnosed with a chronic condition, such as diabetes, cancer or heart disease, you will not only work with a primary care physician, but also with a series of specialists in different facilities. The entire health care system today depends upon referrals.

Not only are the doctors specialized, but the health care facilities have different capabilities as well. For example, most doctors' offices lack the sophisticated equipment necessary to perform a blood test, MRI or X-ray on-site. Instead, they outsource these functions to specialized lab services and imaging companies.

The financial services industry is extremely specialized as well. Firms that were traditionally banks designed to offer savings and loans, now sell a broader portfolio of insurance, investment and retirement services. Most banks did not build their own insurance and investment practices, but instead resell the services of other financial institutions. Many of the life insurance, retirement and college savings plans offered by banks are actually delivered by third parties.

The mortgage industry has become highly specialized as well. The company from which you purchase your original mortgage likely will package your loan with hundreds of others through a process called securitization. These securitized bundles of mortgages are then sold to investors around the world who then become the recipients of your monthly principal and interest payments. As we learned in the 2008 financial crisis, specialization and outsourcing is not always a good thing as it can lead to irresponsible behavior on Wall Street.

Companies in every business sector are becoming more and more specialized as they outsource more and more of their business functions. Customer service is being outsourced to offshore firms, such as Wipro and TCS. IT functions are being outsourced to systems integrators, such as Accenture and IBM. Public relations and marketing are outsourced to large agencies, such as Omnicom and Interpublic. Strategic planning is outsourced to management consultants, such as McKinsey and Boston Consulting Group. Tax and accounting functions are being outsourced to Big 4 firms, such as Deloitte and KPMG. It is hard to find an example of an industry today that has not become highly specialized and highly dependent upon business partners for success.

The Information Supply Chain

For companies to successfully outsource such a broad range of functions so extensively, they must have access to real-time information about the activities of their business partners. Unfortunately, however, this "information supply chain" between business partners is not always as streamlined or efficient as it should be. Less than 50% of all interactions between business partners are performed electronically. The inefficiencies resulting from this lack of automation create a tremendous drag on productivity throughout the world. In fact, many people have referred to the commercial activities that occur between companies—Business-to-Business (B2B)—as the most inefficient part of the global economy. While data flows at the speed of light between computers within the four walls of a corporation, the information flowing between the firewalls of business partners often moves at a snail's pace.

Inefficiencies exist in the financial services market. Hedge funds deploy sophisticated computer algorithms to churn through terabytes of data in order to recommend the best investment strategies for portfolio growth. But when a trade for $500,000 worth of bonds needs to be placed, the hedge fund manager picks up the phone and calls a stock broker that hand keys the order into a computer screen at his desk. After the trade is executed, the broker calls the hedge fund manager back to provide a confirmation. The follow-up call ensures that the hedge fund has an up-to-date view of its position for the three days before the paper trade confirmation arrives in the mail.

The health care system experiences inefficiencies as well. A 45-year old woman might undergo $50,000 of medical procedures and diagnostics in the process of treating a chronic disease. Specialized tests are performed using MRI machines. Expensive consultations are received from industry leading specialists. Minor outpatient surgeries are undertaken at various hospitals. However, the results of these medical procedures are printed out onto pieces of paper, and then stored in filing cabinets at different physicians' offices. When a new doctor needs to review the patient's medical records, he must phone all of the different practices to request that copies of notes, lab results and radiology images be faxed or couriered to his office.

Consumer products companies spend billions of dollars on research and development each year in hopes of inventing the next big energy drink or pain relief medication. When these new potential blockbuster products are ready for sale, the manufacturers blitz television screens with millions of dollars of advertisements. But the availability of the products on the shelves of stores is typically delayed two to four weeks, waiting for the new product to be properly "set up" in the retailer's IT systems. Someone in the retailer's merchandising department must hand-key the new product's size, weight, description and price into various systems before it can be sold.

The commercial sector has successfully generated trillions of dollars in productivity gains over the past few decades by deploying information technology within the four walls of their company. However, efficiency levels drop off a cliff when it comes to B2B processes. Much of the information relayed between business partners is exchanged using people and paper-intensive techniques such as "snail mail," fax machines, phone calls and documents attached to emails.

Introducing B2B e-Commerce

You may be wondering why these widespread inefficiencies in B2B communication exist? Are there not technologies that could be used to automate the exchange of information between business partners that buy or sell from one another? The answer is "Yes," there is an entire category of technology called B2B e-commerce that is specifically designed to facilitate regular communications of data between business partners.

When most people hear the term "e-commerce" they envision visiting the Amazon.com website to buy clothing, books or electronics online for home delivery. We have all become accustomed to paying bills via online banking sites; listing products on Internet auction sites; and buying stocks via electronic trading portals. These are all examples of Business-to-Consumer (B2C) e-commerce technologies. But consumers are not the only ones using the Internet for commerce. Many businesses also have the need to buy merchandise, pay bills and trade stocks electronically. These electronic interactions between businesses are what we refer to as B2B e-commerce.

The first B2B e-commerce technology, Electronic Data Interchange (EDI), was introduced back in the 1960s. EDI continues to be used extensively today in the retail, manufacturing, transportation and health care industries. The company I work for—GXS—is one of the leading providers of EDI and B2B e-commerce services with almost $500 million in annual revenues. Technically, EDI refers to a specific standard for exchanging data between companies, but the term is also used more broadly to describe the entire category of B2B e-commerce technologies.

I like to define B2B e-commerce as a set of technologies that help to facilitate the real-time transfer of information, money, goods and services. However, I think the best way to understand B2B e-commerce is through real-world examples.

Perhaps, the easiest examples to understand are the B2B "e-procurement" applications, which mimic the online shopping experience you are accustomed to, but for business buyers rather than consumers. Large Global 500 companies and government agencies can use e-procurement sites to purchase everything from raw materials for their manufacturing plants to toner refills for their office printers. B2B e-commerce technologies can be used not only to purchase goods and services, but to manage entire supply chains. American, European and Japanese firms can utilize B2B e-commerce networks to track goods manufactured in China, Malaysia and Vietnam as they travel via container ships to their destinations around the globe.

The entire health care system depends upon B2B technologies. When you arrive at a doctor's office, EDI technology can be used to ask your insurance company about your eligibility for medical care. If you visit a specialist, "Electronic Health Records" technology can be used to share copies of your medical history, recent lab tests and X-ray images. The electronic records are typically shared across specialized "Health Information Exchanges." If you are issued a prescription, your doctor's office may send it electronically to the local pharmacy to fill. Once you have left the doctor's office, another series of EDI messages can be exchanged with the insurance company to pay for the care you received. These electronic claims and payment transactions can be exchanged over specialized health care "clearinghouses."

Banks are big users of B2B e-commerce technology also. Most transfers of money that occur between banks around the world are facilitated through specialized B2B e-commerce networks. Another common use case is in the stock market. Professional money managers that buy and sell lots of stocks on behalf of mutual funds, endowments and pension funds can use specialized "FIX networks" to submit electronic orders to their stock brokers. The brokers execute the trades, and then work with the money manager and their bank to clear and settle the trades. At every step of the lifecycle of a stock trade, B2B e-commerce technology can be used.

In some cases there are no humans involved at all. Machines communicating with other machines using B2B e-commerce technologies are assuming responsibility for entire business processes. For example, hedge funds are utilizing "algorithmic trading programs" to execute stock trades. These computer programs automatically monitor the stock market trends, and then decide when to buy or sell stocks. The trade instructions are passed electronically via FIX networks to brokers for execution. Next, the details of the trade are collected, matched and forwarded for clearing and settlement. In this "straight through processing model" no humans are involved. The stock trading is orchestrated completely by computers leveraging B2B e-commerce technologies.

Stock trading is just one example of a business process occurring in what economist W. Brian Arthur describes as the "Second Economy." He is referring to business processes that once took place among human beings that are now being executed electronically. Arthur predicts that in about two decades the digital economy will reach the same size as the physical economy.

Investments in B2B e-Commerce

But we still have quite a bit of work to do before we can realize Arthur's vision of the fully digital Second Economy. One of the key obstacles which must be overcome is the inability of different businesses to exchange information with one another. As we learned from the examples earlier in the chapter, there are numerous cases in which B2B e-commerce technologies are not being used to effectively streamline communications between business partners.

You may be wondering why not. One of the key challenges relates to small businesses which by numbers represent the majority of companies in the world. In industries such as health care, retail and manufacturing, small businesses outnumber large ones by a factor of 1000-to-1. These small businesses lack the budget, resources and expertise to implement sophisticated B2B e-commerce applications.

Imagine a four-person dentist office that runs its entire business on the PC located at the check-in desk. One day the dentist office gets an email from an insurance company requesting that it submit all claims going forward using the "HIPAA EDI 837-D transaction set." Don't know what the 837-D is? Neither does the dentist office.

Imagine a three-man hedge fund startup in Connecticut that doesn't have an administrative assistant to answer the phones or a permanent office space to work out of. One day the hedge fund gets an email from its stock broker requesting that it start sending trades electronically over the Sungard FIX network.

Imagine a 50-person toy manufacturer in China that exports its products to "big-box" stores in the US. One day the toy maker gets an email from its largest retail customer in the US requesting that it place RFID tags on all of its shipments and must send "856 Advanced Shipment Notices" when goods leave the factory. The retail customer also stipulates that penalties will begin to be assessed within 60 days if the supplier fails to comply with the new shipping guidelines.

Hundreds of companies have tried to break down the barriers to electronic commerce with innovative and disruptive technologies. During the dot-com era, venture capitalists invested billions in startups to improve B2B interactions in the health care, financial services, manufacturing and retail sectors. In the past 20 years, over 60% of the Fortune 50 has made direct investments in companies that provide B2B e-commerce technologies. Big industrial manufacturing companies, such as GM, Ford, HP, Boeing, United Technologies and Dow Chemical, have created joint ventures in the B2B e-commerce sector. Each of the major consumer products companies, including Procter & Gamble, Johnson & Johnson, PepsiCo, Kraft Foods and Coca-Cola, have made equity investments in B2B startups. The big banks, like JPMorgan Chase, Citigroup and Bank of America, each own stakes in multiple B2B e-commerce ventures. Even health care companies, such as McKesson, Cardinal Health, Medco, CVS Caremark and Express Scripts, have invested millions in these technologies. But most of these strategic investments in B2B e-commerce have met with only modest levels of success.

Convincing a few thousand of your small business partners to adopt a new B2B e-commerce technology can be a bit like herding cats—at least that is most people's view of the situation. But with the right approach, it is possible to achieve high levels of participation in B2B e-commerce initiatives. So perhaps the idea of herding geese is a better analogy. Herding geese is much easier than herding cats, that is, if you have a scientific approach.

Get the Flock Out of Here

Lack of technology proficiency by small businesses is one of the key inhibitors to further B2B e-commerce adoption. But there are just as many challenges caused by the hundreds of different technology vendors that develop and sell B2B e-commerce solutions. Many of these vendors generate millions of dollars in revenues, but take no accountability for the success of B2B e-commerce ventures. For example, software companies sell big companies the "infrastructure" necessary to build a world-class B2B e-commerce platform and then walk away before the hard work of implementation and onboarding begins.

Another set of challenges is created by the "standards organizations" that operate in various vertical industries. There are hundreds of different B2B standards that companies can use to exchange information electronically with business partners. In fact, many people say that the best thing about B2B e-commerce standards is that there are so many to choose from. The standards industry has become a big business in B2B with hundreds of "industry associations" introducing new e-commerce frameworks every year. Although these associations operate as non-profits the competitive dynamics between them rival even some of the most cut throat activities of for-profit corporations.

There are also some unusual technology dynamics in B2B e-commerce that would qualify for a chapter in the next *Freakonomics* book. In most parts of the consumer and business world, new technologies are adopted over a period of a few years, if not months. But new B2B e-commerce technologies often take decades to be adopted. For example, when consumer products companies place labels on multi-million dollar shipments of products destined for retail stores, they do not use the RFID technology that recently came out of the labs at MIT. Instead, they use barcode labels that were invented back in the 1950s to track railroad cars. When a high tech company, such as Apple, Samsung, or RIM, places an order for chips to put in its next batch of smartphones, they could use the "RosettaNet" e-commerce standards developed in the late 1990s. But these cutting-edge, high tech innovators are three times more likely to send their supplier an order using the EDI technology developed for mainframe computers back in the 1960s. When I share these stories with colleagues in the IT industry they stare at me in disbelief almost as if to say "Get the flock out of here."

Herding Geese is the story of the numerous attempts by venture capitalists, standards organizations, government entities and Fortune 500 companies to create an information supply chain that connects all the business partners within an industry electronically. Throughout the book we will examine attempts to implement B2B e-commerce programs in five industry segments —manufacturing, retail, government, health care and financial services. I think you will be surprised to learn not only of the potential for B2B e-commerce in each of these sectors to enable individual corporations to be more successful, but to solve some of society's greatest challenges. B2B e-commerce is playing a critical role with improving homeland security, reducing sovereign debt, simplifying international trade and reforming the US health care system.

I also think you will be surprised to learn how many of these B2B programs have failed to achieve the desired adoption levels and business outcomes despite the level of enthusiasm and investment applied. In fact, at times some of these programs have appeared more like a wild goose chase than an organized industry-wide initiative. There are unique challenges that exist in B2B e-commerce that are not present in any other sector of the Information Technology industry. Connecting the business applications of two different companies is ten times more challenging than connecting two applications within the four walls of a single organization.

SECTION 2

The Manufacturing Supply Chain

Chapter 2
B2B e-Marketplaces

In 1994, a Harvard Business School graduate named Glen Meakem made a proposal to a group of GE executives that he claimed would change the world of corporate purchasing forever. A *Fortune* Magazine article about Meakem stated,

"His project would do no less than reinvent one of the murkiest, most backward, least sexy processes in industry: the purchase of the parts and materials that go into everything from granola to cars. The idea was as simple as it was radical. Meakem proposed to make suppliers compete for manufacturers' orders in live, open, electronic auctions. No more golf-course schmoozing, no more haggling, no more sealed bids. The market for semi-finished goods from circuit boards to packaging materials would become as efficient as the market for stocks, and prices would drop to levels purchasing managers previously could only dream of."[2]

Although the GE executives were intrigued with Meakem's idea, they viewed the proposal as expensive and relatively risky. Rather than starting a new company to develop the concept, GE's leadership recommended that Meakem leverage the already established GE Information Services division to build an electronic auction platform. For a short time, Meakem pursued the idea as a skunkworks project under the GE executive Gary Reiner, a rising star who eventually became the company's CIO. However, Meakem was so passionate about the idea that he decided to resign from GE and start up a new company himself. The new company, FreeMarkets, was founded in Pittsburgh, which is not typically the first choice for technology startups. However, Pittsburgh proved to be an excellent choice as it was in close proximity to the headquarters of most of America's industrial giants. FreeMarkets quickly gained success with companies such as GM, Raytheon, and United Technologies and went public in November 1999. Although it had only generated $7 million in revenues during the first half of 1999, FreeMarkets valuation quickly grew to over $9 billion.[3]

FreeMarkets revolutionary concept was the idea of a "reverse auction." You are probably familiar with the concept of a traditional "forward auction" in which potential buyers outbid one another by offering a higher price for an item. If you have bid on an item at an art show or on eBay you have participated in a forward auction. Reverse auctions work the opposite way. Instead of the highest price buyer winning, the lowest priced *supplier* wins.

Traditionally, suppliers of raw materials and industrial parts were selected through secretive Request for Proposal (RFP) processes. There were several challenges with the traditional RFP-based process. Most notably, the buyer would never truly know whether they had obtained the minimum price. For example, the three primary suppliers participating in the bid process may have offered a 30% discount from their list price. However, one of the suppliers may have been willing to discount up to 60% in this particular order, as it was struggling to meet its revenue goals. Furthermore, suppliers had no visibility to competitor's bids so they could not be certain if they were pricing too aggressively or not aggressively enough.

A FreeMarkets reverse auction solved many of the traditional supplier selection challenges. An auction could be scheduled to occur over the course of a varying timeframe, like a 30-minute window or an hour. All participants, including the buyer and potential suppliers, had visibility to bids over a shared Internet application. As a result, suppliers could react to competitor bids in real time.

Suppose an automobile manufacturer is seeking to purchase 20,000 units of a particular part in bulk through an auction. The first supplier might offer to sell the parts for $500,000. Another supplier, with lower cost margins and more desire to gain the revenue, could undercut the initial bid with a lower offer of $480,000. The auction participants can continue to under-bid one another until the lowest price is reached. The benefit to the buyer is the assurance that they have obtained the absolute minimum price available in the market.

In many cases, buyers find that price reductions of 20 to 30% can result in millions of dollars of immediate cost savings.

FreeMarkets has a special significance in the history of B2B e-commerce. It was one of the pioneers that revolutionized procurement and catalyzed a new technology sector called B2B e-marketplaces. The purpose of a B2B e-marketplace was to facilitate the real-time transfer of information, money, and goods using newfound Internet technologies. The marketplaces, which were also called "exchanges," supported a wide range of business processes. Some matched buyers and sellers to the Internet for the purpose of developing new relationships, much like an online dating site would do. This process was called "supplier discovery." Some marketplaces specialized in e-procurement models, such as reverse auctions, as described earlier. Still other marketplaces focused on digitizing supply chain processes, such as sales forecasting, inven-

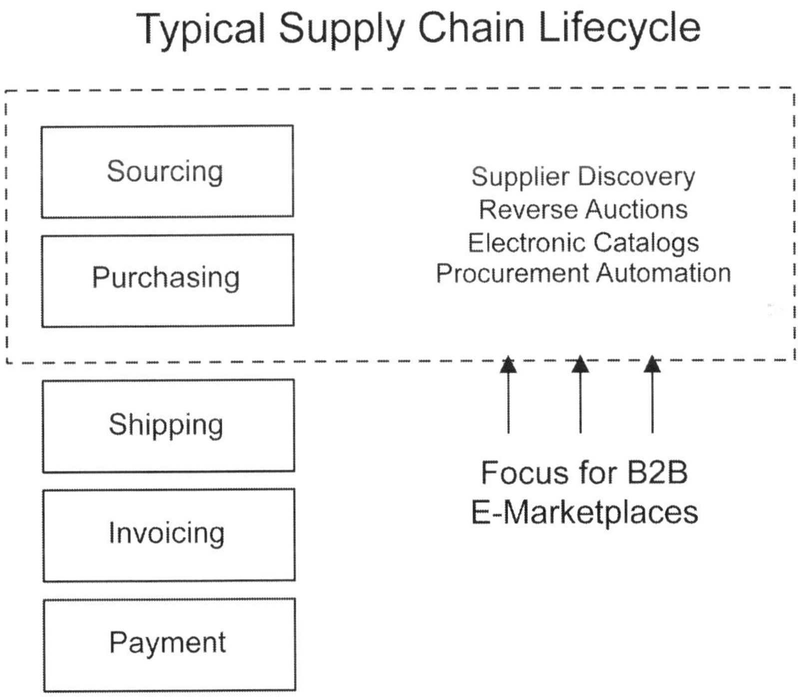

tory management and invoice processing.

The B2B e-marketplaces introduced in 1999 were expected to dramatically transform the way commerce was conducted between businesses. Just like the construction of the Erie Canal in the 1800s substantially reduced freight costs between Chicago and New York, the new inter-company digital links created by the marketplaces were poised to substantially reduce supply chain costs. Some entrepreneurs called it the Second Industrial Revolution.[4]

For the technology segment, B2B e-marketplaces were the second wave of the dot-com bubble. When most people recall the irrational exuberance that dominated the dot-com era, they remember the B2C companies. There were many successes, such as Amazon.com, eBay and Buy.com, which revolutionized the online shopping experience. But there were also many failures. For example, Webvan was a startup that was going to revolutionize the online grocery sector. It proved to be ahead of its time and fell into bankruptcy in 2001. Pets.com, which advertised in the 1999 Macys Thanksgiving Day parade and the 2000 Super Bowl, was another iconic brand that failed when the bubble burst. What most people do not remember were the big B2B e-marketplace vendors such as Commerce One, Chemdex and FreeMarkets.

There were three primary types of marketplaces that emerged in the late 1990s: independent, consortia, and private. Each model had different strengths and weaknesses. Without question the most interesting of the three was the consortia marketplace.

WorldWide Retail Exchange and the Consortia Marketplaces

Starting in late 1999 and throughout 2000 many of the world's largest companies began to join together to build their own electronic marketplaces. One particularly interesting aspect of these new exchanges was that they were formed by companies that had traditionally been cutthroat competitors. Ford, GM, and Chrysler, which battled each other in the US automotive market, united to create a marketplace called Covisint. P&G, Kraft Foods, Coca-Cola, and PepsiCo, which competed for market share in the consumer products segment, joined together to form Transora. Lockheed Martin, BAE Systems, Raytheon, and Boeing, which competed ruthlessly for government defense contracts, formed an aerospace marketplace called Exostar. Toshiba, Hitachi, and Matsushita (Panasonic) were among a group of high tech companies that founded E2open.

In the consortia marketplace model, retailers and industrial companies provided capital in exchange for an equity stake and a governance role in these new exchanges. The idea was that these consortia marketplaces would get a jump start through the instant participation of their owner community.

Perhaps the most interesting consortia marketplaces formed were in the retail industry. In March 2000, a consortium of 17 international retailers founded the WorldWide Retail Exchange (WWRE). The equity investors included Albertsons, Auchan, Best Buy, Casino, CVS, Delhaize, Gap, J.C. Penney, Jusco, Kingfisher, Kmart, Marks & Spencer, Royal Ahold, Safeway, Target, Tesco, and Walgreens. There were two primary drivers for WWRE's formation. First, retailers were concerned that someone else would build a retail exchange. If an independent exchange was developed by a Silicon Valley-based startup, it could become the dominant platform for B2B e-commerce in the retail industry. Retailers believed that such a strategic platform needed to be owned by the industry itself. Second, these retailers were increasingly threatened by Walmart. Not only had Walmart aggressively expanded its market share during the 1990s, but it had gained a technological advantage through its private exchange called RetailLink. Walmart's competitors did not want to spend several hundred million dollars each in building a Retail-Link-equivalent. However, the other retailers wanted access to comparable technology. The WWRE was designed to satisfy both goals.

WWRE offered similar services to other exchanges, including supplier discovery, electronic procurement and reverse auctions. Additionally, WWRE offered services specific to the industry such as the ability for retailers and suppliers to collaborate on forecasting future sales. WWRE was fairly successful in the areas of reverse auctions and collaborative forecasting during its early years. However, it had not delivered the revolutionary impact that its members originally believed possible. To increase its impact, WWRE sought to expand its scale in the industry. As a result, WWRE merged with GlobalNetXchange (GNX) in 2005. GNX was a competitor to WWRE that was founded in early 2000, by a different group of retailers which included Carrefour, Karstadt Quelle, Kroger

Co., Metro AG, Sainsbury, Coles Myer, Pinault-Printemps-Redoute, and Sears.

The merged WWRE-GNX entity was rebranded as Agentrics. I thought the rebranding was an excellent decision as there had always been confusion between WWRE and the World Wrestling Entertainment (WWE) group. Three years later, a Brazilian holding company named M. Abuhab Participacoes (MAP) acquired a controlling interest in Agentrics.[5] Today Agentrics has 15 of the top 25 retailers as customers. However, these retailers also continue to use their own customized versions of supply chain applications run by their internal IT organizations.

Consortia marketplaces like WWRE have a particular significance in the history of business. Competitors rarely collaborate in joint ventures like the marketplaces of the dot-com era. There will always be ongoing collaboration between competitors to lobby government organizations for policy changes, and competitors will always work together on technology standards. However, the levels of financial investment, resource commitment and joint technology development between competitors in the B2B e-marketplaces were on a scale that may never be seen again.

Independent Marketplaces	Consortia Marketplaces	Private Marketplaces
Owned by venture capitalists	Owned by customers (retailers, manufacturers)	Owned by single organization (retailer, manufacturer)
Ventro VerticalNet	WWRE E2open Exostar	GE Marketplace Walmart Retaillink

Three Types of Marketplaces

The idea of competitors collaborating is by definition unusual in a capitalist economy. In fact, regulators are usually suspicious of any joint ventures between competitors due to the potential for collusion on pricing. Consequently, the consortia exchanges had to undergo regulatory review in the EU and US prior to offering commercial services.

Ventro and the Independent Marketplaces

The evolution of the consortia marketplace was a direct response to a series of independent exchanges that had emerged in the late 1990s. Sometimes called public e-marketplaces, these organizations were founded by venture capitalists and managed by entrepreneurs. One of the independents' key strengths was neutrality. Not owned by any specific buyer or seller, the independents were free to develop their technology and their business models as they desired.

One example of an independent marketplace was Chemdex. The founder, David Perry, was a student at Harvard who had created a business plan for an online chemicals marketplace. Perry and his teammates received an award in the first annual Harvard Business Plan contest of 1997. After college, Perry set out to make the vision a reality. He secured funding from the venture capital community, then began to develop the Chemdex e-marketplace.[6]

The original value proposition of Chemdex was to simplify the purchasing of specialty chemicals, bio-chemicals, and re-agents in the life sciences industry. Historically, these specialty chemical products were sold via third-party distributors. The distributors printed massive catalogs that each listed millions of different products available for sale. Government and university labs, the US National Institute of Health for example, used these catalogs to purchase chemicals.

To place an order, the buyer had to search through dozens of catalogs to find a particular chemical, a process both time-consuming and error-prone. To keep expenses to a minimum, distributors only published new versions of the catalogs every 24 months. However, 25% of companies changed their product descriptions annually. As a result, product descriptions were frequently incomplete and out-of-date. Pricing was often incorrect as well. Once the appropriate product was located, a buyer would phone the distributor to place an order, and products were shipped from the nearest warehouse.

Chemdex intended to replace the complex series of print catalogs with an online marketplace. Buyers could have a single website to purchase all of their specialty chemicals, making it easy to compare prices between products. Suppliers could publish complete product descriptions that could be updated regularly. Costs would be substantially reduced. By eliminating the middleman, buyers could purchase at wholesale prices. Chemdex offered real-time inventories of all its cataloged products by integrating with suppliers' Enterprise Resource Planning (ERP) systems. Because products shipped directly from suppliers to buyers, Chemdex did not need to maintain any inventory.

Chemdex was backed by venture capitalists, such as CMGI, Bay City Capital Fund, Kleiner Perkins Caufield & Byers, and Warburg and Pincus Ventures. Services first became commercially available in November 1998 and the company went public just a few months later in July 1999.

Shortly thereafter, Chemdex expanded its business plan. The owners did not want to remain limited to specialty chemicals. Instead, Chemdex expanded into a holding company for a number of e-marketplaces in various vertical industries. In February 2000, the company was restructured and renamed to Ventro in support of its new business model. The new NASDAQ ticker symbol was VNTR, which in the biomedical field was an acronym that referred to the replication of genetic code.[7]

As Ventro, the company launched exchanges in a variety of industries—specialty medical supplies (Promdeix), commodity medical supplies (Broadlane), energy and chemical plant equipment (Industria), food service (Amphire) and office supplies (MarketMile).[8] Stock market analysts loved the Ventro story. The company's stock soared until it reached a peak market valuation of $7.86 billion. However, much like other dot-com companies, the Ventro stock quickly plummeted in late 2000 and early 2001. Eventually, Ventro was trading for less than $1 per share, leading NASDAQ to explore a possible delisting of VNTR. Chemdex was shutdown in early 2001. A group of shareholders sued the management team for securities fraud, claiming that it had issued "false and misleading statements concerning the company's business and financial condition." Eventually Ventro merged with the company Nexprise in late 2001.[9]

During the B2B e-marketplace era there were hundreds of stories like Chemdex—venture-backed startups that were going to change the world in a few months by harnessing the untapped power of the Internet. In every subsector of every industry, exchanges began to proliferate. In the food sector there was Water2Water.com for purchasing bottled water. Agex.com was a specialized exchange for buying and selling nuts and dried fruits. GoFish.com, fishmonger.com, Ralboray.com and Seafood.com were four marketplaces focused exclusively on seafood transactions. In the industrial sector there was a marketplace specifically designed for sales of Ferris wheels and associated parts. Analysts were predicting that each of the sectors represented by the 2,500 SIC codes would have at least two marketplaces each.

Over $48 billion of venture capital was invested in startups during 1999, two thirds of which was related to Internet technologies. Early views of the return on the investment were promising. In March 2000, the market capitalization of the top 64 US Internet and B2B software/e-commerce companies had reached over $200 billion. At the time, new ventures were being announced daily as entrepreneurs exercised their "constitutional right to the pursuit of happiness."[10]

Investment was not limited to venture capital sources. The large "brick and mortar" companies jumped on the bandwagon as well. Tired of watching their own valuations go sideways, while Silicon Valley churned out record-breaking IPOs, the large consumer and industrial conglomerates began direct investments in the consortia exchanges. Even the boards joined in the euphoria as "technical committees" of directors began to emerge alongside the traditional audit and compensation subgroups. Each of these companies had hopes of curing their own "market cap envy" by being "sprinkled with the magic dust of high-tech multiples."[11]

Venture capital investment froze in April 2000 after the NASDAQ began its precipitous decline. The change in stock market performance shut off funding for new marketplaces. However, it did not deter entrepreneurs and consortia that had already obtained investment capital from continuing to execute on their business plans. The number of B2B e-marketplaces peaked in 2001 at just over 1,600. I estimate that more than 1,200 of these failed in the coming years.

Today only a handful of the major consortia marketplaces still exist. A few survivors include Agentrics (formerly WWRE), Covisint and Exostar. These remaining few successfully transformed themselves into viable companies with long-term business plans. Some have enjoyed more success than others. For example, E2open reported 30% growth for its first half 2010 fiscal year and Covisint is planning a $1 billion IPO.[12]

Sadly, nearly all of the independent exchanges that started the revolution like Ventro, VerticalNet, and FreeMarkets were sold off or shut down. The independents were the true source of much of the innovation that fueled the B2B e-commerce revolution of the late 1990s. Some experts say that the independents were ahead of their time. The value proposition provided by these independent marketplaces took a few years to be embraced by the industry, but by then vendors had run out of cash.

In many respects, the independent marketplaces were victims of their own successes. Once industry leaders understood the potential benefits of a marketplace, they chose not to buy technology from a third-party vendor, but to invest directly themselves. Threatened by the potential disruption to historical supply chain dynamics, leading buyers and sellers rushed to build their own private and consortia e-marketplaces. The result was that the largest potential customers of independent marketplaces quickly became equity owner stakeholders in their competitors.

Dummies Books

If the marketplace era emerged today, a series of "Dummies" books would undoubtedly be published to educate novice investors on how to participate in these emerging opportunities. I could envision a four-part book series that would be required reading for most of the venture capitalists on Sand Hill Road. Here are the titles that I think would have been best-sellers:

Internet Marketplaces for Dummies—The book that started the revolution, Internet Marketplaces for Dummies, explains how any startup with just a few million dollars can launch a B2B auction site with the power to fundamentally alter the dynamics of a supply chain. The book is particularly appealing to the hundreds of executives and venture capitalists who have no experience in procurement or buyer-seller relationships in the value chain. Sure to be a *New York Times* Best Seller, thousands of readers seeking to generate "Billions in Profits" would read it cover-to-cover.

Reverse Auctions for Dummies—Required reading in Fortune 500 procurement organizations, this popular title explains how large buying organizations can squeeze 10 to 15% cost savings from strategic suppliers with reverse auctions. Chapter 10, "Shut Up and Bid" features objection handling techniques for suppliers reluctant to participate. Chapter 14, "What to Wear to Your Reverse Auction" is very popular in the retail sector.

Matching Buyers and Sellers for Dummies—Authored by two founders of an online dating service, this title explains how the Internet can create new long-term relationships between buyers and sellers of goods in a variety of industries. Freed from the constraints of the traditional brick and mortar establishment, buyers and sellers can find supply chain happiness with the click of a mouse.

How to Sell Your B2B e-Marketplace for Dummies—The last book of the series, published in 2002, appeals to the hundreds of investors seeking to salvage some nominal value from the billions they squandered in marketplace investments. Additionally, an underground cult of pension fund and university endowment managers purchased the title in a futile attempt to understand where the billions invested in these marketplaces had gone. The book became required reading for partners at bankruptcy law firms and managing directors at investment banking firms.

Why did the e-Marketplaces Fail?

There were a number of reasons why the B2B e-marketplaces were not successful. One major challenge faced by the consortia marketplaces was the governance model. There were many different owners of these exchanges—most being cutthroat competitors—creating an unusually complex decision-making process. For example, the consumer goods marketplace Transora had 49 different equity investors!

Consortia marketplaces such as Transora, Covisint, and WWRE struggled with a perceived lack of neutrality. While many buyers and sellers took equity stakes in marketplaces, other companies stood on the sidelines. For the consortia marketplaces to grow they needed to gain the participation of additional non-owner organizations. But these outside companies were neither comfortable sharing sensitive pricing nor product information on an exchange owned by their competitors. Nor were they interested in paying transaction fees that ultimately flowed back to these same competitors.

Marketplace vendors underestimated the importance of long-standing personal and corporate relationships in the existing supply chain. Buyer relationships with suppliers extended back for decades, or in some cases as long as a century. These buyer-supplier dynamics were unlikely to be disrupted for a 10% price gain through a reverse auction. Middle-aged buyers and suppliers accustomed to negotiating purchases over the phone were reluctant to quickly transition to new, unproven e-marketplaces. There were relatively low levels of transaction volumes and the marketplaces threatened to potentially eliminate the need for the very end-users they aimed to support.

In perhaps the most widely read report about the B2B e-marketplace sector, Morgan Stanley Dean Witter provided a quotation from an anonymous supplier that concisely summed up the challenges: "Let's see, you want me to put all my products and prices online so my customers can beat me about the head and shoulders. Then I can commoditize myself even more to take my razor-thin margins down to microscopic level. Finally, I get to pay transaction fees for this privilege. What am I missing?"[13]

The Golden Age of B2B e-Commerce

The exchange era was marked by an unparalleled infusion of capital from investors who displayed an insatiable appetite for risk. Entrepreneurs around the world engaged in widespread supply chain innovation and experimentation. Some call it the Golden Age of B2B e-Commerce. Others call it the height of insanity. Regardless of your perspective, most agree that there will never be another time like it in the world of B2B e-commerce.

Most people in the supply chain and B2B e-commerce sector do not like to talk about the e-marketplace era. People rarely introduce themselves as former Covisint, WWRE, or Chemdex employees, just as few people reference prior employment at failed B2C companies such as Pets.com, Webvan, or e-Toys. However, I think it is important to study and to remember what happened during the B2B e-marketplace era. As George Santayana once said, "Those who cannot learn from history are doomed to repeat it." As we will discover in later chapters, there are many an entrepreneur and venture capitalist that should open their history book. The cycle of irrational exuberance and investment bubbles has been repeated 10 times in the years following the B2B e-marketplace era.

Chapter 3
The Automotive Supply Chain

The decades immediately following World War II are referred to by many in the automotive industry as the glory days for American automakers. GM, Ford and Chrysler collectively enjoyed a commanding market share as there was relatively little outside competition from foreign brands. However, in the late 1960s a new set of market forces were emerging that would challenge the US automakers considerably. First, the industry was becoming increasingly regulated. The first safety belt and passenger restraint system laws were being passed. There also was a growing awareness of the impact the industry was having on the environment. In addition to the regulations, foreign competition, particularly from the Japanese brands, was increasing rapidly. The 1973 oil crisis complicated matters even further by increasing demand for more fuel-efficient vehicles.

The US automakers needed strategies to reduce costs quickly. Automated computer processing was one strategy favored by the automakers. Computers could not only lower costs, but improve supply chain efficiency. Eliminating time-intensive, paper-based communications between automakers and suppliers—B2B e-commerce—was viewed as an area for opportunity. Many of the large automakers and their suppliers began to use Electronic Data Interchange (EDI) in the 1970s. B2B e-commerce, primarily in the form of EDI, grew steadily throughout the 1980s and 1990s until another series of challenges emerged in the automotive industry. In the late 1990s US automakers and their suppliers were reaching another crisis point. The Big Three (GM, Ford and Chrysler) were continuing to lose market share to competing Japanese and Korean automakers. New designs from import brands continued to gain popularity with American consumers.

Three Big Problems with the Big Three

The US automakers could not seem to create a flexible supply chain that could quickly respond to changing market conditions and volatile consumer demand. Even when the US auto brands had new design ideas, they were challenged to get the vehicles to market quickly due to lengthy product development lifecycles. From concept to first sale, the process to bring a new vehicle could range from 18 to 48 months and cost between $800 million and $1 billion.[14] The four-year turnaround time meant that the US automakers were not able to keep pace with the changing tastes of consumers. The industry viewed better technology as one way to shrink product development lifecycles. If virtual workplaces could be created to allow designers at the automakers and their part suppliers to collaborate online, timeframes could be reduced considerably.

Perhaps a bigger problem than the lengthy product development lifecycles was the challenge automakers faced with demand forecasting. In many cases the Big Three simply produced too many of the wrong types of vehicles. Throughout most of the twentieth century, vehicle production and sales forecasts were based upon internally-driven factors. Each year, automakers would start their sales forecasts with the quantity of each make and model sold last year. While such an approach might seem logical, it often perpetuated a set of overly optimistic forecasts. Prior year sales can be misleading as they distort true end-consumer demand. For example, throughout much of the 1990s high percentages of certain vehicles were held in inventory for long periods of time before sales promotions were utilized to eventually unload the vehicle. In many cases, large volumes of these passenger vehicles were sold to fleet operators, such as rental car agencies or state governments, at substantial discounts from the list price.

To reduce the inaccuracies of sales forecasting the large automakers contemplated shifting to a "Build to Order" (BTO) model. If you have ever purchased a computer from Dell's web site then you are familiar with BTO. With BTO, car buyers could visit a website which would allow them to mix and match the paint colors, fabric interiors, entertainment systems and other options they preferred. The car would be manufactured as ordered in a nearby plant then shipped to the dealership for pickup within 5-10 days.

The benefit of BTO to automakers would be to reduce the need to guesstimate which quantity of each type of vehicle to produce. With multiple choices for everything from the paint color to the entertainment system options, consumers could create thousands of different configurations for each vehicle. If successful, the BTO model would cut dealer inventories by 50%. Profitability would increase by as much as 50% per vehicle.[15] Dealers would benefit from having access to the exact product the consumer desired, which would lead to more sales.

The closest model to BTO that existed in the late 1990s was the "special order" program. However, consumers who placed special orders had to endure 50 to 70 day lead times to receive the cars.[16] Radical changes to the automotive supply chain would be required to implement the new BTO model. Vehicle makers would have to use the same standardized parts in multiple vehicle types to enable more configurability. Real-time inventory data would need to be collected from suppliers to determine "available to promise" dates. New technology platforms linking business partners in the automotive supply chain to share information in new ways were needed.

In addition to long product development lifecycles and inaccurate sales forecasts the third problem faced by the US auto industry was manufacturing efficiencies. The labor unions were often blamed by management as the reason US manufacturers were less cost competitive than the Japanese. Labor unions had a different perspective. Unions blamed declining market shares and cost challenges on poor decisions by senior management. There is no question, however, that the labor costs of US automakers had grown significantly in the decades following the 1960s. Automakers began offering health care benefits and pension programs to hourly employees after World War II. The costs were relatively negligible in the 1940s. However, over time the benefit expenses began to escalate quickly. In 2002, approximately $1,700 of each vehicle GM sold was used to pay pension obligations and health care costs.[17] At the time, GM's per vehicle profit was only 0.5%. Without the pensions and benefits costs, GM would have realized a profit of 5.5% per vehicle.[18]

Some thought leaders proposed that US automakers should abandon manufacturing altogether. Instead the car companies would focus on a new set of core competencies such as brand development, product design and vehicle financing. The assembly and production of the vehicle would be fully outsourced to contract manufacturers such as Magna (of Canada) and Valmet (of Finland). The idea was not as far-fetched as it might sound. Vehicle manufacturers had been pushing manufacturing activities upstream to suppliers for decades.

In the early 1900s, automakers produced each and every part in the vehicle themselves. Over time, increased responsibility for design, manufacturing and assembly of subsystems within the vehicle became outsourced to large Tier 1 suppliers. Automobile companies depend upon an extensive network of suppliers to provide most of the raw materials, parts and subsystems needed to build a vehicle. There is a tier of suppliers that provide component parts, such as lights, sensors and brakes. These component parts are then assembled into subsystems for safety, exhaust, entertainment, heating/air conditioning, by what are called Tier 1 suppliers. Vehicle manufacturers, such as Toyota, GM and Volkswagen, then take the subsystem provided by the Tier 1s to make the finished vehicles.

An outsourced model would enable vehicle makers to quickly respond to changes in demand. Contract manufacturers would be able to better balance demand across different vehicle brands. When one vehicle type is experiencing higher demand you could borrow labor and equipment from the lines of other vehicles with lesser demand. New economies of scale could be introduced by working with multiple customers.

The Birth of Covisint

The answer to these three big challenges was a new automotive technology exchange called Covisint. As mentioned in Chapter 2, the new company was a joint venture of the Big Three US automakers: GM, Ford and DaimlerChrysler. The word Covisint was formed from the first few letters of the words Collaboration, Visibility and Integration. It was said that Covisint was going to bring new Internet-based technology to market that would enable the US automotive community to accelerate product development, enable BTO models and lower manufacturing cost structures.

The Big Three US automakers contributed a collective total of $250 million in funding as well as lending numerous employees to the joint venture.[19] The owners expected Covisint to go public in a few years with a market capitalization of $30 billion to $40 billion on revenues of $3 billion.[20] At the time GM, Ford and DaimlerChrysler spent $238 billion in procurement annually. The thinking was if even a small fraction of transactions were processed by Covisint, the exchange would generate significant revenues.

Confident with the business plan, the Big Three announced their plans for Covisint on February 25, 2000. The announcement came just two weeks before March 10, 2000 the date on which the NASDAQ market reached its all-time peak from the dot-com bubble. However, Covisint's immediate concern following the launch was not the stock market, but the anti-trust regulations in the US and European Union (EU). The Big three automakers controlled 44% of the global auto market. Consequently, anti-trust authorities were concerned about possible collusion and price fixing by the Big Three. Regulators on both sides of the Atlantic conducted thorough reviews before any employees could be hired. The FTC cleared Covisint in September 2000. The EU clearance occurred in July 2001.

A secondary challenge Covisint faced was its governance model. Despite efforts to create a joint venture, Ford, GM and Daimler Chrysler were fierce competitors in the marketplace. The complications only grew as Renault, Nissan and PSA Peugeot Citroen later joined Covisint along with 25 auto suppliers. Covisint had six different CEOs in the first three years. Contrary to popular rumor, Tommy Boy was not one of them. One CEO lasted only 31 days.[21] When the company was founded there were actually three CEOs—one each from GM, Ford and Daimler Chrysler. Perhaps the most pivotal of the early CEOs was Kevin English, who had led TheStreet.com to a $100 million IPO in 1999. Under English's leadership, costs were reigned in and the business plan was formalized. In an interview for a Harvard Business School case study, Kevin English stated, "When I first came to Covisint in April 2001, the spending was out of control. There were approximately 400 consultants working in the company at a cost of approximately $300,000 per day. At times, consultant expenses approached $20M per month. A venture capital friend of mine said that, in the 25 years he had worked in the industry, he had never seen anything like it."[22]

Although Covisint's revenues grew quickly to a respectable level of approximately $60-$70 million in 2002, its costs remained excessive. To bring costs in-line, consulting staff was reduced, travel budgets were cut and employees were repatriated to the vehicle manufacturers or let go.[23]

Covisint had developed almost twenty products ranging from quality planning and asset recovery to virtual project workspaces and web conferencing. However, adoption of these systems by most end-user clients was much slower than expected. The vehicle manufacturers preferred, in many cases, to continue using their own in-house systems which had been customized to meet their business needs. A Yankee Group analyst was quoted as stating, "The expectation that a 100-year-old industry that represents 18 percent of the total economic output within a country would simply change its means of purchasing and interacting with suppliers in a short period of time based on the availability of the Internet was incredibly high."[24]

The most successful of Covisint's products was the reverse auction which represented 90% of revenues by the end of 2001.[25] While the auctions were popular with the buyers, or vehicle manufacturers, the suppliers resented them. Suppliers viewed the marketplaces purely as a mechanism to lower price and squeeze margin out of the suppliers' business. Suppliers believed that with a reverse auction the buyers effectively treated all products as commodities to be judged solely on price. There was no opportunity to differentiate based upon factors such as quality, lead time or customer service.

Starting in 2001, a series of bankruptcies among Tier 1 suppliers began to occur that continued for almost a decade. The economic recession occurring at the time was cited as the root cause for most of the bankruptcies. However, I suspect the price pressure created from auctions did not help the situation.

In 2003, Bob Paul was promoted to CEO of Covisint. He refocused the product strategy to where the company could gain a predictable and growing set of revenues services such as EDI. The company began to shed assets as the realization that activities such as joint product development and BTO manufacturing were not going to occur on the exchange. In December 2003, Covisint divested its sourcing and auction assets, which were the highest grossing product line at its inception, to FreeMarkets. Shortly thereafter, in February

2004, Covisint was acquired by the IT services firm Compuware.

Although, it received most of the media attention, Covisint was not the only exchange in the automotive market. Approximately six months after the formation of Covisint, a group of German automotive suppliers also announced a B2B e-marketplace. The company would be a joint venture of Bosch, Continental, INA/LuK, ZF and SAP. The original focus of the company was e-procurement using online auctions and electronic RFP technologies. SupplyOn also enabled automakers and suppliers to collaborate electronically. In the past 10 years, the company has diversified to focus on aerospace and manufacturing as well as automotive. SupplyOn generated over €20 million of revenue in 2010 from manufacturing leaders such as Airbus, BMW Group, BorgWarner, Bosch, Continental and Textron.[26]

Since 2004, Covisint has continued to diversify its product portfolio and go-to-market strategy following the Compuware buyout. Covisint is now a leading player in the fast-growing Electronic Health Records market, which we will discuss further in Chapter 12. Enjoying a period of steady growth, Covisint announced its intention to launch an Initial Public Offering (IPO) in early 2008.[27] The offering was postponed shortly thereafter due to the widespread distress in the financial markets.

Despite its early struggles, Covisint's business model was making progress towards the original IPO vision of its founders under Compuware's leadership. However, a storm of controversy resurfaced in February 2009 when Compuware's management team made a questionable decision to hire the former Mayor of Detroit, Kwame Kilpatrick. During Kilpatrick's tenure as mayor from 2002 to 2008 he was implicated in numerous scandals. After being charged with 10 felony counts including perjury and obstruction of justice, Kilpatrick eventually resigned. He served a short jail sentence before being released on probation.[28] There is a rather lengthy Wikipedia entry on the accusations against Kilpatrick which provides some interesting reading. After 15 months, the relationship between Covisint and Kilpatrick was terminated in May 2010. Although the controversial decision to hire Kilpatrick may have damaged Covisint's reputation in the media, its business strategy continued to reward the company with new accounts. Health Information Exchanges (HIEs) in the states of Montana,[29] Vermont[30] and Pennsylvania[31] each awarded contracts to Covisint. The company is expanding its industry focus to include oil and gas and the defense sectors. Discussion of a potential IPO resumed in 2011.[32] However, at the time of the publication of this book, no definitive IPO date has been set.

The story of Covisint's transformation is perhaps one of the most amazing turnaround successes in the history of B2B e-commerce. While Covisint was successful in its transformation, the same cannot be said of the automotive industry it was created to rescue. In the years following 2000, the US automakers costs continued to rise steadily. By 2007, GM covered one million people on its health care budget at a cost of $4.6 billion annually.[33] There was a 4:1 ratio of GM retirees to active employees. At one point, overall pension and health care benefits represented a $47 billion liability on GM's balance sheet.[34] The Big Three share of the US market steadily declined from 70% in 1998 down to 53% in 2008 when a crisis emerged.[35] The price of oil had skyrocketed to $150 a barrel during 2008. Rising oil prices deeply hurt the sales of US automakers which had become dependent upon high volumes of Sport Utility Vehicles (SUV) sales. As gasoline prices soared, consumers shifted to more fuel-efficient vehicles. To make matters worse, the collapse of Lehman Brothers in September 2008 resulted in a global credit crisis. Many consumers were not able to obtain the credit necessary to finance a new vehicle purchase. Other potential buyers, who did have credit, postponed purchasing decisions due to uncertainty over the economic climate. The US automotive industry, which at its peak sold 17 million vehicles, declined to a rate of less than 10 million in the midst of the crisis. The situation worsened until Chrysler filed for bankruptcy in May 2009. A month later, GM entered a Chapter 11 bankruptcy restructuring as well.

Chapter 4
E-Procurement

In Chapter 2 we discussed the rise and fall of the B2B e-marketplaces. Looking back it is easy to call into question the judgment of venture capitalists and Fortune 500 CEOs who invested so heavily in these technologies. However, during the time period there was a tremendous amount of pressure to participate in these initiatives. In fact, large corporations that did not invest in marketplaces were criticized as being "old-school" thinkers and technology laggards.

One of the major forces underpinning the hype surrounding B2B e-marketplaces was the technology vendor community. There was a small group of companies that fully exploited the irrational exuberance of the era. Lots of executives and sales representatives at these companies made millions of dollars selling technology platforms to the owners of independent, consortia and private exchanges. When the market collapsed, the stock prices of these technology vendors dropped precipitously. Over the 36 months following the NASDAQ peak in March 2000, technology companies lost $5 trillion in market value. The value of many individual stock portfolios and retirement plans declined significantly. However, many of the former sales representatives and corporate executives of these B2B startups were newly minted millionaires having cashed out before the bubble burst.

Arriba, Arriba, Andale

One of the most successful B2B e-commerce vendors to emerge from the dot-com era was a company called Ariba. I first heard the word "Ariba" growing up in the 1970s watching cartoons. Speedy Gonzales would exclaim "arriba, arriba, andale, andale," which seemed to mean "speed up." As it turned out the company was aptly named. Ariba was founded in 1996 by a group of seven colleagues that were frustrated with the cumbersome and time-consuming process associated with buying goods and services. While sitting at a cafe in Menlo Park, the group sketched out an automated e-procurement solution using some crayons and a paper tablecloth.

Historically, the procurement process at a large organization worked as follows. A group of buyers would thumb through printed catalogs, provided by vendors searching for raw materials, component parts or finished goods that needed to be purchased. For regularly purchased items, the pricing, terms and conditions for these goods were negotiated in advance. Once the items were selected, the buyer would create a purchase requisition for the goods. The requisition would be printed out and circulated via interoffice mail for approval and release to the supplier. A purchase order could be phoned in, faxed or transmitted via EDI to the supplier. The process was very time-consuming and paper-intensive.

Ariba had a better model. Their vision for an Internet-based e-procurement application was, "It would have a walk-up user interface. It would integrate with enterprise financial systems. It would hook right up to the suppliers. It would run on this new thing called the Internet. And it would fundamentally change business models."[36]

Ariba's first buy-side e-procurement application was launched in 1997. Catalogs were published electronically by suppliers into a single repository that buyers could view. As suppliers changed the attributes or prices of their products the updates were published to the buyer's e-procurement application. As a result, buyers never had to worry that the information being used to make a purchasing decision was out-of-date. Complex forms were replaced with user-friendly wizards which guided buyers through the requisition process. A bottom line savings of $10 to $20 per purchase order could be achieved. The savings were realized by eliminating the keying of data from paper requisitions into applications; eliminating the mailing of orders to suppliers, and reducing the errors that resulted from highly manual processes.

Ariba was originally privately funded by venture capitalists such as Crosspoint Ventures and Benchmark Capital. However, the ownership model quickly turned public as Ariba became among the first of the B2B e-commerce vendors to IPO in June 1999. The stock price tripled on opening day raising the company's market capitalization to $6 billion.[37] During 1999, Ariba signed a number of high profile contracts with industry leaders such as Nestle, GM, Motorola, Andersen Consulting, Charles Schwab and Morgan Stanley Dean Witter. While 1999 was a great year for Ariba, 2000 was even better. The company reported over $80 million in revenues for the second quarter of 2000, nearly a 600% increase over the same quarter in 1999.[38]

The One for Commerce

Ariba was not the only one enjoying success in the B2B e-commerce sector during the year 2000. Its archrival, Commerce One, also reported phenomenal growth. Commerce One, also a provider of e-procurement and marketplace technologies, reported over $60 million in revenues for the second quarter of 2000, which was nearly a 1400% increase year-over-year.[39]

Commerce One was started a few years before Ariba in 1994 under the original name of Distrivision. However, the company's growth did not accelerate until Mark Hoffman was named CEO. Hoffman, previously the CEO of Sybase, had a vision for the young company. He wanted to develop an Internet powerhouse that would simplify commerce transactions between businesses in the same way that Amazon.com had revolutionized consumer shopping. Hoffman renamed the company Commerce One in 1997 and quickly raised additional funding from companies such as MCI Systemhouse and GE Capital.[40]

Commerce One's IPO closely followed Ariba's in July 1999. The stock skyrocketed, increasing its price 1,000% by the end of the year. On news of a strategic partnership with GM, Commerce One's market value increased by $2 billion overnight. At its peak, the market capitalization of Commerce One reached $21.5 billion.[41] Employee stock options rose to be worth hundreds of thousands of dollars. The executives became multi-millionaires in just a few months. But perhaps the fastest money was made by the sales organization.

Commerce One and Ariba focused on two primary sectors. The first opportunity was to sell e-procurement software directly to large enterprise accounts that wanted to automate their purchase order requisition and approval process. The concept of e-procurement software was relatively new, which meant that very few large companies had existing software packages. Consequently, it was a green field opportunity to generate millions in license and services revenue from all of the world's largest companies. But that's not really what excited the sales teams at Commerce One and Ariba in the year 2000. Instead, they were focused on selling B2B e-commerce platform technology to the hundreds of newly formed B2B e-marketplaces and exchanges popping up all over the world.

Most of the marketplaces preferred to license technology from vendors rather than build the capabilities themselves. In 2000, no one could afford to risk the delay in market timing that building an in-house platform would require. The Internet operated in dog years—meaning that the events, which would normally occur in seven years in any other industry, were compressed into one. Ariba and Commerce One each sold their technology to 150 different marketplaces. The opportunity was so large that both vendors formed a consortium with other technology powerhouses to maximize their sales efforts. Ariba teamed up with IBM and another fast growing technology startup called i2. Based in Dallas, i2 had a suite of supply chain management applications that were complementary to Ariba's e-procurement and marketplace capabilities.

SAP and Commerce One

Threatened by the Ariba-i2-IBM "dream team," Commerce One sought out a partnership to solidify its position in the industry. Hoffman reached out to SAP, but was turned down by one of its Co-CEOs. SAP quickly reconsidered and re-approached Commerce One to start negotiations on what became one of the largest joint product development efforts ever undertaken in the technology sector.[42] The Commerce One/SAP partnership announced in 2000, called for 14 joint engineering teams representing 400 personnel. There were two different development teams and one joint marketing team. As part of the deal, SAP also provided $250 million in cash in exchange for a 4% equity stake. The deal was widely applauded, especially by Commerce One's customers, 75% of which already used SAP.[43]

Commerce One enjoyed an unprecedented level of fame in 2000. It spoke at almost every supply chain and B2B e-commerce conference, including its own event which attracted 2,500 attendees. Much like Apple in 2010, the only thing Commerce One had to do to make the news was to issue a press release.

The competition between Ariba and Commerce One was intense. At one of Commerce One's sales conferences, the executives had T-shirts printed with the phrase "Aribanator" and Arnold Schwarzenegger's photo on them.[44]

In addition to SAP, Commerce One established channel relationships with Compaq, Microsoft, Intel, PeopleSoft, Sterling Commerce and GE's Global eXchange Services. Perhaps most noteworthy was the deal with automotive exchange, Covisint. Commerce One was part of the joint venture between GM, Ford, DaimlerChrysler, Nissan and Renault to form the new automotive exchange. Commerce One would supply its e-marketplace technology platform. In return, it would receive a revenue share from Covisint for 10 years as well as 2% equity stake in the exchange. Also, as part of the deal, GM and Ford were granted a combined 14% ownership stake in Commerce One.[45]

The competition to become the technology foundation for e-marketplaces such as Covisint was intense. Vendors were approaching the situation like a Monopoly game, seeking to acquire as much property as they could on the first trip around the board. It was a land-grab based upon the premise that exchanges were the future of commerce. Technology providers that received a revenue share of the transaction fees charged by the exchanges were sure to make millions in profits.

With their market valuations reaching astronomical heights, both Ariba and Commerce One used their stock as a currency to fund acquisitions to build out their portfolios. Ariba acquired TRADEX in 1999 and SupplierMarket.com in 2000.[46,47] Commerce One acquired companies such as Veo Systems and Appnet.[48,49] Even after the acquisitions, both companies ranked on "the top ten list of highest market capitalization per line of code."

The Commerce One/SAP partnership delivered its new platform in 2001, but by then the market had shifted. The stock market had collapsed. Business executives reacting to the recession stopped investing for growth and began focusing on cost reductions. "People were buying vision in 2000. In 2001, they were looking for return on investment," said Robert Kimmit, then Commerce One's president.[50] The SAP partnership was overall a success for Commerce One, representing up to 50% of revenues at one time.[51] However, the partnership began to fall apart when Commerce One's financials began to deteriorate.

With the economy in a deep recession, Commerce One was not able to meet its forecasted sales projections. The company declared losses of $2 billion in a single quarter in 2001 on revenues of only $100 million. The company cut 50% of its staff in 2001. At first SAP was supportive. Despite the precipitous decline in revenues, SAP doubled its investment in Commerce One. It increased its ownership position to 20%.[52] Rumors were rampant that SAP was going to acquire the floundering e-commerce vendor. However, Commerce One's financial situation continued to worsen and the deal never materialized. SAP began to distance itself from Commerce One, investing further in its own Supplier Relationship Management software as its primary e-procurement offering.

The Fall of Commerce One

The collapse of the SAP partnership was the beginning of the end for Commerce One. In April 2002 the company reported an 80% decline in quarterly revenues year-over-year.[53] A one-to-ten reverse stock split was issued, followed by another massive staff reduction. In 2002, Commerce One sold off three businesses to an e-procurement marketplace called eScout.[54] By November 2003, the company only had 100 remaining employees, each of which was given a mandatory two week furlough to reduce expenses. On October 6th, 2004 Commerce One filed for Chapter 11 bankruptcy.[55] On the day of the announcement, the Motley Fool stated, "This is going to be a sad one, folks."[56] Bruce Richardson, Chief Research Officer at AMR, commented, "It's too bad that Commerce One won't be around to see the industry it helped create."[57]

Commerce One was divided up in bankruptcy court. A portfolio of patents were packaged and sold to a subsidiary of Novell for a nominal amount of money.[58] The remainder of the company was sold to a new group of owners, which operated it independently for about eighteen months. In February 2006, another B2B vendor, Perfect Commerce, acquired the remaining Commerce One business. It has since been assimilated into Perfect Commerce's operations.[59]

Ariba experienced similar struggles during the dot-com collapse. However, in 2001 and 2002, Ariba's financials began to stabilize. And in the following years Ariba began to grow again as did its market capitalization. One of the questions I have often wrestled with is why Commerce One failed and Ariba succeeded. I have never seen a third-party analysis that attempted to explain the root causes for each company's success or failure. Both seemed to have similar product strategies and financial challenges. However, Ariba appeared to have responded faster to the changing market conditions. It refocused its product strategy on enterprise-class applications for e-procurement and sourcing. Ariba also enjoyed a strong, loyal customer base which provided foundational revenue and growth opportunity. Another factor could have been the promotion of Ariba's CFO to CEO, which undoubtedly led to a focus on financial discipline. Whatever magic was used, in the end Ariba emerged victorious over Commerce One.

Spend Management

In the wake of the e-marketplace decline and dot-com collapse, the e-procurement vendors refocused on servicing the needs of individual enterprises with a broader array of applications. Although Commerce One had all but disappeared, Ariba found itself competing with an even fiercer set of rivals in SAP and Oracle. No longer dependent upon Commerce One, SAP aggressively invested in building out its Supplier Relationship Management capabilities. Oracle, which had been developing its purchasing capabilities independently for several years, continued to invest in its iProcurement suite. A battle began to emerge in manufacturing sectors such as automotive, high tech, consumer products and pharmaceuticals. The manufacturers in these industries had heavily invested in SAP and Oracle to run their business. Tight integration, between procurement, finance, accounting and supply chain management features of the ERP system, was critical.

By the time the B2B e-marketplaces had collapsed, most of the large companies in the world had implemented some form of e-procurement application to automate their requisition process. The industry then began to shift towards a broader goal of identifying opportunities to reduce corporate spending. If you work in a large corporation, chances are you are already familiar with this process. Corporate travel agencies offer the best examples. Companies are always trying to reduce the corporation's spend on travel. As a result, CFOs and purchasing departments will contract with a third-party travel agency, such as American Express or Carlson Wagonlit Travel. The agency will analyze the travel patterns of your employees then negotiate favorable discounts with key travel providers on your behalf. For example, if your company has headquarters in Chicago and satellite offices in Los Angeles and Dallas, then you should choose an airline partner that has hubs in these cities such as American Airlines. The travel agency may negotiate with several hotel chains and rental car agencies to find the best deal. Employees are required to perform all travel requisitions through the agency which ensures the preferred, negotiated rates are enforced. The agency may perform a quarterly or annual analysis of travel patterns to ensure that the vendors selected are offering the best mix of services for your employees actual needs.

The same process can be used for other types of goods and services being purchased. However, in most cases the procurement organization rather than a specialized third-party agent performs the analysis, negotiation and requisition functions. The process begins with spend analysis to determine what the company is buying and from whom. To obtain the information, companies will aggregate all their purchasing data from procurement and accounts payable systems for the past year. Spend analysis software from vendors such as Ariba will group the purchases into categories, and then show spend by item, category, supplier and business unit.

The outcome of spend analysis is usually an opportunity to identify cost savings. Consolidating spend with a single vendor is usually an area that can provide short-term savings opportunities. For example, a company may be using DHL for 50% of its international shipping needs, FedEx for 30% and UPS for the remaining 20%. By consolidating all of its international shipping with one of these three companies, the company may be able to obtain an additional volume discount of 10-15%.

Further benefits can come from standardization of the goods purchased. For example, an automobile manufacturer may purchase 20 different types of brake pads from 10 different suppliers to place on its various vehicles. By redesigning the vehicles, the car manufacturer may be able to standardize on three different brake pads from only two suppliers. Through standardization, the car manufacturer may be able to negotiate further volume discounts with the two suppliers. The automobile company can also simplify its inventory management process and reduce the supply chain costs of managing so many different parts and suppliers.

The cost savings opportunities described above can be identified using specialized spend management applications, but to implement a new purchasing strategy companies use another application called e-sourcing. These e-sourcing applications can identify a list of potential suppliers and all the criteria used to evaluate the purchases. Just as when you shop at home for a new TV, dishwasher or car, corporate buyers evaluate products on more than price alone. The evaluation criteria are extended to include payment terms, lead times, inventory policies, performance specifications, quality metrics and customer service capabilities. Once the suppliers and purchasing criteria are identified, sourcing tools can generate electronic Requests for Proposal (RFP) or Requests for Quote (RFQ), offering a variety of mechanisms to stimulate a competitive bidding process between potential suppliers. One model is the reverse auction scenario discussed in Chapter 2. E-sourcing applications can also support a traditional buying model in which suppliers submit proposals with prices which are then compared and negotiated further until a winner is chosen. Of course, procurement organizations start with the largest spend categories which offer the greatest opportunity for savings.

Ariba's Second Wave

One of the most challenging aspects of selling e-purchasing applications is the sophistication of the customer you are selling to. The buyer for an e-purchasing application is, of course, someone in the procurement organization. These groups are made up of professional negotiators whose primary mission is to obtain goods and services at the absolute minimum price for their company. In a recessionary period like the one experienced in 2000-2002, the pressure to negotiate aggressively became even more compelling. In fact, it was during this period that purchasing departments first used e-procurement technologies to negotiate with the companies that developed the applications. In 2001, America West Airlines used a reverse auction hosted by FreeMarkets to identify the lowest cost provider of auction services for its procurement department. Despite its inside advantage, FreeMarkets did not win.[60]

The combination of the challenging buyer, recessionary pressure and stronger competitive dynamics with SAP and Oracle created a challenging environment for Ariba. But Ariba successfully overcame these hurdles. It added new products in the areas of spend analytics and e-sourcing. And in January 2004, Ariba acquired reverse auction pioneer, FreeMarkets from Covisint, for $500 million.[61] The combination brought additional product capabilities as well as a more diversified customer base.

ERP vendors were not the only ones chasing the e-purchasing sector. A number of the former technology marketplaces and e-procurement vendors had also transformed their business models to focus on the broader e-purchasing landscape. For example, Perfect Commerce, Emptoris and Procuri, which had also survived the e-marketplace collapse, rebounded with an expanded presence. Other survivors included SciQuest, which specialized in purchases of laboratory products for universities and research organizations; and cc-hub-woo, a French vendor, which specialized in the oil and gas segment. cc-hub-woo, which now goes by just Hubwoo, has the best name of all the vendors in the space. I'm not sure how it is pronounced in French, but I like to slowly draw out the last few letters "wooooooooooo." Perhaps, most threatening about many of these niche competitors, was their Software-as-a-Service (SaaS) delivery model which differed from the traditional enterprise license approach taken by Ariba and others. With SaaS, customers rent applications, rather than buy them. Unlike traditional software models in which IT organizations manage the technology themselves, SaaS offers a model in which the vendor hosts the application in their own data center providing all the upgrades and support.

Sensing that a shift in business models was on the horizon, Ariba decided to build a SaaS version of its product in late 2005. Very few enterprise software companies have attempted to transform themselves from the traditional license and maintenance model to a SaaS model. The SaaS model provides a more predictable, recurring revenue stream; however, it offers lower margin opportunities. Most enterprise software vendors, including Microsoft, SAP and Oracle, have not attempted to transform into SaaS models due to the significant change that would occur in their financial reporting results. Although the SaaS model is favored by investors due to its predictability, the largest enterprise software vendors fear that changes to their revenue and earnings patterns will meet with short-term resistance from shareholders. Ariba did not appear to be constrained by these fears.

Ariba's acquisition strategy changed to reflect the SaaS focus as well. In September 2007, it acquired a competitor named Procuri for almost $100 million. Procuri offered similar functionality to Ariba with sourcing, spend analysis and contract management. However, Procuri offered a SaaS model that included a significant installed base of mid-sized companies.[62] The transformation continued as Ariba rolled out additional SaaS offerings and began a renewed focus on building out its supplier network. In November 2010, Ariba acquired Quadrem for $150 million. Quadrem was a former e-marketplace that was founded by 18 metals and mining companies including Alcoa, BHP Billiton, Rio Tinto Alcan, Glencore and De Beers (yes, the diamond guys). Quadrem's model was also network-centric with a portfolio of SaaS applications.[63]

Today, 88% of the Fortune 500 use Ariba for sourcing, procurement, contract management or other purchasing functions. On an average day, Ariba conducts more than 100,000 B2B e-commerce transactions representing $450 million worth of goods and services.[64] The company has the number three position behind SAP and Oracle in many of the e-purchasing analyst rankings. Ariba is generally considered one of the most successful SaaS vendors.

Someone really should have written an entire book about the evolution of Ariba and Commerce One. Ariba offers a rare story of a vendor that not only survived the dot-com collapse and ruthless competition from ERP vendors, but then successfully transformed into a SaaS vendor. Although it did not succeed, Commerce One made an unforgettable impact on the technology used in the supply chain. I have often wondered whether Commerce One would have survived if the economic recession following the dot-com collapse had not been quite as sudden or far-reaching.

Chapter 5
Private Marketplaces

There is an adventure tale you may have read called Ali Baba and the 40 Thieves. In the story, Ali Baba, is an honest man pursuing a career in woodcutting. One day Ali Baba overhears a group of forty thieves discussing a treasure cave that holds all of their gold and riches. The mouth of the cave is sealed by magic and only opens to the words "Open Sesame." One day when the thieves are gone, Ali Baba enters the cave to collect some of the treasure. He also shares the secret with his greedy brother who visits the cave to collect riches for himself. But, in his excitement, the brother forgets the magic words to get back out of the cave. He remains trapped in the cave until he is discovered by the thieves and killed. The rest of the story chronicles the thieves' attempts to track down the others who know the secret including Ali Baba. In the end all forty of the thieves are killed while Ali Baba's life is spared. He lives on being the only one who knows the secret of the treasure in the cave.

Why am I recounting this story? You probably assume that there is a message in here about the greed of the Internet pioneers who founded the B2B e-marketplaces. Perhaps there is. However, I included this reference because there is a company called Alibaba.com that developed a B2B e-marketplace in China. Surprisingly, Alibaba has enjoyed a very different outcome than the exchanges of the Silicon Valley dot-com era.

The Alibaba Story

One of the three primary propositions of the B2B e-marketplaces was the idea of online discovery. In Chapter 2, I compared this value proposition to online dating sites such as eHarmony or match.com. Suppliers seeking to sell their products and services to new customers listed their profiles online. Buyers in need of new sourcing options would browse these online profiles to find potential suppliers. Using these online directories, buyers would find the perfect matches for their needs. And the two would unite online, living happily ever after.

These online discovery services were not very successful in the US and Europe. Experts blamed the failures on the lack of appreciation for the cultural dynamics that exist in buyer-seller relationships. The theory was that buyers would never be comfortable purchasing goods from an anonymous source on the Internet without performing appropriate levels of diligence and relationship building. However, Alibaba.com has proved these theories to be untrue, at least in several regions of the world.

Alibaba allows Chinese suppliers to create online storefronts which list their products and services. Foreign and domestic buyers can search through these directories to identify potential suppliers. Alibaba.com currently offers a selection of 5,000 different product categories from 30 different industries.[65] There is no cost for suppliers to create storefronts to list their products. However, for an additional fee, suppliers can purchase a membership package which offers preferred placements in directories and search rankings. Buyers do not have to pay any fees. Alibaba is similar to Google in that suppliers can either pay for placements or compete in the natural search results. Alibaba generates all of its revenues from the approximately 1% of suppliers who pay for preferred listings associated with keywords.[66]

Unlike the B2B e-marketplaces of the dot-com era, Alibaba.com has been amazingly successful with online discovery. It has become the world's largest online B2B trading platform for small businesses, claiming 60 million registered users.[67] Alibaba consistently ranks as the most visited site in the Chinese "e-Commerce, Business and Trade segment." The company has expanded beyond its original international English language that was designed to unite Chinese exporters with Western buyers into four different marketplaces. There is a Chinese marketplace called www.1688.com for domestic B2B trade in China. There is a Japanese marketplace called www.alibaba.co.jp that focuses on Japan-related trade. Recently, the company also introduced www.aliexpress.com which allows smaller buyers to buy small quantities of goods at wholesale prices.

Grandfather of the Chinese Internet

Alibaba.com was founded by a man named Jack Ma, who is now known as the grandfather of the Chinese Internet. Alibaba was actually Ma's second attempt at an Internet-based supplier directory. His initial venture into the space, an online directory called China Pages, was quickly sold to China Telecom. He then took a job working for the Chinese government helping to resolve international trade disputes. In that role Ma traveled several times to the US.[68]

In 1995 Ma traveled to California to resolve a trade dispute between a Chinese firm and its US partner. The negotiations did not go well. Ma claims to have been held at gunpoint for two days before talking his way out of the situation. But from California, Ma traveled north to Seattle where he was first exposed to the Internet.[69] While visiting, one of his friends showed him how to perform a search on the web. Ma searched for Chinese beer, but found no results. Disappointed, but inspired, Ma had the idea to create a site which would help foreigners find Chinese companies on the Internet.[70]

With Alibaba, Ma views himself as the champion of small proprietors. Alibaba was founded on the premise that small businesses have a limited capability to develop customer and supplier relationships outside of their home territory. Small businesses represented 70% of the Chinese economy. Ma viewed helping small and medium businesses to grow as the next big wave of growth for China.[71]

The Alibaba.com site was originally launched in 1998 as an electronic bulletin board for businesses to trade leads. To support the growth, Ma raised $25 million from Goldman Sachs, Fidelity, and Japan's Softbank during the years 1999 and 2000. Alibaba became profitable in 2001. The growth continued until November of 2007 when the company raised $1.7 billion in its IPO on the Hong Kong Stock Exchange. At the time, Alibaba was one of the largest Internet IPOs ever, second only to Google.[72]

In addition to the various e-marketplace sites, Ma's empire holds a number of other assets. In October 2005, Alibaba took over the operation of Yahoo! China, which at the time was the second largest search engine in the world's most populous nation.[73] Why would Yahoo sell this asset? Yahoo was under heavy criticism for providing the Chinese government with access to the email accounts of two pro-democracy advocates. The advocates were tracked down and arrested by the Chinese government, creating a strong backlash against Yahoo in the international human rights community. Google withdrew from mainland China a few years later to avoid confrontations with the government over similar issues. For Alibaba, Yahoo! provided best-in-class search capabilities which were a critical component of any e-commerce function, B2B or B2C.

Where Discovery Works

Alibaba.com is not the only company that has enjoyed success with an online supplier discovery model in China. Global Sources, its primary competitor, has grown quickly as well. Global Sources is a $200 million company that was founded in 1970 as a trade publication focused on consumer products manufactured in Asia. Historically, Global Sources' primary business focused on printed directories of suppliers and exhibitions designed to match buyers with suppliers. Global Sources began to shift its strategy towards online marketplaces and catalogs in 1996. Much like Alibaba, it began to make supplier and product information available on the Internet. Global Sources' community includes 800,000 buyers and 200,000 suppliers, offering over 4 million products.[74]

Why are online discovery services so popular in China but struggling in the US and Western Europe? Is the value proposition provided by its online discovery site unique to China? Alibaba.com does not seem to think so. It has been expanding internationally, especially in the US. In July of 2010 it acquired its first American company—Vendio Services. Vendio offered technology to enable small businesses to sell through eBay and Amazon.com.[75] The following month Alibaba acquired Auctiva, a leading third-party developer of tools for eBay sellers. It does make you wonder why companies such as eBay, Google, and Amazon.com have not offered a similar service to Alibaba.[76]

Were the discovery ideas introduced in the late 1990s fundamentally flawed due to the unique purchasing dynamics within the United States? Or were they merely ahead of their time? I have posed this question to numerous industry insiders, but no one has a clear answer.

Before we end the discussion I should clarify that the name Alibaba does refer to the story of the forty thieves. Founder Jack Ma tells the story:

"One day I was in San Francisco in a coffee shop, and I was thinking Alibaba is a good name. And then a waitress came, and I said 'Do you know about Alibaba?', and she said 'Forty Thieves.' And I said, 'Yes, that is the name!' Then I went onto the street and found 30 people and asked them, 'Do you know Alibaba?' People from India, people from Germany, people from Tokyo and China... They all knew about Alibaba. Alibaba—forty thieves. Alibaba is not the thief. Alibaba is a kind, smart business person, and he helped the village. So...easy to spell, and globally known. Alibaba opens sesame for small- to medium-sized companies. We also registered the name Alimama, in case someone wants to marry us!"[77]

GE and the Private Marketplaces

In Chapter 2 we discussed the challenges confronted by the independent and consortia marketplaces of the dot-com era. But not all of the B2B e-marketplaces in the US and Western Europe failed. In fact, there was an entire category that grew rapidly starting in 2000. This third category of marketplaces was formed privately by individual corporations. For example, Walmart did not join any consortia. Instead, it continued to enhance its self-developed Retail Link portal that remains one of the leading B2B e-commerce platforms today. GE also developed its own private marketplaces. Although GE chose not to invest in the reverse auction model that FreeMarkets founder Glen Meakem championed back in 1994, GE quickly began to realize the disruptive potential the Internet could have on its business. In fact, during the last few years of Jack Welch's tenure as CEO at GE, e-business was one of his four strategic priorities for the company.

During GE's annual Operating Managers Meeting in January 1999, Welch announced a new initiative to his top 600 executives. It was called "Destroy your business.com." Welch feared that new market entrants would be able to cannibalize GE's existing businesses much as Amazon.com had done to Borders and Barnes & Noble. Each GE division was tasked with evaluating how a hypothetical Internet company could potentially take its market share. Once vulnerabilities were identified the businesses were tasked with designing pre-emptive strategies to defend their positions.[78]

As time progressed, Welch prioritized the e-business strategy stating that the Internet was "the biggest change I have seen at GE." Each GE division developed a website to display product catalogs and facilitate online orders. For example, GE Plastics created a transactional website that grew from $100 million in sales during 1999 to $1.2 billion in 2000. As time passed, GE determined that there was no credible threat to its businesses from new dot-com players. Consequently, GE shifted from reinventing its business model and refocused on using e-marketplaces to grow its existing business.[79] Additionally, GE embraced B2B e-commerce technology on the buy-side of its business. It deployed e-purchasing and reverse auction technologies with its suppliers. Perhaps, the most impressive accomplishment of GE's e-marketplace strategy was its placement atop Internet Week's "Internet 100 list."[80] There was a bit of irony in GE's recognition by Internet Week as it occurred in July of 2000 during the middle of the dot-com frenzy. GE, an iconic brand of the "old economy," was ranked above all the dot-com start-ups and high tech companies for its e-commerce programs.

There were a few aspects of GE's e-marketplace strategy that provided it with a competitive advantage. First, GE focused primarily on the sell-side of its business before migrating towards the buy-side. GE was centered on using the Internet to grow revenues, build customer relationships, and extend customer loyalty. Most other large companies had focused their e-marketplace strategies on the buy-side initially seeking to lower costs. Second, GE refused to join any of the independent or consortia e-marketplaces. For example, GE was invited to join the Omnexus e-marketplace founded by the plastics industry companies DuPont, Dow Chemical, BASF, and Bayer. But GE believed that no one should come between their relationships with their customers. Consequently, not only did GE not join consortia, but it did not list its products on independent marketplaces either.[81] The Global Healthcare Exchange was the only notable exception. GE, along with Johnson & Johnson and numerous other medical device companies, invested in a consortia marketplace to streamline the health care supply chain.

There were a number of advantages to the private marketplace strategy. GE and others that formed private marketplaces gained instant critical mass as their community of supply chain partners were immediate and captive participants. Additionally, most private marketplaces were built upon existing supply chain transaction systems rather than based upon completely new designs. As a result, these private marketplaces were integrated into legacy systems that already exchanged high volumes of data. Private marketplaces also had goals more aligned with the priorities of their end-users. The goals of private marketplaces were simply to improve supply chain efficiency rather than to generate transaction fees or grow towards an IPO. Funding was provided as part of the traditional IT budget rather than through the capital markets or external equity investments. Private marketplaces avoided many of the governance and intellectual property issues that hampered the independents and consortia. The buying hub could control the marketplace's roadmap and security of all transactions exchanged.

SECTION 3
The Retail Supply Chain

Chapter 6
VANs and Internet EDI

The first Walmart store opened in 1962 in Rogers, Arkansas. In the following years, Walmart expanded aggressively, not only in Arkansas, but in adjacent states, including Kansas, Louisiana, Missouri and Oklahoma. Ten years after its formation in 1972, Walmart became listed on the New York Stock Exchange. Following the IPO, the expansion continued into more states, including Tennessee, Kentucky, Mississippi and Texas. By 1979, Walmart had reached over $1 billion in sales, becoming the first company to reach the financial milestone in such a short period of time.[82]

Throughout the 1980s, Walmart continued to expand into more states and introduced new store formats. First was the warehouse-style Sam's Club in 1983. A few years later, Walmart introduced its first SuperCenter, combining its traditional discount stores with a grocery store.[83] By 1990, Walmart had become America's largest retailer, surpassing both Sears and K-Mart. The company then introduced its own private label brands, such as Sam's Choice and Ol' Roy. It expanded outside of the US, first into Mexico and then into Canada. In 1996, Walmart opened a joint venture in China. The following year, Walmart eclipsed $100 billion in annual sales. Its stock was added to the Dow Jones Industrial Average. International expansion efforts continued with the acquisition of ASDA Group in the UK during 1999. Shortly thereafter, Walmart took a minority stake in Seiyu, one of Japan's largest department store chains.[84]

By 2002, Walmart had nearly $220 billion in revenues, making it the world's largest corporation. Walmart was ranked number one on the Fortune 500 list, a position typically reserved for manufacturing and oil companies such as GM, Ford, GE, Exxon, Mobil, and Texaco. The company had a workforce of over 1 million employees. In fact, Walmart had grown so large that it represented 2.3% of the US Gross National Product.[85] Economists postulated that Walmart's ruthless pursuit of cost savings was driving so much efficiency across the US that it was effectively suppressing inflation. Independent studies found Walmart's Everyday Low Prices were saving consumers $20 billion per year.[86] A key part of its strategy was sourcing lower cost goods from overseas. In 2002, Walmart alone purchased $12 billion worth of Chinese merchandise representing 10% of all US imports from the Asian giant.[87]

Walmart's influence on the supply chain was unparalleled. In 2002 Walmart controlled 30% of the US market for products such as diapers and hair care as well as 20% of all toothpaste and pet food sales. Walmart was the dominant distribution channel for Hollywood record labels and movie studios. Between 15 to 20% of all CD, video, and DVD sales occurred through Walmart stores. With the rapid growth of its SuperCenters, Walmart became the nation's largest grocer with 19% market share. It was also expanding so quickly into new categories, like magazines and prescription drugs, that it had rapidly established 15% and 16% market shares respectively.[88]

Many of the largest consumer products companies were critically dependent upon Walmart for success. At the time, 28% of Dial Corporation's sales were through Walmart. Del Monte depended upon Walmart for 24% of revenues, and its expansive channels provided 23% of both Clorox and Revlon revenues.[89] The high concentration of revenues that Walmart owned gave the retail superpower unparalleled influence over its supplier community. Walmart was able to drive not only aggressive price discounts, but also demand its own unique packaging and product designs.

Walmart also had considerable influence over the technology standards used in the supply chain. The retailer was a significant driving force behind barcode labels in the 1980s. In 1983 Walmart was among the first retailers to use barcodes to speed up the checkout process. It also invested aggressively in barcode technology to track inventory in its warehouses and stockrooms. Walmart introduced its RetailLink web portal in 1992 to share inventory positions and sales trends with suppliers. In 1996 RetailLink was extended to the Internet many years before the idea for WorldWide Retail Exchange was even originated. In the early 2000s, Walmart was a key advocate of both RFID and data synchronization technologies that are explored in later chapters.[90]

AS2 and the Shot Heard 'Round the World

Perhaps the best example of Walmart's influence over technology in the supply chain was Internet-based EDI. On September 9th, 2002 Walmart announced that it had selected software from a small company called iSoft to power its new Internet-based EDI system.[91] This was the shot heard 'round the world in the EDI industry. The new Internet EDI technology, called AS2, would circumvent the VANs, enabling businesses to exchange transactions directly over the Internet. Walmart's announcement had catastrophic impacts to the EDI VAN business that had a virtual monopoly on supply chain B2B transactions for decades.

During the 1980s and 1990s, the public Internet was in its infancy and by no means a viable conduit for multi-million dollar B2B transactions. As a result specialized, private telecommunications networks were formed to enable companies to exchange B2B transactions. The first of these Value Added Networks (VANs) was launched in 1975 by a company called Telenet. It was considered the commercial equivalent of the Department of Defense's ARPA-Net which was the predecessor to the Internet. If two businesses needed to exchange data electronically during the 1980s and early 1990s, they shared the files over a VAN. The VANs were used for electronic bulletin boards, email messages, and EDI.

Retailers were some of the earliest and fastest adopters of EDI VANs. Grocery retailers that placed a high frequency of smaller orders needed a standardized mechanism for communicating with suppliers. Department stores and general merchandisers ordered less frequently but from a wider range of suppliers, creating a strong need for EDI transactions. There were two different EDI standards introduced for usage in the retail industry. In the US, the American National Standards Institute (ANSI) EDI set was launched. In Europe and Asia, the United Nations Electronic Data Interchange For Administration, Commerce and Transport (EDIFACT) standards were used.

Suppose a company such as Walmart, Carrefour or Metro needed to place an order for $1 million from a clothing supplier. Perhaps the order consists of an assortment of "basics" such as black socks and white t-shirts for the men's departments of its stores in the US. The merchandising team at the retailer first analyzes the various brands, colors, sizes, styles, prices, and packaging to select an appropriate assortment for their stores.

Once a decision is made to purchase a particular set of products from a vendor, the retailer issues a Purchase Order (PO). In the US, the PO is routed to the supplier as an ANSI 850 EDI transaction. The supplier assesses the quantities, timing and terms of the retailer's PO to determine if they have the capacity and resources to fulfill the request. If so, the supplier acknowledges the order using an EDI transaction called the 855. Buyers may adjust the order quantities or compositions later based upon changes to their sales forecasts. A Purchase Order Change will then be issued to the supplier in the form of an EDI 860 transaction.

The supplier then routes the confirmed order to its warehouse. For most basic products, apparel suppliers keep inventory on hand to fulfill retailer purchase orders. However, if sufficient inventory does not exist, then the supplier forwards the order to one of its manufacturing plants requesting that additional quantities be produced.

Once the goods have been packaged for delivery, the supplier forwards an Advanced Shipment Notice (ASN) to the retailer. The ASN—an EDI 856 transaction—provides details about the goods shipped such as the descriptions, quantities, weights and packaging configuration. The ASN will also provide an estimated delivery date and the name of the trucking company carrying the load. As the goods are transported the trucking company may provide a shipment status update electronically to the buyer and/or supplier. When the goods arrive at their final destination, the transportation carrier typically sends an electronic proof of delivery back to the supplier as a confirmation.

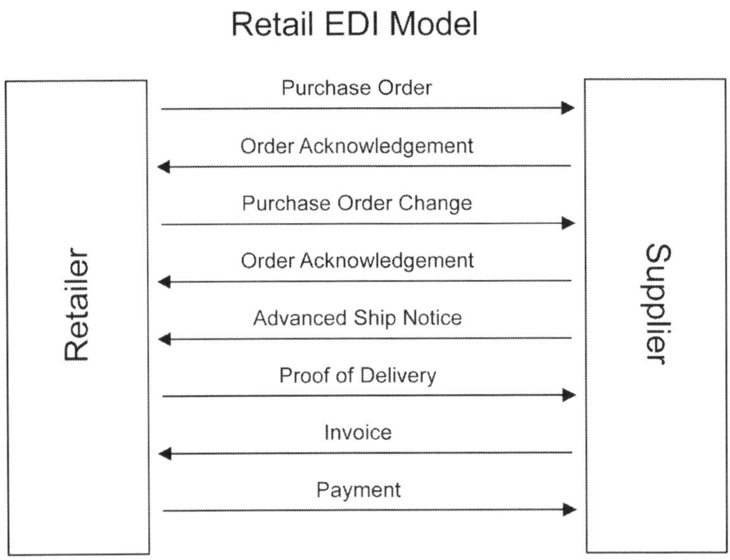

The process can be slightly more complex for goods manufactured overseas. In such a case, the EDI VAN might be used by the supplier to submit export declarations to its local customs agency. There are also EDI transactions that can be exchanged with ocean freight carriers to arrange for transportation of goods.

All of the transactions described including the product catalog, PO, PO acknowledgement, PO change and ASN were historically exchanged over VANs. AS2 enabled the same type of business processes between retailers and suppliers by transmitting the documents directly over the Internet rather than the specialized private network of the VAN.

A simple way to think about AS2 is that it emulates the way a web browser communicates with a webserver to support B2B communications. The "http" that you see preceding website addresses refers to Hypertext Transfer Protocol. HTTP is the transport protocol that all of the content in a website page is packaged into for distribution over the Internet. As you know from viewing web pages, HTTP can include video, audio, images, text, or games. The creators of AS2 said, "if web content can be stuffed into an HTTP communication, why not an EDI or XML message as well?"

AS2 Kills the VANs

Walmart's September 2002 announcement was a game changer because it effectively created a market for Internet-based substitutes to VANs. Walmart used its considerable purchasing power and supply chain influence to drive Internet EDI into its supplier community. However, Walmart's supplier community was so large and diverse that this effectively meant that much of the manufacturing industry needed to begin using Internet EDI.

Walmart suppliers found the technology to be inexpensive, highly reliable, and easy to use. A viral effect emerged in which suppliers began to ask other business partners to consider using AS2. The most prominent adopters of AS2 were other US retailers who quickly followed Walmart's lead in migrating towards the new standard. Meijer, Kohl's, Home Depot, and Lowes were among the first to embrace AS2. The phenomenon spread to Europe when Walmart introduced AS2 to the UK via its ASDA brand. Over the following years Carrefour, Tesco, Metro, Macys, Sears, and nearly every other major retailer in Western Europe and North America shifted traffic away from VANs to AS2.

In the late 1980s and early 1990s the EDI VAN sector was a big business backed by some of the world's largest companies. For example, IBM had a large EDI VAN called Information Exchange. GE's Information Services division had a VAN called EDI*Express. Each of the major telecommunications vendors including AT&T, MCI, Deutsche Telekom, France Telecom, and British Telecom had VANs. There also were smaller niche firms like Sterling Software and Harbinger that had developed EDI networks.

Even Sears launched a commercial VAN service called Sears Transport Electronic Data Interchange (STEDI) in 1989. Sears had been a significant user of EDI for 20 years through a proprietary network it developed called Senden. Sears new STEDI offering was not proprietary to Sears and its suppliers. It was open to anyone wishing to exchange EDI messages with one another.[92] It is hard to imagine the Sears we know today operating an EDI service, but in the late 1980s it was a diversified conglomerate whose reach extended far beyond retail stores. Sears owned the Allstate insurance business, the Coldwell Banker real estate business, the Dean Witter brokerage business, and the Discover credit card network. Prior to developing STEDI Sears was one of three founders of the Prodigy Internet dial-up service.

Herding the Geese

It is fair to say that most of the B2B e-commerce networks were caught off-guard by the rapid adoption of Internet-based connectivity models. Most of the B2B networks had not viewed AS2 or the other Internet-based communications protocols as a significant threat. Even in 2002 many of the VAN providers believed that the Internet was not a secure medium for electronic commerce. When I arrived at Global eXchange Services (GXS) in early 2004, the Internet was still viewed as a security threat and a distraction rather than a medium for business. The GXS IT organization had placed highly restrictive filtering on the websites that employees could view. For example, employees could not visit corporate websites from companies such as Disney, Walmart, or Ford Motor Company. The reasoning was that employees should not be shopping or surfing the web during business hours. Ironically, companies such as Disney, Walmart, and Ford were the target accounts to whom GXS was selling our EDI and B2B e-commerce services. Sales representatives who wanted to research their accounts could not even access to their company's website. Most of these unproductive policies were removed shortly after I arrived at the company by Gary Greenfield who was named CEO and President in 2003.

In 2002, GXS was headquartered in a large campus outside Rockville, Maryland. The building was reminiscent of those seen in nearby Washington, DC, with an architectural style similar to the Kennedy Center. In fact, scenes from the movie *Body of Lies* with Leonardo DiCaprio and Russell Crowe were filmed at the GXS headquarters in 2007. The resemblance to US government buildings made the location appealing to cinematographers. The interior looked like the basement of the Pentagon. The walls were covered with sea foam green colored wallpaper that was really brought to life by the fluorescent lighting throughout the building.

The grounds surrounding the facility included a large man-made lake that was home to a large flock of geese. All the employees complained about the geese because they would stand on the road blocking traffic. When you honked your horn, the geese would scatter in different directions or walk slowly to the other side of the street. The geese also painted the parking lot with a colorful array of their digestive by-products. Before I joined GXS, the company would pay for a dog to come chase the geese away from the roads and building.

In fact, the dog was the true inspiration for the name of this book. Professional "Geese Police" have become a big business at golf courses, school playgrounds and corporate campuses across the US, each of which is seeking to rid their grounds of these flocks.

When Bob Segert, the company's second post-GE CEO, joined in 2008, one of his top priorities was moving to a new headquarters building, which GXS has occupied since 2010. Needless to say, it took a few years to find another tenant for our former quarters. Prior to joining the company I had a great deal of respect for GE. However, I was mystified by some of the business practices that had been institutionalized during the GE ownership period of GXS. For example, there was a Six Sigma project initiated to determine how GXS could reduce Accounts Payable (AP) costs. Analysis revealed that the most frequent calls into the AP Call Center were customers inquiring about how to cancel their services. The study concluded that these calls should be routed to Customer Service, not AP. A solution was devised which reduced the volume of inbound calls to AP thereby allowing for staffing reductions. Printed at the bottom of each GXS invoice in large font were instructions on "How to Cancel Your EDI Service." There's no greater return on investment than making it easy for your customers to leave!

As can be seen from the examples above, the EDI VANs were hardly blazing a trail of innovation when AS2 and Internet alternatives emerged. AS2 is a classic example of an Internet technology that disrupted industries and transformed traditional business models. Of course the EDI VAN sector was not the only industry impacted by the Internet.

The Melting Ice Cubes

In 1999, Napster disrupted the traditional music distribution business with its free, peer-to-peer file sharing applications. A few years later, Apple transformed the music industry again with a legitimate paid download model based upon its iPod device. As a result music retailers like Tower Records experienced dramatic sales declines which ultimately led to their insolvency.

In recent years, startups such as Netflix and Redbox have created a similar disruptive effect in the video rental market. A significant percentage of consumers have switched to mail-order subscriptions, kiosk rentals, and Internet downloads for movie watching. As a result, multi-billion dollar chains, like Blockbuster Video, have fallen into bankruptcy and liquidation.

The Internet has also disrupted the book publishing industry. Online book sellers like Amazon.com emerged in the late 1990s offering significant discounts on books that could be shipped in 2-3 days from a network of distribution centers around the world. More recently the introduction of e-books, read through devices such as the Kindle or the Nook, has caused even further market disruption. Book retailers like Borders have been forced into bankruptcy or liquidation.

The newspaper industry experienced similar challenges due to the Internet. Advertising revenues plummeted when online sites such as Craig's List started listing classified ads and eBay began directly auctioning goods. Subscription revenues also suffered with the availability of free news sites on the Internet. The Tribune Company, the Minneapolis Star Tribune, and Philadelphia Newspapers have all filed bankruptcy in the past few years. Other newspapers such as the Detroit Free Press, the Seattle Post-Intelligencer, and the San Francisco Chronicle have made significant cut backs to avoid insolvency.[93]

Similar transformations have occurred in film and photography space. The popularity of digital cameras and photo-sharing websites has been devastating to companies like Kodak and Fuji. The shift to digital led to rapid declines in film sales and photo processing services.

The investment banking communities refer to business models such as newspapers, CDs, video rentals, book stores, and photo finishing services as "melting ice cubes." The metaphor refers to the inevitable demise of business models that have been disrupted by new technologies entering the market.

Perhaps, the best example of a melting ice cube in the technology sector was the Internet Service Providers (ISPs) sector. Most ISPs in the late 1990s were dependent upon dial-up connections to provide consumers with access to content. At its peak, AOL was the largest ISP with 30 million members. But in the early 2000s telecom providers, cable companies, and satellite television providers began to offer low-cost broadband access to consumers.[94] For the same price as dial-up service, consumers could access the Internet at speeds up to 100 times faster.

No company suffered more from the emergence of broadband than

AOL. After growing at exponential rates in the 1990s, the company began to struggle in 2001 with the growing perception that dial-up connectivity was slow and cumbersome. AOL's competitors also criticized the company for not providing consumers with access to the "real Internet." AOL had developed a "walled garden" model that was designed to keep the majority of its users engaged in its own content versus that of third-party websites. It is hard to imagine a time when Internet users would willfully submit to a closed community with applications managed by a single company. Today, we call this model Facebook.

In my opinion, no other company was in a better position in 2004 to develop a social networking platform like Facebook than AOL. However, AOL chose a different path pursuing new advertising-centric business models and attempting to salvage its subscription business with broadband-based offerings. Neither approach has been particularly effective as the company now counts just over 5 million subscribers. However, it is possible to keep a melting ice cube from evaporating even though the heat is rising. But the focus must shift from selling just ice cubes to the need of keeping drinks cold.

Consider the market trends in some of the categories described previously. It is not that book sales have declined. Today consumers are reading more books than ever. The difference is they are buying the books through a broader range of channels (online and in store) and reading them in different formats (both digital and print). People are not taking fewer pictures. Instead consumers are taking more photos than ever. Today pictures are captured on new devices (smart phones and digital cameras) and shared via different formats (both online and print).

Borders, Blockbuster, and Tower Records failed to change from their traditional retail formats fast enough to avoid bankruptcy. Others like Kodak and AOL have managed to shift their models, but not quickly enough to cash in on most of the growth from new digital channels. Most newspapers have failed to find sustainable business models based upon digital content which has led to numerous bankruptcies. However, *The Wall Street Journal's* subscriber base has actually increased in recent years, illustrating it is possible to reverse the trend in declining industries.

Get Off the VAN

Most analysts would place the EDI VAN sector in the category of a melting ice cube. In fact, in 2002 experts predicted that EDI VANs would be dead by the year 2010, if not 2005. However, the EDI VAN business is still a $1 billion sector in the year 2012. Only one EDI VAN declared bankruptcy in the period between 2000 and the publication of this book—Peregrine and its bankruptcy was unrelated to distress in the EDI VAN sector. Peregrine was charged with massive accounting fraud by the SEC in 2003.

Another interesting fact is that no companies grew big by replacing the EDI VAN. The companies that most aggressively promoted AS2 were two startups called iSoft and Cyclone Commerce. Most have never heard of either of these companies because neither went public. Neither of the companies were the target of a big acquisition by IBM, Microsoft, Oracle, or SAP. iSoft was acquired by nuBridges in May of 2006.[95] NuBridges was a company formed by the spinoff of MCI's EDI VAN. Cyclone Commerce was acquired by an integration software company called Axway for an undisclosed sum.[96]

Despite the disruptive effect caused by AS2 and other new Internet technologies, the B2B industry never produced an Amazon.com, iTunes nor a Netflix. There were no $1 billion Internet-based B2B e-commerce companies to emerge from the Internet era. There were no $100 or $50 million companies to emerge either. As discussed in Chapter 2, most of the B2B e-marketplaces failed. Those that did survive have not grown to more than $50 million in revenues.

Ten years later there are still several VANs which generate $100 million or more in revenue. And there are still B2B e-commerce companies such as Hubspan running marketing campaigns encouraging customers to "Get off the VAN."[97] So how is it that the VANs managed to survive?

Most retailers started their AS2 programs with their top 20 suppliers. These larger suppliers such as P&G, Nestle, Kraft Foods, and Kimberly Clark quickly switched their traffic off EDI VANs to a direct Internet connection. Having met with great success for the top 20 suppliers, retailers then moved to the next tier of business partners. A new set of challenges emerged with the second and third tier suppliers, particularly with smaller companies. Many of these smaller companies did not have the budget, skills, or resources to establish an AS2 infrastructure. In order to switch off the VAN these companies needed to purchase AS2 software as well as a server to run the technology. Additionally, the suppliers needed to hire someone with AS2 skills or send their EDI manager to training courses. As a result, many suppliers put up a type of passive resistance. These business partners did not say "No," but used stall tactics to delay a switch to AS2.

Not all small suppliers avoided AS2. Some were already using AS2, particularly those that sold to Walmart and were forced to adopt the technology. These AS2 users formed a second wave in AS2 adoption. The net effect of the first two waves of adoption was a yield of 20% of suppliers switching to AS2. These 20% of suppliers were the biggest users which represented an impressive 80% of overall transaction volume. But, convincing the remaining 80% of the suppliers to switch from the VAN to AS2 proved quite challenging. Some retailers simply gave up, satisfied that they had significantly reduced VAN fees. Other retailers persisted with the AS2 rollout. Slowly but surely they would get another 5% of the supplier community to adopt annually.

Cream Skimming

The software vendors who promoted AS2 were satisfied with the outcome. They were able to deliver 80% of the value from 20% of the effort. Similar "cream skimming" or "cherry picking" practices have emerged in other types of networks when a new group of competitors entered the sector. For example, in the 1980s when the US Airline industry was de-regulated, many of the new market entrants focused only on the most lucrative, highest volume routes. Whereas the traditional airlines strived to build the broadest network with widest reach, many new startups focused only on transporting passengers between Boston and New York; Los Angeles and San Francisco; or Houston and Dallas. These routes have consistently high demand patterns allowing for a predictable cost structure. New airlines could simply undercut the incumbent airline operators' prices to quickly gain market share. The result was that legacy airlines had to compete more vigorously for the most popular routes and at considerably lower margins. They also had to continue to fund expensive operations in less populated regions to maintain the breadth of their networks.

Similar models emerged in the telecommunications sector that was deregulated in the US during the 1990s. Telecommunications vendors were required by the government to provide "universal service." Every household, even in rural, hard-to-reach areas, had to be wired to ensure equitable access for all. However, competitors who entered the telecom sector following deregulation did not have a universal service requirement. Instead, these new startups could focus on acquiring the lucrative customers in the highest areas of density. There was an influx of new telecommunications providers that targeted metropolitan areas such as New York City and Los Angeles. These telecom providers simply wired a line to a large office or apartment complex then sold discounted services to tenants of the buildings. For the relatively low cost investment of establishing high capacity lines to densely populated regions, telecom providers could cherry pick the best customers. Meanwhile, the legacy telecom vendors had to continue to service customers in rural, low density areas such as farms or forested regions. In response, the government established a "Universal Service Fee" that is collected from all customers to cross-subsidize the legacy telecom providers and fairly compensate them for continuing to provide service to less densely populated regions.

The cream skimming phenomenon emerged in the airline, telecom, and B2B e-commerce industries because new entrants learned that it was very time-consuming and expensive to build a large network. Instead, these new competitors achieved a higher return on investment by simply picking off the most trafficked links and allowing the remainder of transactions to stay on the legacy networks. As it turns out the value proposition of the VAN was not the ability to electronically interconnect two companies. The Internet enabled such connections. The true "Value Add" from the VAN was that it provided retailers with a simple way to reach tens of thousands of suppliers through a single connection.

Retailers benefit from the same principles in the area of credit card processing. There are millions of retailers around the world that accept credit cards as forms of payment. Most people refer to the cards in their wallets by the brand name of Visa or MasterCard. However, Visa and MasterCard just refer to the network utilized. The actual credit is being issued by a bank. If the borrower defaults on payment obligations it will be the issuing bank, not Visa or MasterCard that is responsible for reimbursing the affected parties. There are tens of thousands of issuing banks around the world. Some of the bigger ones might include Citigroup, Chase, HSBC, and BNP Paribas.

Imagine if Visa and MasterCard did not exist. In order for retailers to accept a credit card as a form of payment they would have to establish direct connections with the tens of thousands of issuing banks that sponsor the cards. Most retailers are small- and medium-sized businesses and lack the resources to establish secure connections with tens of thousands of banks. Without a network like Visa or MasterCard acting as an intermediary, the option to use a credit card as payment would be limited to very large retailers. *Note: Retailers using Visa and MasterCard actually connect to a "merchant-acquirer" bank rather than directly to the card networks. But there are still tens of thousands of acquiring banks creating the same need for a network.*

The Network Effect

The value proposition created by Visa and MasterCard is an example of a concept that economists refer to as "the network effect." The principle is best described through "Metcalfe's Law," which states, Network Value = n^2 (where n refers to the number of participants on the network)[98]

If there are 1000 participants in a network, then the maximum number of other members that each participant can connect to is 999. The number of total potential connections is equal to the 1000 members times the 999 connections that each member can connect to. 1000 times 999 is approximately 1000 squared or n squared.

Venture capitalists and entrepreneurs fell in love with Metcalfe's Law due to its economic applications. Metcalfe's Law asserts that in order for networks to deliver value, a certain critical mass needs to be achieved. But once that inflection point is reached, the value of the network grows exponentially while costs remain linear. The concept makes sense if you apply it to telephony networks, instant messaging or today's social networks. A network with 1, 10, 100, 1000 people is of limited value. But once an instant messaging or phone system or social network becomes connected to hundreds of thousands, if not millions of people, the utility is significantly increased.

Social Networks—Facebook, Friendster, MySpace, LinkedIn and Twitter—have grown principally due to the benefits of network effects. Significant incremental value is created with each new friend that is added. These sites have proven to be a good source for new relationships, new jobs and networking opportunities.

Wikipedia offers another good example. Over 16 million articles have been published collaboratively to Wikipedia by volunteers around the world. The more contributors author content and publish new articles, the more the site becomes a preferred destination for neutral, crowdsourced information.

During the dot-com era, Metcalfe's Law became an article of faith with entrepreneurs, venture capitalists and stock market analysts. Network effects offered a quantitative justification for all types of new strategies such as "build it and they will come," "first mover advantage" and "Internet time." Metcalfe's Law has been described as one of the most "dangerously influential" concepts of the dot-com era as it drove a mad rush for growth and a neglect for profitability.[99]

There were a few lucky dot-com startups that were able to benefit from network effects. Consider the case of eBay. The value of its online marketplace grew dramatically as the number of buyers and sellers on the site increased. A reinforcing network effect was clearly experienced in the site's auction capabilities. The more bidders there were for a particular item, the higher price that could be achieved, which attracted more sellers. The broader the range of merchandise available for sale, the more buyers joined the site. However, there were only a handful of winners, such as eBay, AOL and Amazon.com that emerged successful from the dot-com bust and thousands of others that failed.

Should We Blame Metcalfe?

Robert Metcalfe was the original inventor of the Ethernet protocol. He spent his early career working at Harvard University and at the Xerox Palo Alto Research Center (PARC), where many other technology innovations, such as the Graphical User Interface (GUI) and laser printing, were conceived. Metcalfe went on to found the networking equipment vendor 3Com in 1979. 3Com became a leading supplier of switches, routers and wireless access points growing to over $1 billion in revenues before being acquired by HP in April 2010. Following the launch of 3Com, Metcalfe remained in the technology sector as a venture capitalist and the publisher of the magazine, InfoWorld.[100] The interesting part about Metcalfe's Law is that although he postulated the concept of network effects in the 1980s, it was another person, George Gilder, who institutionalized the concept and named it.

Despite the enthusiasm about Metcalfe's Law in the technology sector, there remain many skeptics. You can find numerous essays on the Internet about why Metcalfe's Law is Wrong. Critics find fault with the assertion that all new network connections have an equal value. In many person-to-person or business-to-business networks, certain groups of members may add no new value at all.[101] For example, suppose you connected a community of 200 million Mandarin-speaking Chinese members with a community of 50 million English-speaking Americans in a social network. Although these groups may share common interests the language barriers prohibit the realization of benefits. In the B2B e-commerce sector, connecting a network of apparel manufacturers with a community of grocery retailers may have limited value as the two groups do not buy and sell from one another. So there is something to be said of quality versus quantity in network connections.

Critics also state that the value of a network cannot continue indefinitely. At some point the network becomes over-saturated or overwhelmed with noise. In other words, there is a point at which negative network effects begin to emerge and new entrants do not offer a noteworthy benefit. Consider file-sharing networks such as Kazaa or Napster. At some point all of the popular music and movies on the market will be available on the network and new users will contribute very little.[102]

Another limitation of networks is caused by clustering. In other words, most members consistently use only a subset of the relationships and network services available to them.[103] Most Facebook users interact with a relatively small percentage of the overall community, shielding their status updates from the majority of members. Clustering dampens the network effect in B2B e-commerce. Most buyers and sellers only interact with business partners with which they have pre-existing relationships.

There have been attempts by thought leaders to alter the formula behind Metcalfe's Law to more accurately represent the true benefits of network effects. However, there has been no agreement on the best way to represent the value of network growth. There does seem to be universal consensus of the fact that the value of a network does grow at a nonlinear rate after reaching critical mass. The question is how fast? The answer is somewhere between linear and quadratic growth.

The network effect can be observed in most of the B2B e-commerce scenarios we will review throughout the book. For example, the reverse auctions discussed in Chapter 2 can benefit from the network effect. The price savings that can be obtained through a reverse auction are dependent upon the number of participants. If only the two to three largest suppliers in a particular category participate in a reverse auction there will not be much benefit. These suppliers have little to gain by undercutting one another's price. However, if a group of 10 or more suppliers bid in the auction then the odds of significant price reductions increases. Ideally, such reverse auctions would include some smaller players seeking to aggressively capture market share through price concessions.

E-procurement vendors can also benefit from network effects in the supplier discovery process. Ideally, buyers would like a choice of a few different vendors in each purchasing category since competition leads to better choice and price. An e-procurement network with 500,000 suppliers like Ariba will have substantially more value than a network with 50,000 or 5,000 suppliers.[104]

VANs are Dead. Long Live the VANs.

There are no EDI VAN companies today. While several companies still operate large VANs, none depend on these networks as a standalone business. Most of the owners of VANs have a broader portfolio of B2B software and outsourcing services. In other words, these companies are focused on keeping the drinks cold not just making the ice cubes.

For example, Sterling Commerce, now owned by IBM, made significant investments in its B2B software portfolio. Sterling grew to over $600 million in revenue, approximately half of which was derived from sales of software to corporate IT organizations.[105] EasyLink, another large EDI VAN operator, expanded its network to allow companies to exchange information in a variety of formats. Not only could businesses exchange EDI documents, but they could also send faxes and telex.

GXS shifted its focus beyond just operating a VAN to a variety of services that help to make a company's B2B programs more successful. Whether exchanging information directly over the VAN or Internet protocols like AS2, GXS helps with onboarding of business partners, translating data from EDI to XML standards, and providing technical support for end-users. Although most large companies are not expanding the use of traditional VAN services, the number of businesses using the GXS EDI network continues to be a significant factor in selecting a B2B e-commerce provider.

Chapter 7
XML and B2B Standards

You may have guessed by now that if there is an AS2 there must have been an AS1. You would be correct. AS1 was the first in a series of four Internet-based communications protocols introduced by the Internet Engineering Task Force (IETF). In simple terms, AS1 emulated the technology used to send email messages between individuals, but for the purposes of exchanging EDI documents instead. AS1 caught the industry's attention, but it was not until AS2 that the concept of EDI over the Internet really gathered meaningful adoption.

There was also an AS3. Although AS3 followed AS2, it was not meant to be a replacement or successor. AS3 attempted to harmonize the many different flavors of a standard called FTP or File Transfer Protocol. FTP is the most popular protocol for transmitting B2B e-commerce transactions. It is not used as much in the retail industry as it is in manufacturing, banking, and other sectors. FTP was invented back in 1971, but its popularity peaked in the 1990s when Internet protocols became mainstream networking standards. During the course of its history there have been numerous derivatives of FTP created.

Much of the justification for these various different flavors of FTP is that the plain old version of FTP is actually not very secure. All data being transferred via FTP is in "clear text." That means that a hacker monitoring network traffic could potentially view the information being transmitted. To solve the problem, the industry created a series of "secure" FTP protocols.

The secure variants of FTP include "Secure" FTP (SFTP) which uses the Secure Shell (SSH) protocol. However, SFTP should not be confused with FTP over SSH, which is a different protocol. Sometimes the "S" is used after the letters "FTP" to form "FTPS." However, it is necessary to determine whether it is referring to "implicit" or "explicit" versions of FTPS. Plain old FTP can also be used with something called PGP which stands for "Pretty Good Privacy."

One of my favorite FTP derivatives is called 9P that refers to the Plan 9 Filesystem Protocol. It is also referred to as Styx, not to be confused with the 1980s band. Plan 9 is used by the Inferno operating system which I suspect is the brains referred to in the song, "*Mister Roboto.*" In addition to the many FTP "standards," there are also 150 different software packages that enable you to use FTP. My favorites are the ones with funny names such as Filezilla, cURL, Captain FTP, cuteFTP, CyberDuck, Fetch, and Yummy FTP.

Confused yet? Imagine a small business whose customer asks if the business can send EDI transactions via FTP. How confusing would it be to determine to which version of FTP the customer is referring? An Internet search would reveal that there more variants of FTP than there are flavors of Baskin Robbins ice cream. Two business partners that agree to exchange information using FTP have not really reached any agreement at all.

Unfortunately, AS3 failed to achieve any meaningful adoption. Among GXS's 40,000 customers I am not aware of a single one who has seriously entertained using AS3 for B2B communications. An AS4 has also been introduced to standardize another Internet protocol called SOAP. But thus far, AS4 has not been successful in cleaning up the protocol mess either.

FTP is just one example of the proliferation of standards that has occurred in the B2B e-commerce sector. In the past 10 years there have been hundreds of XML standards introduced each with the goal of replacing EDI. XML promised to offer unparalleled flexibility to model new transaction types and business processes. Throughout the 1970s and '80s B2B e-commerce standards were managed by a small group of government agencies and industry associations, such as the American National Standards Institute and the United Nations. What effectively occurred during the dot-com era was a democratization of standards. The power to create B2B e-commerce standards shifted from a few centralized organizations to a new group of non-profit organizations which I like to call the dot-orgs.

The dot-orgs brought capitalism to the standards development process. Soon different standards were competing with one another for market attention. The dot-orgs took a different approach to the market than the prior generation of government committees. Rather than developing mass market standards, such as EDI that could be used across multiple industries, the dot-orgs introduced dozens of new XML-based standards designed to meet the specialized needs of different vertical industries. There was the Petroleum Industry Data Exchange (PIDX) standard that allowed manufacturers of oil exploration and production equipment to share catalogs with customers. A dot-org named RosettaNet introduced a new set of XML standards to the semiconductor and high tech industry. The Chemicals Industry Data Exchange (CIDX) standard was developed to support the chemicals supply chain. Even the paper companies, that you would think would have a vested interest in not using electronic documents, created a new standard called papiNet.

B2B e-commerce standards were being developed not just for major industries, but for specific sub-sectors within industries as well. The US National Association of Convenience Stores (NACS) developed a set of standards specifically for convenience chain retailers to exchange product catalogs, price books and invoices electronically with their suppliers. NACS' Petroleum Convenience Alliance for Technology Standards (PCATS) XML offers specific business templates for managing unique processes to support state lottery tickets and motor fuel purchases.[106]

Perhaps, my favorite new standard to be introduced in the past 10 years was Shortsea XML. Short sea refers to shipping that occurs between points on the same continent. Short sea vessels are preferable to trucks because they lower carbon emissions, alleviate road congestion and reduce transportation costs. Some short sea shipping occurs via inland waterways on rivers, such as the Mississippi, the Yangtze or the Rhine. Other short sea shipping occurs around the coastal perimeter of continents. For example, a cargo barge might travel from Lisbon to Rotterdam or Melbourne to Sydney. Shortsea XML is a messaging standard specifically designed for the ocean lines, agents, ports and manufacturers that utilize this fast growing mode of transportation. Customers wishing to utilize short sea shipping can utilize the XML standard to view shipping schedules; book orders with carriers; submit cargo documentation; track in-transit cargo and view damage reports.[107] Why can't the short sea shippers use the same EDI standards that the long sea ocean liners, air cargo, rail and ground transportation companies use? That is a good question.

Betamax versus VHS

B2B e-commerce is not the only industry to experience competition between different standards organizations. One of the most studied standards wars in the history of business occurred in the home entertainment industry during the 1980s between Betamax and VHS. Although Beta was introduced to the market first and offered superior picture quality, it quickly was displaced by VHS. Beta's 100% market share in 1975 was reduced to less than 25% by 1981.[108]

One of the key factors behind VHS success was its distribution channel. JVC which developed the VHS technology licensed it to other consumer electronics manufacturers much more aggressively than Sony licensed Beta.[109] With many different manufacturers pushing VHS-format machines into the market, more competition emerged. Competition leads to lower prices which make the devices more appealing to consumers. Lower prices had a self-reinforcing effect. Lower prices led to increased sales volume that enabled higher economies of scale in manufacturing.

Another key differentiator that drove consumers towards the VHS format was the longer recording time. Sony Betamax for the US market could only record up to one hour. While one hour may be suitable for a TV sitcom, it is too short to record a typical Hollywood movie or an NFL football game. VHS was willing to compromise picture quality in exchange for extended recording times. Sony refused to extend the recording length of its tapes, thinking that consumers were more concerned about the picture quality.

The availability of extended play attracted the attention of the movie studios, which began to release hundreds of films onto home video. The films were originally priced prohibitively. To purchase a single movie originally cost as much as $89.99. As a result, the rental industry for videos boomed by offering a lower-cost mechanism for consumers to watch movies at home. However, the rental shops had to choose whether to stock Beta, VHS or both. With VHS growing in popularity and offering lower price points, it became the choice for most rental chains. By 1986 Beta's market share was less than 10%. The battle continued until 1998, when Sony conceded and began to sell its own branded

VHS machines.[110]

In addition to the VHS format created by JVC and the Betamax format created by Sony, there were other early contenders for the original home video standard. Philips introduced Video 2000 which had tapes that could be flipped over to extend playing time.[111] Sanyo introduced V-Cord which had a sideways-loading mechanism for tapes.[112] There was also "The Great Time Machine" from Quasar which was based upon a VX format.[113] Unfortunately, the VX home video standard floundered, but an extremely toxic nerve agent with the same name remains a popular choice for chemical weapons.

Another series of format wars occurred just recently in the high-definition home video sector between HD DVD and Blu-ray. The battle was started over which home video format would accompany the rapidly growing high-definition television market. Both sides agreed that a divided market with two dominant technology formats would stunt growth and frustrate consumers. As a result, the two camps began negotiations towards a converged standard. However, before an agreement could be reached, the market picked a winner. Companies, such as Target, Blockbuster, Warner Brothers, Netflix, Best Buy and Walmart, began to shift exclusively to Blu-ray. Shortly thereafter Toshiba stopped development of HD-DVD in February 2008, effectively conceding the battle.[114]

In between the HD DVD-Blu-ray battles and the VHS-Betamax war there were several other smaller scale conflicts. For example, you may remember the DVD versus DIVX battle. DIVX refers to the Digital Video Express format created by Circuit City. DIVX allowed consumers to purchase a DVD which could be played in a home player, but with limited viewing rights. Consumers would pay $4 for a DIVX which could be watched for a 48-hour period after purchase.[115] To extend viewing time, consumers could watch the video again by paying a continuation fee. The DIVX machines required connections to a phone line to authorize continuations. At the time many consumers thought the idea of connecting their home video machine to the Internet just to watch a movie was ludicrous. Today, millions of consumers are streaming Netflix rentals through Internet connected video game consoles and set-top boxes.

CDs versus Internet Downloads

The music industry also has experienced similar format wars. In the early days of records back in the 1920s, the 78 Revolutions Per Minute (RPM) album became the dominant standard. However, the 78 had to battle with various other speeds between 72 and 96 RPM before becoming effectively a standard. In the 1940s, slower speed technology was introduced to phonographs. The 33 1/3 RPM, 12-inch format was introduced which allowed for four to five tracks to be recorded on each side of an album. The 45 RPM, 7-inch format replaced 78s as the preferred format for singles.

During the 1970s, the 8-track tape emerged as a popular format. The 8-track format was quickly abandoned with the introduction of the cassette, which gained majority market share throughout the 1980s. However, cassettes peacefully co-existed on the shelves of music stores for some time along with records and the newly introduced CD format. CDs quickly gained dominance in the 1990s, while cassettes were relegated to use primarily for "mix tapes."

Today CDs are facing rapidly declining sales due to competition from purely digital formats such as MP3. But while MP3 is the most widely known audio file format, it is only one of many. There are at least 50 popular audio file formats in use today by online music sites. There are a few legitimate reasons why multiple digital music formats exist. For example, the music files on your iPod are not the original studio recordings created by the artist. The original recordings are compressed into smaller files so that more can be stored on a 16GB or 32GB device. Some audiophiles prefer to have access to the original uncompressed recording files. The industry has also created a middle tier that it calls "lossless" compression.

That explains the need for at least three different formats—uncompressed, compressed lossless and compressed lossy. But why do we need the 47 others? These standards do not exist to satisfy the different needs of consumers. The primary beneficiaries are the record labels, online music stores, software developers and hardware device manufacturers. Each has their own favorite format.

Is the existence of different file formats a hindrance to most consumers? Not really. The popular software players for audio content, such as RealPlayer, Apple's iTunes and Windows Media Player, each support a diverse range of standards. Open your Windows Media Player on your PC and scroll through the list of supported file formats for video and audio content. You will see a list that includes MP3; MP4; MPEG; AVI (video); CDA (CD audio); AIF (AIFF); WAV (wave sounds); WMA (Windows Media Audio File Format); WMV (Windows Media Video File Format) and MOV (QuickTime Movie Format). These are just a few of the many different digital audio and video formats in widespread use around the world.

It is interesting to note that while physical music media such as CDs, records, cassettes converged to one or two single dominant standards during most periods, the exact opposite has happened with audio formats on the Internet. There has been an explosion in competing standards introduced to the market, but with minimal inconvenience or confusion to consumers. Similarly, physical video media such as DVDs and VHS converged to a dominant standard over most periods, but the exact opposite has happened with video formats on the Internet. The technology introduced in the Internet era has enabled industries to support a much wider base of standards than were traditionally possible.

EDI and Darwin

So in many respects the evolution of B2B e-commerce standards has followed a similar path to audio and video standards in the home entertainment industry. Both have proliferated in the Internet era. However, one major difference between B2B e-commerce versus the home entertainment industry is that the new B2B standards have not rendered the old ones obsolete.

VHS and Betamax battled for domination during the 1980s. Both became irrelevant with the picture quality enhancements introduced by DVD. The DVD had a relatively short lifespan of less than 10 years before being upended by the Blu-ray format. And today the retail shelf space devoted to both DVDs and Blu-ray is quickly disappearing as on-demand Internet or cable alternatives become more popular.

However, in the B2B e-commerce sector a different phenomenon has occurred. In B2B it is the legacy standards and older technology that continue to dominate the market. For example, recent studies have shown that EDI continues to represent more than 80% of all B2B e-commerce transactions. Few would argue that the newer XML standards are not technologically superior. However, adoption of XML remains relatively low. The continued dominance of standards such as EDI is a topic that mystifies outsiders to the B2B industry. People cannot comprehend how a technology dinosaur has managed to remain so popular and prevalent through an era that has witnessed the birth of unprecedented levels of disruptive technology. If Charles Darwin were alive today, he might enjoy studying the characteristics that have led to EDI's survival, despite the introduction of genetically-superior species to its ecosystem.

There are several factors that have led to the continued prevalence of EDI over XML. First, EDI is mature. It has been in use for over 40 years, resulting in its reputation as a proven, reliable, mission-critical technology among its widespread users. EDI is ubiquitous. EDI had the advantage of being the only B2B standard in the supply chain for almost two decades. During that time, EDI became pervasive in a number of industries, such as manufacturing, high tech, automotive and retail, as well as segments of banking and health care. As a result, companies that choose to utilize EDI have a high level of confidence that their business partners will be able to receive their documents. By contrast, businesses that try to standardize on XML face significant headwinds, as their entire business partner community must become XML-enabled.

EDI is working well and has been for several decades, which begs the question, "Why fix what is not broken?" EDI is successfully supporting mission-critical processes for many of the world's largest companies. Corporations need a compelling business benefit to migrate to XML. The business plan would need to account not only for the expense to perform a migration, but also the opportunity cost as compared to other alternative investments.

One way to think about the competition between EDI and XML is to compare it to the ongoing battle between the metric and imperial (English) system in the US. The metric system is much easier to learn and use as it is grounded in the base 10 system. As a result, all but three countries including the US have switched to metric units of measurement. There would be significant benefits to international trade for such a conversion. Nonetheless, the US has continued its use of the legacy imperial standards.

There was actually an Act of Congress passed in 1975 that officially enacted the change to metric.[116] However, the conversion process was voluntary with no definitive timeframe. Education was the primary means used to influence private sector adoption. In the early 1980s, during the Reagan administration, the metrication process was abandoned completely.[117] There have been a few attempts at revival such as the Omnibus Trade and Competitiveness Act of 1988 that stipulated the metric system as the preferred model for US trade and commerce.[118]

In effect both systems are being used in parallel within the US today. Speed limits are listed in miles per hour. Lumber is sold with 2-inch by 4-inch cross-sections. Television screens are sold with diagonal measurements of 50 inches. Airplane altitudes are 30,000 to 35,000 feet. However, Americans regularly purchase two liter bottles of Coke from the store. Film for cameras is sold in 35 mm format. Wine is sold in 750 milliliter bottles. The 100 meter dash and 5 kilometer races are very popular track events. Even the drug dealers are going metric, as cocaine is typically distributed in kilos.

There is a definitive economic impact from the US decision to not standardize on the metric system. Any US company that exports goods or services must maintain two systems to support its domestic and international operations. Furthermore, any company importing to the US, whether in China, Japan, Korea, Canada, Mexico or Europe, has to maintain dual systems in manufacturing plants. Goods produced for US consumption must be labeled and packaged in standardized imperial sizes.

In addition to the inefficiencies created through management of two parallel systems, the use of two measurement standards creates opportunities for error in both industry and government. For example, the dual measurement systems caused the destruction of the Mars Climate Orbiter spacecraft in 1999. Although NASA had specified metric units be used for all calculations, one of the subcontractors, Lockheed Martin, had provided certain figures in imperial units. As a result the orbiter descended too low into Mars atmosphere, causing it to burn up.[119]

The US is not the only country to struggle with migration to the metric system. The UK still has not fully converted either. For example, you still order beers by the pint at a pub. Road signs on the highways continue to use miles, yards and feet rather than metric units. One of the primary reasons the UK has not switched fully to the metric system is the cost involved. Switching two million road signs in a short period of time was forecasted to cost between £500 and £700 million.[120]

Corporations have taken a similar attitude towards EDI. Although XML is unquestionably a superior model, there is little economic incentive to make a change. You will not find many CFOs or CEOs that will approve a multi-million dollar project to switch out fully-functional EDI systems with newer XML-based applications simply to enable a more elegant technology model. Today's IT initiatives are driven by business value, not technology standards preferences.

However, there remains great hope for XML as it is the preferred choice for new projects. In situations in which there is no existing legacy system, XML is often the standard of choice.

Chapter 8
Data Synchronization

In April of 1985 the Coca-Cola Company performed what is probably the most legendary and controversial new product introduction of all time. I am referring, of course, to the introduction of New Coke. Coca-Cola had been losing market share to its archrival Pepsi for 15 consecutive years. Coke's share had declined from a post-World War II high of 60% down to 24% in 1985.[121] Pepsi was beginning to outsell Coke even in supermarkets. The Coca-Cola management team was faced with a formidable challenge. How do you revitalize consumer interest in a product that had been on the market for almost 100 years?

The decision was to introduce a new formula for Coke's iconic soft drink. The formula promised a smoother, rounder, bolder taste that it was hoping would help to lift sales. Coke did extensive taste tests on the product with nearly 200,000 consumers.[122] The majority of the test results indicated that consumers would embrace the new product after a short adjustment period. In many of the blind taste tests that were performed consumers actually preferred the taste of New Coke over Pepsi. When the new product hit the shelves early sales results were promising. Noteworthy increases in purchases occurred in regions such as New York and Washington, DC.[123]

However, shortly after the launch a public uproar began to grow in the Southeastern US. Residents in these states did not approve of Coca-Cola tampering with its secret formula. A vocal minority of consumers began a public protest against Coca-Cola. Boycotts were organized and bottles of New Coke were being emptied into the streets of southern cities. Over 400,000 letters were sent to Coke headquarters from customers expressing their frustration with the formula change.[124] Loyal Coke buyers began hoarding cases of the old products in their basement. One San Antonio man purchased $1000 worth of Coca-Cola from a local bottler in Texas.[125] Fidel Castro spoke out against the New Coke, calling it a sign of American capitalist decadence.[126] Bill Cosby ended his contract to perform advertisements for Coca-Cola, claiming that he had lost credibility by promoting the new product.[127]

After 79 days of controversy, Coca-Cola finally succumbed to public pressure. The company announced that it would re-introduce the old formula to the market under the name Coca-Cola Classic. When the news broke, Peter Jennings of ABC News interrupted the popular daytime soap opera General Hospital to share Coca-Cola's decision.[128] The following day, Coca-Cola's decision was featured on the front page of every major newspaper. Needless to say Coca-Cola Classic significantly outsold the new formula after its re-launch. Coca-Cola chose to keep both products on the market for an extended period of time. The Coca-Cola Classic name was retained until 2009. The new formula was renamed Coke II in 1992; however, it never gained significant market share in the US. In 2002, the New Coke was effectively withdrawn from the shelves of American grocery stores. Local bottlers still have the rights and capability to produce New Coke, but only a few do. For example, Coke II is very popular in American Samoa and a Micronesian state called Yap.[129]

A few conspiracy theorists thought that Coca-Cola's miscalculations with New Coke were not a mistake at all, but rather a deliberate strategy to attract attention amongst consumers. Although Coca-Cola Company received a significant amount of negative publicity over the New Coke decision, the company ultimately benefited. The reintroduction of Coca-Cola Classic effectively revitalized the brand and reattached its consumer base to the product. Another conspiracy theory surrounded the US Drug Enforcement Agency and Coca-Cola. Some believed that the Coca-Cola Company was collaborating with the DEA to discourage the harvesting of coca plants used to create cocaine. The new Coke had no coca derivatives in the formula, reducing the need for South American countries to raise these plants.

Pepsi failed to gain many new customers despite Coke's marketing disaster. In fact, a few years later PepsiCo struggled with a new product introduction of its own. In April of 1992, Crystal Pepsi was introduced. It was a clear soda that was caffeine free. Pepsi hoped that consumers would equate the new product with purity and health. However, sales did not grow as expected leading Pepsi to quickly withdraw the product from the market.

The challenges faced by Coke and Pepsi are common among manufacturers of food, beverage, and consumer packaged goods. Few companies in the consumer products industry are satisfied with steady year-over-year sales. Instead most companies are seeking to expand their market share by taking away business from competitors. Consumer products companies utilize numerous strategies to try to increase market share and increase sales. But, how do you generate consumer interest in brand name products that have been sold for 10, 20, or 100 years?

New Product Introductions

In addition to pricing and promotional incentives, consumer brands have also focused on introducing new products. Both New Coke and Crystal Pepsi were examples of new product introductions. Most new consumer products do not attract quite as much attention as New Coke and Crystal Pepsi did. Some new product introductions are simply new packaging configurations or derivations of existing SKUs. In an attempt to grow market share or stimulate sales, consumer products manufacturers will introduce new sizes, colors, flavors, fragrances, and price points for their offerings. Others are completely new products designed to fill a void in the marketplace.

In 2009, there were 50,000 new SKUs introduced to the market.[130] What types of new products could food, beverage, and consumer packaged goods companies possibly introduce that don't exist today? There are new types of laundry detergent for high efficiency machines or with new stain fighting formulas. There are new types of energy drinks for athletes and vitamin waters for health-conscious consumers. Various different types of yogurts with digestive aids have been introduced in recent years. Many new product introductions come from the pharmaceutical industry. For example, there have been several new over-the-counter heartburn medications, pain relievers, and sleep aids introduced in the past few years.

My favorite examples of new product introductions come from the toothpaste category. Innovation in the dental-care products has exploded in recent years. Procter & Gamble, GlaxoSmithKline, and Colgate-Palmolive have each introduced pastes with new features such as tartar control, whitening, baking soda, and anti-gingivitis formulas. There were almost 70 new toothpastes introduced in 2010. However, that is a significant decline from 2007 when 100 new SKUs reached the market.[131]

Consider the Procter & Gamble line of Crest products. There are SKUs specially designed for kids including Spiderman, Sesame Street, and Hello Kitty branded toothpastes. There are specialized SKUs which provide focus on "Sensitivity," "Whitening," "Flavor Experience," "Fresh Breath," and, of course, there are classic formulas. At the high end are "Dentist Inspired" SKUs such as "Crest Pro-Health Clinical Gum Protection Toothpaste with Invigorating Clean Mint." I am a real sucker for these Dentist Inspired SKUs and purchase whatever appears to be the highest end paste believing it will reduce the likelihood of new cavities.

The rate of new product introduction in the consumer products industry doubled in the years between 1998 and 2008.[132] The typical grocery store carries 45,000 different SKUs today, twice as many as compared to 1996. In 2008, the industry reached a saturation point at which SKU proliferation began to decline. Some consumers have expressed frustration with the overwhelming number of choices. Do we really need 10 different types of Oreo cookies to choose from? Do we really need 25 different choices of superglue at a drug store, or would 2 suffice? In an effort to reduce costs and boost margins, many retailers are limiting the number of SKUs they would continue to carry in inventory.

In addition to pricing, promotions, and new product introductions, manufacturers also change the packaging of popular SKUs in order to stimulate consumer interest in their brands. Some packaging changes are financially motivated. In times of rising ingredient prices many food and beverage companies will introduce smaller sized packages. The strategy is to introduce a package with 5 to 10% less product while keeping prices the same. For example, in response to rising commodity prices, Coke's China division switched from its standard 600 milliliter bottle to a smaller 500 milliliter size in 2011.[133] Manufacturers prefer selling packages with lesser contents over trying to raise prices. Most consumers notice a 5 to 10% price increase but very few notice the slightly smaller packaging configurations.

Other packaging changes are driven by corporate social responsibility initiatives. For example, bottled water manufacturers such as Nestle, Danone, Coca-Cola, and PepsiCo have focused efforts to reduce the environmental impact of packaging. Bottled water has been heavily criticized for its Polyethylene Terephthalate (PET) packaging. Although PET is recyclable, only one in four bottles is properly disposed.[134] With approximately 200 billion bottles of water consumed each year globally, even a small decrease in packaging materials could have a big impact. Manufacturers have changed the shapes and dimensions of the bottles to utilize less PET. Plastic lids have been re-engineered to weigh less. In some cases the corrugated cardboard at the bottom of case packaging has been removed entirely.

Supply Chain Issues with New Products

Packaging changes and new product introductions do influence consumer behavior and drive increased sales, but the changes wreak havoc on the operations of retailers and distributors. Before a new item can be sold by a retailer it must be "set up" in the appropriate computer systems, warehouses, and stores. There must be a place for the product to be displayed on the shelf, and a slot is needed in the warehouse to store inventory. The item must be registered in the Point of Sale (POS) application to ensure that it scans properly at check out.

For most retailers the new item setup process takes two to four weeks longer than it should. Delays to new product introductions are a significant source of frustration among consumer product manufacturers. Billions of dollars in research and development are invested every year to bring new products to market. Being first to market with a new health food, energy drink, or laundry detergent can have a tremendous influence on short term and long term sales. For example, in 2010 the best new food product introduction was Powerade's ION 4 which generated over $190 million in new sales.[135] The best non-food product introduced was Crest's 3D White strips which generated $150 million in new sales.[136] The first to market in a category enjoys a rare period with no competition. As a result, manufacturers can charge a price premium that allows for higher levels of profitability. Furthermore, history has demonstrated that the first two companies within a new category generally benefit from market leadership throughout a product's lifecycle.

One of the root causes for delays in new item setup is the lack of an automated process for manufacturers to provide retailers with information about upcoming product launches. Historically, the manufacturer sales representative emailed or hand delivered a product data sheet to the buyer at the retailer. The data sheet included information such as the brand name, product description, packaging configuration, price schedule, and total weight. The product information from the data sheet was rekeyed into the retailer's merchandising, warehouse, transportation, and accounting systems prior to the launch. The manual data entry process was not only slow but it led to problems as human error was inevitable. Imagine typing a series of 14-digit SKU identifiers into a merchandising system. The odds of mistyping one of the numbers are fairly high. Hand keying dimensions of a case or pallet is also problematic because the height and width can be easily transposed.

Many of the 40,000 new products introduced each year are "new and improved" versions of existing SKUs. These product replacements can cause significant disruptions in the supply chain if not communicated in advance. Suppose a soup manufacturer introduces a new version of its traditional Chicken Noodle SKU. The change is introduced in October to capitalize on the anticipated the seasonal demand increase for the soup. The new version of the soup contains 20% more soup than previously. A marketing strategy such as that is sure to capture the attention of consumers and lift sales. The introduction of the new soup SKU can also cause challenges for the retailer's operations, for instance, the new soup might have a 10% price increase and a 20% larger can.

If the new soup SKU is not properly set up in the retailer's systems, then a number of exception scenarios occur. First, retailers may continue to place orders for the old SKUs. Since the manufacturer discontinued the old SKU, they will likely replace it with the newer, larger cans. When a pallet of the new cans arrives at the retailer's distribution center it will not match the corresponding purchase order in the warehouse management system. The larger pallet configurations may not fit in the appropriate warehouse slot, requiring a special accommodation to be made. The same number of larger pallet configurations may not fit on the truck that carries the product to the store. Previously 50 of the old pallets may have fit, but the new weight and height may only allow 40 pallets per truckload. When the goods arrive at the store the cans may not fit on the store shelf. As a result, the inventory may sit in the back room until a store associate can reconfigure the shelves during off-hours. The overall result of the new product introduction may be an out of stock or as the famous Seinfeld character would say, "No soup for you!" Pricing issues can also result since the new soup is 10% more expensive than the original SKU. When the invoice is submitted to the retailer's accounting department a mismatch will occur with the original purchase order. The retailer classifies the new SKU an "unauthorized substitution" and therefore will not honor the price increase. In other words, the supplier ships the larger, higher cost items but is reimbursed based upon the older, lower price.

Examples such as this are all too common in today's retail supply chain. Small changes that are designed to improve the consumer experience may end up causing out of stocks or product launch delays due to poor communication in the supply chain.

To overcome these supply chain challenges the retail industry developed a new technology called data synchronization. The idea was to build a set of registries which would catalog all the consumer products available for sale in a particular market. In addition to the registry, a series of "data pools" would be created to store the latest product information for each individual SKU. When a manufacturer wished to make a change to the dimensions or price of a particular SKU, the company would publish the change to the data pool. Retailers would subscribe to updates for each of the SKUs sold in their stores. As a soon a change occurred for a particular SKU, the retailer would be notified electronically. Upon receipt of the update the retailer would have to confirm its acceptance of the change back to the manufacturer.

The goal of data synchronization was to eliminate many of these supply chain inefficiencies. Data sync would ensure accurate, complete, and up-to-date product information for all SKUs shared between retailers and manufacturers. Improving notification about new introductions and product discontinuations would result in fewer incorrect orders and returns. Accurate weights and measures would lead to optimal use of trucks and warehousing space. New product introduction timeframes could be shortened by two to four weeks. Finally, sales representatives would spend much less time resolving issues related to product data.

One of the best case studies conducted on the benefits of data synchronization came from the US grocery retailer Wegmans. With data synchronization, Wegmans was able to reduce coupon scanning errors by 40%, resulting in 400,000 fewer disruptions at the point of sale annually. Wegmans accelerated new product introductions by seven days. Accurate weights and dimensions for pallet configurations enabled Wegmans to eliminate 10% of its outbound shipments, resulting in $1 million profit annually. The retailer was also able to optimize inbound transportation resulting in $2.5 million of savings, which represented 5% of logistics costs.[137]

The Beginnings of Data Sync

The initial sponsors of data synchronization were the non-profit groups that managed product numbering activities like Universal Product Codes and barcode labels. In the US, the organization which championed data synchronization was the Uniform Code Council (UCC). Outside the US, there were European Article Numbering (EAN) associations in each respective country that led the efforts.

One of the first data synchronization initiatives to emerge was the UCCnet project in the US. Sponsored by the UCC standards organization, UCCnet was championed by industry heavyweights such as Walmart, P&G, and Coca-Cola. In the same year a similar initiative was started in the UK. However, the British data synchronization service was initiated by a venture capital-backed startup called UDEX rather than the local EAN organization.

Retail industry focus towards data synchronization grew quickly between 2002 and 2004. Numerous reports were published by industry associations such as the Grocery Manufacturers of America (GMA) and the Food Marketing Institute (FMI) extolling the benefits of data sync. Systems integrators and management consultants such as AT Kearney and Kurt Salmon Associates were recruited to document the return on investment. In the following years a number of country "data pools" emerged offering synchronization services for local retailers and manufacturers. Most of the local data pools were sponsored by the respective EAN organizations in each country. For example, the EAN Canada group created ECCnet. The EAN organization for Australia and New Zealand created EANnet. Germany created a data sync service called SINFOS.

In January 2004, Walmart announced its desire to have all its suppliers synchronize data electronically. Other major retailers including SuperValu, Home Depot, and Lowe's had also initiated data synchronization programs. In the US market, the industry decided that data synchronization adoption could be accelerated by introducing a number of competitive data pool services. In addition to UCCnet, both of the former retail e-marketplaces, World Wide Retail Exchange and Transora, launched data synchronization services. Independent technology vendors also were introducing data sync services. For example, there was a company called Big Hammer that specialized in data synchronization for the home improvement sector.

By the end of 2004 it was official. Data sync was the new cool thing in the retail supply chain. The B2B e-marketplaces had failed to achieve the groundbreaking impact they had promised. Most of the companies that were going to adopt AS2 had already done so. As a result when Walmart showed a strong commitment to data sync all of the supply chain and B2B e-commerce vendors redirected their efforts towards the new initiative.

Data Synchronization Network

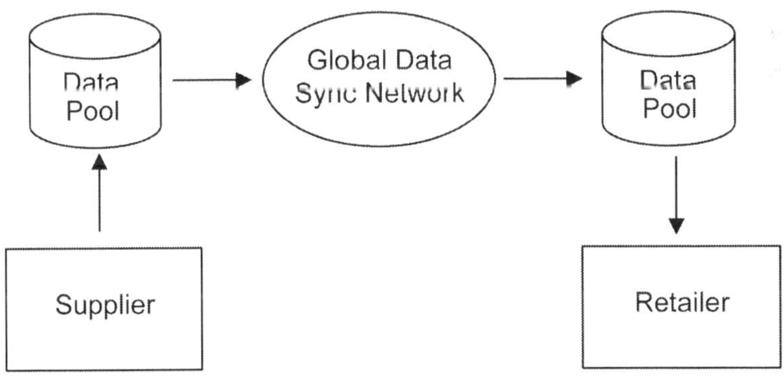

The Rise of the Data Pools

Witnessing the surge in activity in the US and Western Europe, EAN organizations in countries around the world began to launch their own data pools. New ventures were starting all over the world by EAN organizations in the Netherlands, Argentina, Slovakia, Croatia, Russia, Taiwan, and Hong Kong. No vendor was more caught up in the hype surrounding data synchronization than GXS. With EDI prices declining rapidly GXS sought a growth market to offset revenue declines. One of the key tenets of GXS' strategy was to catalyze the development of the local country data pools.

GXS had a small sales team travelling the world to speak with EAN organizations about the business case for developing a data pool. The company had developed a hosted platform that could be leveraged as a turnkey solution for new countries seeking a data pool. GXS would operate the service while the local EAN organization would market and sell to its retail community. To encourage adoption GXS asked for no upfront fees from the EAN organizations. Instead, GXS asked the EAN organizations to share a percentage of the revenues generated from the data pool as compensation for our efforts. The sales team earned handsome commissions based upon the projected revenues of what the future data pool would generate once operational. If a country had 10,000 companies in its retail supply chain, each paid $50 per month, then the total potential value was $500,000 per month or $6 million per year.

There was an incredible amount of excitement about data synchronization within GXS and the industry. Almost everyone involved with data synchronization is extremely passionate about the subject. Discussions about the strategy were debated with energy levels only seen in the most sensitive of political and religious conversations. The enthusiasm and attention placed on global data synchronization in 2005 was surprising given that the total revenue generated from the sector could not have been more than $5 million. Nonetheless, you would have thought the data sync pioneers were building the next Amazon.com. In hindsight perhaps they should have—this was the period during which Facebook launched and Google went public.

Sync or Swim

The number of products registered on the various global data pools has grown rapidly since its inception. There were over 7 million products registered in 2011, compared to only 60,000 in 2003.[138] The registration of 7 million items within such a short timeframe is impressive. However, the adoption is relatively low compared to other types of electronic catalogs used in adjacent industries. For example, the e-procurement vendors discussed in Chapter 3 require suppliers to publish electronic catalogs into their applications. Ariba, the third largest vendor in the e-procurement sector behind SAP and Oracle, boasts over 80 million items in its catalog alone.[139] These e-procurement applications originated just a few years before UCCnet was formed but have over 10 times the number of products registered.

Another reference point comes from the US apparel and general merchandise sector including companies such as Macy's, Nordstrom, Sears, and JCPenney. This community of retailers and suppliers chose to develop a product catalog exchange model based on EDI. These EDI-based catalog standards were developed in the 1990s long before UCCnet emerged, but have achieved very high levels of adoption among both retailers and suppliers. A handful of technology vendors like GXS offer specialized catalog publication services for the apparel and general merchandise sectors. The GXS Catalogue has almost 140 million items registered by 150 retailers and 5000 suppliers in the US and Canada. In other words, this one vendor catalog primarily used in the US has 20 times the products registered globally in the GDSN.

Why hasn't GDSN achieved greater levels of adoption? One of the root causes was a stall in the technology rollout by the data pool operators themselves. In 2005, the various EAN organizations and UCC started bringing some much needed alignment and harmonization to the market. EAN International, including all of its country member organizations, merged with UCC to form a new company called GS1. Each of the respective country organizations took on the GS1 brand. Instead of EAN Canada, EAN Australia, SINFOS, and UCC there were GS1 Canada, GS1 Australia, GS1 Germany, and GS1 US.

Around the same time GS1 organized the fragmented country data pools into a framework called the Global Data Synchronization Network (GDSN). The GDSN would interconnect each of the country data pools as well the independent services such as WWRE, Transora, and UDEX. The GDSN used a common set of XML standards for publishing and subscribing to product data. A consistent set of models were used to represent all of the product information such as brand, description, weight, pricing, and packaging.

Harmonizing the disparate data sync efforts of various countries under the GDSN model was the right long term strategy, but it did introduce delays to the broader rollout of data sync platforms. The data pools that had already been developed in countries such as the US, UK, Germany, Canada, Australia, and Columbia had to migrate to a common technology model in order to connect to the GDSN. The migration was a considerable effort for most of the data pools. The early adopters of data sync were forced to focus their investments on migrating to GDSN standards rather than promoting greater adoption.

The migration issues were further compounded when several of the leading data pool providers decided to merge. First, UCCnet and Transora combined into a new venture called 1SYNC.[140] Shortly thereafter, WWRE merged its data pool with SINFOS to create SA2 Worldsync.[141] These mergers further stalled adoption as the data pool vendors focused on consolidating their platforms.

During the multiple years of the consolidation and migration efforts, the retail industry's interest in data synchronization began to wane. Several key vendors withdrew from the market. Many of the leading retailers and manufacturers began to re-evaluate their strategies for data synchronization. Achieving the promised return on investment was proving more challenging than originally anticipated, especially for manufacturers.

With decreased customer adoption some of the data pools began to have problems. Many failed to ever achieve any meaningful levels of adoption. For example, the data pools in Taiwan, China, Croatia, and Latin America (CABASnet) each have fewer than 10,000 products registered each as of early 2011.[142] Canada, Hungary and Hong Kong have fewer than 1000 SKUs.[143] The Mediterranean, Middle East, and Africa data pool disengaged from the GDSN process as did respective organizations in Slovakia, Greece, and Korea. The operators of the original Russia data pool simply disappeared one day never to be heard from again. A new data pool has been formed in Russia since then.

With so many compelling business benefits and such strong support from major retailers and manufacturers, why has the data synchronization initiative fail to achieved greater adoption? In the next chapter we discuss both the reasons why data synchronization has not been more successful and the reasons why it should be wildly successful in the coming years.

Chapter 9
Product Information

Although Christmas is supposed to be a time of joy, my holiday spirits are often dampened by a little mid-morning angst. I suffer from a disease known as "Wrap Rage." This disease affects millions of people around the world and there are no medications to manage the symptoms. My outbreaks are usually triggered by the un-wrapping of gifts my children receive. With two youngsters in my household many of the gifts we exchange every year are toys. Most of these toys are manufactured by evil companies who deliberately create the most complex, elaborate packaging systems they can imagine. These toys are housed in plastic clamshells cases and secured with wire ties that are reinforced by plastic bindings. As a result, it takes 5 to 10 minutes to open up a toy that should be unwrapped in 30 seconds. Not only does this frustrate the parents, but it is cruel to the children who have to wait for 5 to 10 minutes before they can play with the toy. Many of us had given up hope until recently we discovered a cure—Amazon.com's Frustration Free Packaging (FFP).

What is Frustration Free Packaging?

FFP products are designed to be opened quickly and easily using a box cutter or a knife. There are no evil wire ties or plastic clamshells. I had always assumed that these elaborate toy packaging strategies were a necessary evil to prevent damage during shipping. However Amazon.com has proved that this is not the case. Amazon collaborated with manufacturers to design alternative packaging materials that are just as secure but hassle-free. Not only is FFP consumer-friendly, but it is also environmentally-friendly. Only recyclable materials are used.

Amazon.com launched FFP in 2008. In the first year of the program Amazon successfully enrolled over 30 vendors in the FFP program. The merchandise consists not only of toys, but also a wide range of categories including beverages, consumer electronics, health, and personal care. Suppliers participating in the program include Mattel, VTech, Microsoft, Garmin, Kingston, Seagate, and Western Digital among others. Consumer response has been very positive. Amazon claims that negative feedback on product pages has been reduced by 70% for the FFP SKUs.[144]

FFP is a differentiator that can lead consumers not only to change where they buy products but the prices paid for the items. I would certainly pay 5 to 10% more to avoid the pain of breaking open those plastic clamshells. Who would have thought that packaging approaches could be used to differentiate one retailer from another? And how can we promote this idea to a broader set of retailers to limit holiday wrap rage incidents?

Data synchronization technologies could play a critical role in building awareness of new packaging options among retailers. The GDSN working group could simply add FFP fields to the list of required product attributes for toys and electronics. For example, the following true or false attributes could be added for each item: Plastic_Clamshell_Casing (true or false); Plastic_Binders (true or false); Wire_Ties (true or false); and Evil_Toy_Manufacturer (true or false).

Merchandise buyers at retailers could then easily assess which manufacturers offer FFP versions of their products and choose to make those SKUs available in their stores.

FFP is just one of many examples of how product information could improve the consumer experience. Having access to a greater range of product data on a retailer's website, mobile device, or via an in-store kiosk would greatly improve the shopping experience for connected consumers. Furthermore, robust product information would create opportunities for retailers to differentiate themselves in the marketplace. One of the challenges with the original data synchronization proposition was that it was highly focused on logistical and supply chain benefits to retailers. Yet some of the greatest advantages to be obtained through synchronization of product data are found with improving the consumer shopping experience.

Online Retail Stores

Nowhere is the demand for more robust product information greater than online shopping sites. US online retail sales are growing 10% annually. Although only 8% of sales occur online almost 50% of purchases are now influenced by online information.[145] Where is the first place that you go when you want to purchase a new car, computer, or television? Most consumers research products online before visiting a store to inspect the product and complete the purchase. In online research and purchasing scenarios, the quality and quantity of product information becomes critical. In the online sale, product content on a website replaces the discussion with a store associate. If the product data is inaccurate, incomplete, or out-of-date there will be a negative impact to the consumer shopping experience.

Perhaps the most interesting category of online sales to study is consumer electronics. Over 50% of all computer hardware, software, and peripherals are now purchased online.[146] Cutthroat competition has emerged between electronics retailers to win the sales of gadget-hungry consumers. Hundreds of websites have emerged with price comparison capabilities and technical product reviews designed to influence consumers.

One of the best features of online websites is the ability to quickly filter search results. Both consumer electronics retailers and independent price comparison websites allow consumers to specify which features are most important in a product search. Suppose you went online to purchase a camcorder. You might only want to view a particular brand of product such as Sony, JVC, or Panasonic or a particular price range such as under $200 or between $500 and $600. Or you might only be interested in high definition models or those with a touch screen LCD. If you are a SCUBA diver or outdoor enthusiast you might want to only view waterproof models. If the color of the camcorder is a key feature, you might request to view only black, silver, or red models. The retailer may also offer you a choice of viewing those with free shipping or free add-on accessory bundles. Filtering technologies allow you to quickly narrow your search results, but are critically dependent upon high quality product data.

Another cool feature of today's retail websites is comparison shopping. You can select between two and five different products that appeal most to you.

The retailer will then display a very detailed table of features and specifications that enables easy comparison between products. For example, with camcorders the website might provide you with a tabular view to compare the storage mechanism, recording speeds, PC software, warranty terms, product dimensions, or availability for store pickup. Of course, all of the product feature data referenced above must be provided by the manufacturer to the retailer.

Data Quality—The Inhibitor

The GDSN would be the ideal means of capturing the product information. However, the ability to synchronize the data depends on the manufacturer having access to it. You would be surprised to learn that many manufacturers lack a central repository containing the complete set of product information consumers seek. Instead, much of the data is scattered across various internal systems. A highly manual process must be performed to identify, cleanse, and aggregate the information necessary to perform data sync. Experts state that for every dollar invested in data synchronization, the cost is 10 times higher to aggregate the necessary data. The cost associated with manually collecting, cleansing, and completing product information was one of the key obstacles to greater data synchronization adoption.

To understand the issues you need to think differently about product information—as a manufacturer rather than as a consumer. For example, suppose you were to ask a Pepsi Bottling Group (PBG) employee to describe the dimensions of a 12 ounce can of soda. You might be surprised to learn than many employees don't know the answer. PBG would tell you that they don't sell individual cans of soda. Instead, PBG sells pallets of soda cans. Each pallet might have 40 cases, each with 48 cans. Retailers and manufacturers buy and sell goods by the pallet, which is the focus of most pricing and logistical discussions between the two. As a result, the data on individual cans of soda may not be well organized in a manufacturer's system.

How do retailers obtain product level information for their websites if manufacturers do not have it readily available to supply? In many cases, the retailer is responsible for capturing the product data digitally. Marketing personnel at the retailer will use digital cameras to take photos for publication on the website. Tape measures are used to capture dimensions of the product both in packaged and unpackaged form. Scanners are used to convert paper versions of warranty documentation, instruction manuals, and assembly guides into digital format.

Some retailers using data synchronization will take such an approach because they cannot rely on the information provided by manufacturers. Best Buy has conducted extensive studies on the accuracy of product data supplied by manufacturers. The company found that 20% of dimensional information provided by manufacturers was incorrect.[147] Imagine that you purchased a refrigerator to fit into your newly remodeled kitchen. You have measured the exact dimensions of the refrigerator spacing between your cabinetry that you compare to the hang tag on the product in the store. Yet when the refrigerator is delivered to your home you discover that it is 1 inch wider and 1/2 inch taller than the label in the store indicated. As a result you request that the delivery truck return the product to the store. Returns are a lose-lose-lose proposition for the retailer, manufacturer, and the consumer. The retailer incurs additional expense to transport and restock the item. As a consumer you had a negative experience with both the brand and the retailer. After the product is returned you might choose not to purchase from either company again. Dimensional problems are not limited to refrigerators. Similar data accuracy issues exist for dishwashers, microwave ovens, high definition televisions, and other electronics.

Completeness is another challenge with product data. Suppose that you are comparing three different digital cameras online. However, one of the manufacturers has not provided information about the tripod mount, video outputs, or battery life. Comparison website functions do not offer much value if many of the table fields are not populated. If features such as tripod mount, video outputs, or battery life were important to you, then you would likely choose a different model. An even worse scenario than incomplete product data is inaccurate product data. Suppose you purchased an HDTV that listed two HDMI ports on the website, but only has one. With only one HDMI port you may not be able to connect both your cable set-top box and Blu-ray player, leading you to return the item.

"May Contain Nuts" No Longer Unacceptable

The categories of data needed by consumers to make informed purchasing choices are expanding every year. The demand for more robust product information is not limited to consumer electronics or appliances. Consider food and beverage products sold in a typical grocery store. Today's consumer is also more health-focused and socially conscious than ever. These educated consumers are demanding more information about the health and environmental impacts of the products retailers offer before making a purchasing decision. Environmentalists want green products with a low carbon footprint. Locavores want locally grown fruits and vegetables. Health enthusiasts prefer organic foods or those with natural ingredients. Diabetics need sugar-free versions of products. Those with known food allergies need SKUs that do not contain nuts.

Food manufacturers have responded by introducing new SKUs specifically designed for those with diabetes or heart disease. Retailers have responded by redesigning store layouts to create entire sections of the store devoted to organic products or locally grown produce. Government regulators have passed legislation requiring more detailed labeling on trans-fat content and known allergen notices by manufacturers.

The growing demand for environmentally-friendly and health-oriented products are challenging retailers in numerous areas. Not only must retailers offer a wider assortment of products, but they must also be able to respond to consumer's need for information about each SKU. Today's health-conscious consumer wants to understand not just the brand, price, and size of each SKU, but they also want to know: Is it organic? Is it locally grown? Is it carbon neutral? Is it fresh? Is it heart healthy? Is it diabetic friendly?

Places that consumers want this product information represented are on a product labels or store shelf displays. However, in-store information is not sufficient to satisfy the full needs of today's multi-channel grocery shopper. What about the consumers who research recipes online? A growing number of consumers are participating in formalized weight loss programs. These diet-conscious buyers are researching the caloric impact of foods online before making a weekly shopping trip. Other consumers are not visiting the store at all, choosing instead to purchase groceries online from retailers such as Peapod, Ocado, or Tesco. Online consumers expect complete item attribute data to be displayed at all steps of the decision making process.

Going Mobile

In today's retail market it is important to not only have product information on your own website, but third-party data sources as well. Consumers are using an increasingly diverse range of social networks and mobile devices to research product pricing and features. Even the largest retailers cannot assume that all its shoppers will visit their site before making a purchasing decision. Retailers must publish product data to third-party shopping sites offered by Google, Yahoo!, and Bing. Food manufacturers must provide ways for weight loss, health, and nutrition portals to display information about their products on their sites. The consumer electronics segment is particularly competitive with hundreds of different price comparison sites ranging from CNET, PC World, and PriceGrabber.

Best Buy has introduced a number of innovative technologies that make it simpler for third-party websites to access its product catalog and content. Starting in 2000, Best Buy began to offer feeds of product data such as SKU numbers and item descriptions to third-party sites. In 2009, the consumer electronics retailer introduced a new game-changing technology called Remix. Social networks and price comparison sites can use Remix to pull Best Buy product data such as specifications, images, user reviews, and sales rankings into their website. Believing that the quantity and quality of information a retailer can provide about a product is a key factor in every online sale, Best Buy is striving to become the authoritative source for data about consumer electronics SKUs. If Best Buy could become an information source for online conversations occurring among gadget enthusiasts, then it could begin to shape and influence consumer demand for its products.

Perhaps more important than social media and price comparison websites, are the growing number of mobile applications that provide consumers with access to data in the store. Armed with an iPhone, Blackberry, or Android-powered mobile phone, consumers can look up prices, check inventory and read user reviews from within a store. The mobile applications use various approaches to identifying products. Many of the apps require the consumer to use the phone's camera to take a picture of the barcode label. Some phones now include barcode scanners that can read the product's label directly. Other applications offer speech recognition. The consumer says the product name aloud then a list of potential matches is then displayed. Of course, there are also old-fashioned applications that allow users to simply key the product name in using a keypad.

After the product is identified, the mobile application will provide a list of comparative prices at various retailers. For a small price difference most consumers will not hassle with traveling to another store. However, for higher priced items such as an HDTV or kitchen appliance, consumers may find a $100 difference compelling enough to drive to another location. Some retailers, who have no brick and mortar stores, are offering mobile applications to lure away customers. For example, Amazon.com's mobile application allows you to quickly look up a product's price then purchase it on your phone. In other words, through mobile devices retailers now have the ability to target consumers while they are standing in a competitor's stores.

The new levels of pricing transparency exposed through mobile applications present a significant threat to retailer profit margins. Historically, large chains would advertise promotional pricing on popular items to lure customers in the store. The hope was that the customer would buy a mixed basket of products that were mostly purchased at regular list prices. Many retailers sell the items in their stores at higher prices than they list online.

Pricing inconsistencies between stores and web sites are another source of challenges for retailers. In 2007, the Connecticut State Attorney General conducted an investigation into Best Buy's pricing practices. The retailer offered customers access to an in-store kiosk that featured the same design as www.bestbuy.com, but only listed the higher prices available in the store. Confused consumers complained that they were being misled. Best Buy stated the purpose of the kiosks was not for price-matching, but for navigating the store.[148]

Trustworthy Data

Most users of mobile phones have probably never stopped to question the data source for their shopping applications. Where is the pricing and product information being offered via mobile applications coming from? Would you trust the dimensions of a refrigerator provided on a mobile application? Would you base a purchasing decision for a camcorder on the feature comparison table provided by a mobile application?

Pricing information delivered from a specific retailer's mobile application such as Amazon.com is guaranteed to be correct. Product information is likely to be more reliable on retailer applications as well. However, third-party applications unaffiliated with any specific retailer or supplier might have a wide range of data. As you may have guessed, these third-party mobile application vendors are not sourcing the product data from the GDSN, nor are they obtaining it directly from the manufacturers. Instead, the data is being aggregated from various public websites which may or may not be accurate.

Suppose you were searching for a freezer. The mobile application on your iPhone suggests that the price Home Depot is offering the freezer for is $100 less than the nearest Lowes store. When you arrive at Home Depot you find out that the cheaper price actually refers to a different model of freezer. Such errors are likely to be widespread with applications that do not use standardized identifiers for products or manufacturer-sourced data for attributes.

The rise of mobile shopping and price comparison applications has a number of implications for retailers. First, retailers now have to ensure that the pricing advertised by third-party applications is, in fact, accurate. Second, retailers need to ensure that the prices they are paying manufacturers are as accurate as possible. Suppose HP lowers the pricing for a popular laser printer by 10% in an effort to move excess inventory that has accrued in its supply chain. If Staples updates its consumer-facing price to reflect HP's discount several days before Office Max, then it will enjoy a temporary competitive advantage in the market.

As you learned from the examples above, consumers have an almost insatiable appetite for product information. Consumers want information about prices, packaging and product features accessible to them in the store, on the web and on their mobile phones. The stakes are high for both retailers and their suppliers. A simple pricing error on a third-party mobile application has the potential to drive hundreds or thousands of shoppers to a competitive store or brand. The only way to ensure that complete, accurate, up-to-date product information flows through the supply chain is through a standardized B2B e-commerce model. As a result I do think we will witness resurgence in the demand for data synchronization in the near future.

Chapter 10
RFID

Frederick Smith, the Founder of FedEx, once stated, "*Information about a package is as important as the package itself.*"[149] Whether or not you agree with his statement probably depends on what the content of the package is. However, Smith does raise an interesting point that is reflective of the importance of technology in today's supply chain. In many respects, the supply chain is becoming as much about technology as it is trucks, warehouses, airplanes and containers.

Information about inventory can help move goods faster through the supply chain. For example, the majority of goods received into distribution centers are not destined to stay there for very long. Often, shipments are taken in only to be relayed onto another location, such as a nearby manufacturing plant, retail store or customer location. Armed with the knowledge of which shipments are to arrive in the coming days, warehouse personnel can arrange in advance for outbound transportation for each incoming load. The ideal case is for inbound shipments to be received, inspected and then quickly loaded onto trucks for routing to their final destination. This "cross-docking" process is used by retailers, such as Walmart, to accelerate the flow of goods through distribution centers. Once again, however, being able to receive highly accurate and reliable information about inbound shipments via B2B technologies is critical to success.

The statement, "information replaces inventory", has become more popular among supply chain experts at leading research institutes.[150] To illustrate the concept, consider another example. Suppose you want to send some flowers to your mom on Mother's Day. Your mom lives in Seattle, but you live in Atlanta. You contact your local florist in Atlanta requesting that a Mother's Day bouquet be sent to Seattle in the next few days. The florist could create an assortment of flowers in its store, then ship them via express freight to Seattle. However, a more efficient model is to forward the order on to a florist in Seattle who can fulfill it locally. In this scenario, an expensive material flow is being replaced by a cheaper information flow. It would not be possible without an information exchange about inventory between the two florists via B2B e-commerce.[151]

Excellence in inventory management can provide a competitive advantage in customer service, cost structure and even the corporate balance sheet. For example, most manufacturers and retailers hold buffer inventories in their supply chain as a hedge against potential delayed shipments. While these safety stocks appear as assets on a company's balance sheet, supply chain professionals view these buffer inventories more as liabilities. Ideally, manufacturers and retailers want to minimize inventories, operating in a "lean" supply chain model. If a company can obtain reliable, high quality information about the locations of shipments in the supply chain, it can confidently reduce its inventory buffer. The challenge, of course, is that identifying the quantity and location of inventory in the supply chain is no easy task.

Wouldn't it be great if inventory could "check in" at different locations as it traversed through long-distance, international supply chains? The process could work similarly to the way mobile phone users can check in with Foursquare, Gowalla or Loopt? Auto check-in would ensure that supply chain managers could monitor inventory movements almost effortlessly. Of course, there would certainly be different check-in points for inventory than for people. Whereas, "twenty-somethings" might check in to local bars, restaurants and concert halls on Foursquare, freight containers would check in to ports, steamships and rail yards. While social moms might check in to shopping malls or neighborhood parks on Foursquare; pallets of goods would check in to distribution centers and retail stores. High-volume suppliers would be able to compete for the honor of becoming the mayor of the Desoto, Texas Walmart Distribution Center or Pier G of the Long Beach Port Authority.

A Foursquare-like, check-in capability would solve numerous supply chain problems. But is it feasible given today's technology? The key requirement would be the empowerment of "dumb products" to automatically check-in to various locations. And the process should work without having a human perform a manual activity, such as scanning a barcode label. It is interesting to note that many of the goods traversing supply chains actually come equipped with auto-identification or geo-location technologies. For example, most high tech goods are equipped with GPS locators, Wi-Fi antennas and Bluetooth capabilities. Of course, while in transit these devices are powered off, rendering the communications functions useless for location-based tracking services. Even if high tech products could leverage their embedded communications capabilities while in transit, these products only represent one category of goods. A broader tracking capability would be required for raw materials, apparel, pharmaceuticals, fast-moving consumer goods, automotive parts and defense equipment, to name just a few.

For automatic inventory check-in to work, the goods would need to be equipped with a transmitter that required no embedded power source. Inventory detectors would have to be installed in retail stores, manufacturing plants, distribution centers and cargo ports to capture the movement of products. The system I am describing is similar to RFID or Radio Frequency Identification. RFID technology includes electronic tags that can store data about the identification, location or condition of a physical item. The data on the tag is communicated via radio frequency waves using an antenna wrapped around the chip. RFID technologies provide an excellent model for self-check-in as the tags can broadcast through most packaging materials, avoiding the need to unpack goods to determine the contents

The Barcode

The technology that has historically been used to track inventory as it travels through the supply chain is the barcode. If you have used self-check-out at a grocery store recently, you are probably familiar with the idea of a barcode. Shoppers aim the barcode label on the product at a reader in the check-out aisle. Once scanned, the barcode uniquely identifies the product and its price. Barcodes play the same role when you check out with a retail sales associate. Whether it is a department store, convenience store or home improvement center, the clerk at the cash register scans the barcode on the item which automatically identifies the item and its price.

You probably have not given much thought as to how the barcode works—because it is so common in our everyday lives—and works almost flawlessly. The key to the barcode is the variable width, parallel lines that represent machine readable data. In the case of an item sold at a grocery store, the lines represent a Global Trade Identification Number (GTIN). GTINs are not as well-known as their predecessor, the UPC or Universal Product Code that was widely used in North America. And if you live in Europe or Asia you may have heard of EANs or European Article Numbers. GTINs were recently introduced as a global standard to replace UPCs and EANs. The GTIN is a 14-digit code that uniquely identifies a specific product. Some barcodes also include the GTIN in printed text below the black and white lines. The human readable format is used the event that the barcode will not scan. The item's identification can then be typed into a cash register or other system manually.

The numbers stored on an RFID tag are more specific than the GTINs on a barcode. RFID tags store an Electronic Product Code or EPC. The EPC numbering scheme was created to provide a unique identifier for every physical object in the world. One of the first applications of EPC was to identify objects in the supply chain. In other words, the EPC is created by taking a GTIN for the specific product type and appending it with a unique serial number. Today, EPCs are managed by an organization called EPCglobal which is owned by the GS1 organization and GS1 US. The ownership model makes sense when you consider that GS1 also administers the allocation of the GTINs used in barcodes.

While barcodes and RFID have many similarities, there are also many differences. For one, RFID tags do not require line of sight to be read as a barcode scanner does. A barcode can only store "static data" such as a product identifier, manufacturing location or expiration date. An RFID tag can store all of these static data elements as well as dynamic data that changes during the transportation or warehousing process. RFID tags can capture information about environmental factors, such as temperature and humidity, as well as packaging integrity and security. Such a feature is useful when tracking medical vaccines or seafood products that are highly sensitive to changes in temperature. The ability to track the environmental characteristics of these "cold chain" products throughout their lifecycle can help to identify potential incidents of contamination. RFID tags can monitor whether the items were exposed to temperatures or humidity levels outside the specified range.

How RFID Works

The process starts with a manufacturer tagging a specific product. Most RFID tags are so thin that you would not even notice that a packaging label had an RFID tag unless someone pointed it out. Your may not be aware but it is likely that your passport probably has an RFID tag embedded in the cover. In the presence of a hardware device called a reader, the tags emit an electromagnetic frequency. The tag effectively broadcasts the data stored on it, such as an EPC code. Readers can be handheld devices that move around with a person. Alternatively, readers can be mounted onto fixed locations, such as the loading dock of a distribution center. When placed in a busy distribution center, RFID readers can capture massive amounts of raw data from the tags. Many of the "reads" are duplicates that must be filtered before the data can be used. Specialized middleware software called a Savant is used to capture and filter the data from the readers. Savant is one of my favorite terms used in the B2B e-commerce space. Why such a fancy name was awarded to a fairly mundane piece of software is something I have never understood. I mention Savant in my conversations at least once a day just to impress people. Once filtered, the data can be routed by the Savant to supply chain management applications, such as a warehouse or inventory management system.

One of the biggest benefits of RFID is to share data with business partners in the supply chain about the location of products and the quantity of inventory. Suppliers who are increasingly responsible for managing inventory on behalf of their customers are particularly interested in visibility to stock positions at distribution centers, manufacturing plants and retail stores. And if the appropriate technology infrastructure was in place, RFID could make sharing this information almost effortless.

How RFID Tagged Me

RFID is actually the reason that you are reading this book. RFID was the "killer technology" that attracted me to the supply chain and ultimately

GXS. I first learned about RFID at a Forrester Research Consumer Products Conference in Chicago, IL on October 21st, 2002. It was at this conference that the power of the supply chain really became clear to me. The theme of the conference was "Winning in a Walmart World." Christine Spivey Overby, Forrester's lead Consumer Products analyst at the time, gave the keynote presentation on Walmart. The presentation was remarkably timely, as Walmart was in the middle of an unbelievable growth spurt. The mass merchandiser had grown from $118 billion annual revenues[152] in 1998 to just under $218 billion in 2002.[153]

October 2002 was a fascinating time to be in the retail supply chain. The B2B e-marketplace shakeout was almost completed—leaving only Transora, WWRE and GNX standing. UCCnet was beginning to gain adoption as a data synchronization platform for the grocery industry. Walmart had just announced its plans to switch to Internet-EDI away from traditional VANs. And a new wave of disruptive technologies was beginning to enter the industry in the form of RFID.

Without question the technology I was most interested in was RFID. Another speaker at the Forrester event was Kevin Ashton, Director of the Auto-ID Center at the Massachusetts Institute of Technology. Ashton was formerly an assistant brand manager at Procter & Gamble who had left the consumer products giant to focus on developing RFID technologies. The Auto-ID center was funded by the Uniform Code Council, P&G, Gillette and 100 other organizations around the world.[154] Its mission was to develop an Electronic Product Code which would supersede the barcode as the primary auto-identification technology in the supply chain.

Changing Retail Forever

The retail and pharmaceutical segments were targeted as having the highest potential for savings from RFID. There were numerous retail scenarios that were appealing, but one that seemed to have universal value was measuring promotion effectiveness. Consumer products manufacturers spend up to 15% of annual revenues on trade promotions. There are hundreds of different types of promotions. The most common example is the manufacturer's coupon, which you may have clipped in a Sunday circular, then redeemed at your local store. Most trade promotions, such as coupons, involve a discount to the end consumer. Increasingly, however, trade promotions require less of a premeditated act on the part of the consumer. Instead, promotions are designed to generate impulse purchases of items that may not have been on a consumer's shopping list. The promotions may be as simple as a short-term price discount. Alternatively, a promotion might entice a consumer with the offer of additional product at a reduced price. Buy-One-Get-One Free (BOGO) is a common example as are value packs and bonus packs.

Despite the billions of dollars manufacturers spend on trade promotions, retailers often fail to execute on these marketing programs. In many cases, promotional displays or product inventory are not moved to the sales floor in a synchronized timeframe with the advertisements. You may see an advertisement for discounted paper towels in the Sunday circular, but arrive at the store only to find there is no such deal. Instead, both the product and display may be sitting in the "back room" of a store during a promotional period. Of course, manufacturers have no way to monitor retailer execution of promotions unless they dispatch a sales representative to check the merchandise displays at each store.

RFID could help track the retailer execution of promotions. Manufacturers could install RFID tags on promotional displays and inventory prior to shipping. Retailers could install fixed RFID readers in the doorways leading from the back room to the sales floor. When displays and inventory are moved onto the sales floor, the timing and quantities could be automatically recorded, then communicated to the manufacturer. Visibility to in-store product movements could quickly identify retail chains and individual stores that are not executing promotions effectively. Real-world implementations of RFID by Kimberly Clark and P&G's Gillette division have found that one third of all stores don't execute promotions properly.[155]

Stopping Counterfeit Drugs

The pharmaceutical supply chain was also believed to be an area of significant opportunity for RFID. In the pharmaceutical supply chain, prescription drugs need to be tracked closely since they are expensive and tightly regulated during distribution. However, the drugs are packaged in small containers, making tracking via barcode or other line-of-sight technologies cumbersome due to the need to unpack and physically inspect shipment contents. The most significant challenge with pharmaceuticals relates to counterfeit drugs. Fake pills, which are prevalent in many markets, may contain incorrect ingredients, improper dosages or hazardous ingredients. Counterfeit drugs are often sold under a false brand name. Unsuspecting users of counterfeit drugs may experience side effects, allergic reactions or worsening of medical conditions.

Counterfeit drugs are big business. Experts estimate that 10% of drugs worldwide are counterfeit. Certain countries have counterfeit levels as high as 50%.[156] The World Health Organization estimates the annual earnings from counterfeit drugs were over $32 billion.[157] Distributors of these products can generate significant margins because they do not have to incur any R&D expenses to develop the drugs, nor do they have to pay the full costs for the medicinal substance called the "active ingredient." Egypt, China and India are known to be among the leading suppliers of these fake products.

Efforts to identify counterfeit drugs in the supply chain have focused on establishing a "pedigree" for pharmaceuticals. The pedigree would include the name of the manufacturer, distributor and pharmacy that handled the drugs. Specific details, such as the manufacturing lot number, drug potency and expiration date, could be tracked as well. At each step in the distribution process, supply chain participants would add to the pedigree until it reaches a point of care or point of sale. Numerous US states and the FDA have proposed regulation that would require manufacturers, distributors and retailers to maintain an electronic pedigree for all drugs sold. RFID is viewed as the ideal solution to track the pedigree for pharmaceuticals.

By tagging pharmaceutical products with RFID, participants in the supply chain could quickly inventory all products in the case without having to unpack and manually scan barcode labels on each bottle. RFID tags with serialized identifiers would be more challenging to counterfeit, thereby enabling law enforcement officials to quickly differentiate authentic products from fakes. RFID also provides additional benefits for products which are sensitive to changes in the surrounding environment. As mentioned earlier, these active RFID tags can track and store changes to temperature or humidity, indicating a product may have been mishandled, and therefore not safe for use.

The Walmart Effect

Although the technology had been under development for years, RFID activity did not pick up until Walmart mandated it in 2005. The announcement from Walmart required its top 100 suppliers apply RFID tags to all shipments destined for three Texas distribution centers. Later that year the University of Arkansas conducted a study on the impact of RFID on reducing out-of-stocks.[158] It was demonstrated that product availability issues were reduced by 21% by the introduction of RFID into retail stores. The US Department of Defense (DOD) followed Walmart as the second entity to request RFID tagging by its suppliers. The US DOD and Walmart have two of the largest procurement organizations in the world, each with annual spending budgets larger than the GDP of most countries. It was believed by many, the Walmart and DOD mandates would act as a tipping point for RFID adoption, leading to high volume demand and lower pricing. However, unlike other technology mandates from Walmart, RFID adoption was not as fast as expected.

Chapter 11
Barcode

Despite the fanfare RFID enjoyed in the media following the Walmart and US DOD announcements, there were major challenges with RFID in 2005. Tag failure rates were unacceptably high at 30%, particularly when placed near metals and liquids. Many consumer products have metal packaging or liquid contents which interfered with RFID transmissions. Consumer privacy advocates waged a publicity campaign against RFID tags, claiming retailers had some Orwellian conspiracy to use the tags to track the purchasing patterns of consumers and their movements post sale.

Without question, the most significant challenge for RFID was cost, particularly for low value items. It was believed that if RFID labels could be reduced to five cents each, then a retailer could tag every item in a supermarket. The ROI was questionable to many; however, given that five cents is often more than the margin a retailer makes from selling a low-priced item. A magic number of 10 million tags per order was discussed as the threshold at which the chips became affordable in mass. But in 2005, not even the most wildly optimistic forecasts showed demand for such volumes for yet another five to ten years. Forrester Research and other analysts published research clearly stating that such price points would not be realized in the near term, but the hype continued unabated.[159] IBM announced a $250 million commitment to RFID at the end of 2004.[160]

IBM was not the only believer. There were thousands of other believers who thought RFID was going to be the biggest disruptive technology the supply chain had ever seen. Many of the believers were from the vendor community that produced the RFID technology and had the most to gain from its success.

The first category of vendors sold RFID hardware, such as readers and tags. Specialized players, such as Zebra Technologies and Alien Technologies, that focused purely on auto-identification technologies such as barcodes and RFID were among the leading hardware vendors. Larger semiconductor manufacturers, such as Philips Semi and Texas Instruments, quickly joined the tag manufacturing sector, seeking to exploit the massive opportunity. Companies, such as IBM, Sun, Intermec, ThingMagic and Symbol Technology, manufactured the RFID readers.

There were also software vendors that created the Savant middleware to exchange data between the readers and business applications. Many of the traditional integration companies, such as Microsoft, IBM, webMethods and TIBCO, offered Savants. Application vendors from the ERP and Supply Chain Management segments began to develop RFID-specific modules, including SAP, Oracle, Manugistics, Red Prairie and Manhattan Associates. And of course, the large systems integrators such as Accenture, IBM, Capgemini and Deloitte developed practices focused on RFID.

Vendors were not the only ones drinking the RFID "Kool-Aid." Other believers included companies such as Intel and Procter & Gamble, each of which had Vice President-level executives responsible for RFID Research and Development. Johnson & Johnson, Gillette, Walmart, Tesco and Metro were also strong advocates.

Perhaps the peak of the insanity and hype was the EPCglobal US 2004 conference held in Baltimore, Maryland. I did not attend the event, but several of my colleagues did. There were over 2,000 attendees present and 100 exhibitors onsite. What no one seemed to recognize was that the actual end-user companies that would buy the technologies represented only a small minority at the event. There were few real-world case studies for RFID at the time. Outside of the handful of consumer products companies that invested in the Auto ID Labs, not many businesses were using the technology.

Lots of bizarre behaviors occurred during the RFID Hype Cycle that no one seemed to question at the time. For example, China was not actively involved in the standards development for RFID, which is ironic, considering that the majority of the products to be tracked using EPC are manufactured in that country. Early RFID efforts focused primarily on the consumer products and pharmaceutical sectors. The high tech industry, that had the most to gain from the sales of RFID tags, readers, and associated IT infrastructure, was not active in RFID pilots.

Lacking the adoption rates forecasted by technology vendors, the data sync movement began to seek out more compelling techniques for demonstrating ROI. The data synchronization community chose to ride on the coattails of RFID, evangelizing that the benefits of EPC could not be realized without data synchronization. The idea behind EPC was that a tag read would not only identify the product, but also provide the associated attribute data such as weight, dimensions, storage and transportation requirements simultaneously. However, the tags did not store product information. The EPC on the tag was just a 14-digit GTIN and a serial number. Instead, the source of the product attribute information was the data pools of the GDSN. Without the GDSN being populated and linked to the EPC, there would be little value. A house of cards began to develop with several technologies of questionable ROI becoming co-dependent upon each other for adoption.

Needless to say, the RFID bubble burst. After peaking in 2005 and 2006, the noise surrounding RFID quieted to a whisper by early 2007. Suddenly no one was talking about RFID. The media abandoned the concept. Analysts avoided discussions about it. Technology vendors moved on to the next new thing. The fallout of RFID resembled the dot-com collapse, but without the stock market impacts. And the world continued to use barcodes for product identification as it had been doing for thirty years.

The Barcode Almost Failed

Although barcodes are nearly ubiquitous in today's commercial environment, the technology struggled to gain adoption in its early years. The first work on barcode technologies started back in 1948 at Drexel University. Ironically, the actual usage of RFID predated the ideation of the barcode by almost 10 years.[161] The original RFID technologies were developed by the defense community for use during World War II. The UK developed IFF (Identify Friend or Foe) transponders that were used to distinguish allied war planes from enemy fighters.[162] In the early 1950s, IBM was among the first technology firms to investigate the technology. However, IBM concluded that practical widespread adoption would not be feasible for several decades. They were correct. The grocery industry did not adopt barcodes for two more decades.

Earlier in the chapter, I discussed several examples of where RFID failed, but barcodes were successful. It is interesting to note that in many cases where the barcode failed, RFID succeeded. In the 1960s, several US railroads tested barcodes to track the location of individual rail cars. While the need for such an auto-identification technology for rail cars was not disputed, the industry was struggling with financial distress and widespread bankruptcies during the evaluation period.[163] As a result, making a business case for implementing barcode label technology was challenging for the railroads. There were also technology limitations that the barcode could not easily overcome. For example, the dirt that accumulates on the side of box cars prevented barcode readers from working properly. Today, North American railroad operators use RFID tags to track locomotives and rolling stock. The tags identify the owner, car number, equipment type and number of axles.

Also in the 1960s, toll collection facilities were interested in using barcodes to automate the scanning of cars that had purchased a monthly pass. Of course today, RFID technology is widely used for prepaid toll passes on highways throughout the world.

Although barcodes are best known for their use in the retail sector the first commercial use of the technology occurred in the US automotive industry. GM used barcodes to monitor the production of automobile axles at a Buick factory in Flint, Michigan during 1969.[164] Yet Flint is better known as the home of controversial filmmaker Michael Moore. But barcode usage did not accelerate until the next year—1970—when the National Association of Food Chains established a committee to develop uniform grocery barcodes. Much like RFID, the original barcode development project was very high profile within the retail sector with high ranking industry executives on the committee. The President of H.J. Heinz and Vice Chairman of Kroger were dedicated to the effort. In 1972, Kroger started an 18-month pilot program to test barcodes in one of its Cincinnati stores.[165] However, the first official UPC barcode scan did not occur until June of 1974. A 10-pack of Wrigley's gum was the first item sold with the help of a barcode at a Marsh Supermarket in Ohio.[166] In the decade that followed, adoption by retailers soared. By the early 1980s, a third of all retail products had barcodes.

During its early years, the barcode experienced similar adoption challenges to RFID. There was pushback from consumer privacy groups worried about the tracking of purchases. In fact, TV host, Phil Donahue, described barcodes as a "corporate plot against consumers."[167] Organized labor groups were concerned about staffing cuts and potential health hazards of laser usage in the workplace. Religious factions claimed that the codes hid the demonic number 666.

Much as with RFID, the barcode was challenged to demonstrate ROI. An IBM analysis suggested that grocery retailers would not break even until 70% of all products had barcodes printed by the manufacturer. The up-front investment required by retailers was substantial. Each grocery store had to spend $120,000 on new barcode scanning equipment. But the benefits proved to be real. Within five weeks of installing barcode scanners, most grocery stores experienced a 10 to 12% increase in sales. Retailers were able to better track inventory with barcode scans contributing to fewer out-of-stocks. Furthermore, stores experienced a 1 to 2% decrease in operating costs, allowing for the flexibility to lower prices.[168] Real quantitative benefits could be achieved simply by improving the checkout process.

The original McKinsey & Company study on barcodes estimated that the retail industry would save $150M per year. However, in 1999 PriceWaterhouseCoopers conducted a study that found the UPC barcode's value exceeded the original forecast by a multiple of 45.[169]

One important thing to note is that the barcodes found on items do not actually include the price. Instead the barcode only contains the GTIN or unique product identifier. Why not embed the price in the barcode? It is not a technology limitation. In fact, more advanced types of barcodes can represent much more than a product identifier. Retailers want the flexibility to be able to change price without having to touch the individual price labels on tens of thousands of items in their stores. Price changes can be much more easily implemented by updating the data in their Point-of-Sale systems which control the cash registers.

Imagine if we did not have barcode technology today. Employees at Walmart or Target stores, which can be as large as 100,000 square feet, would have to stick price labels on each individual product in the store. Believe it or not, there are some US states that have not fully embraced the idea of barcode lookups for price discovery. Both Michigan and Massachusetts have statewide laws which require retailers to affix a price sticker to each and every item in the store. These price stickers are applied in addition to barcode systems as a means of ensuring the price for each item is clearly identified. The laws are designed to protect consumers against scanner errors and potential pricing scams. Theoretically, an unscrupulous retailer could put a lower price label (e.g., $0.50) next to an item on the store shelf, but actually charge more (e.g., $0.75) when the item is scanned at the point of sale. Think about the last time you actually matched all the prices on your grocery store receipt to the price you saw in the aisle.

Consumer protection laws in states like Michigan enable a consumer to sue retailers for $250 in damages plus court costs, if the price scanned at checkout is different from what is marked on the sticker. Labor unions are strong advocates of the price sticker laws. For example, the United Food and Commercial Workers of Michigan estimates that without the price sticker law up to a third of store employees would be out of work. Most retailers find price stickers to be highly inefficient. Prices change frequently in the retail sector, particularly for "Fast Moving Consumer Goods" sold through convenience and grocery stores. A study underwritten by the Michigan Retailers Association found that the price sticker law adds $2.2 billion of increased costs per year for stores. Keeping the stickers on items can be particularly challenging in categories such as frozen foods. Moisture in the freezers loosens adhesives that end up clogging drains of refrigeration units.[170]

Barcodes are Everywhere

Today, nearly everything you can buy in a store has a barcode, even if the retailers in specific states choose not to use barcodes to look up the price within their systems. Barcodes cost less than a penny to implement, which remains less than RFID. In fact, use of barcodes for consumer applications has grown even faster since the mainstream introduction of RFID. If you have gone to a concert or sporting event recently, you may have noticed barcodes on your ticket. Many entertainment venues now scan the barcodes prior to admittance. Barcodes help entertainment companies identify fake tickets. If you have been admitted to a hospital recently, you may have received a wristband printed with a barcode label. The barcode can not only uniquely identify you, but also can provide details about known allergies and medical history when scanned. If you have checked a bag with an airline recently, you may have noticed that a barcode is printed on the luggage tag. Barcode readers are used throughout airline cargo management systems to route and track luggage. You also may have noticed a barcode on your last boarding pass. The airlines scan the barcode to verify you are on the correct flight before admittance onto the jetway. Even rental cars have barcode labels on the windshield. When returning your car to the lot, attendees will scan the barcode to identify the vehicle and your rental contract.

Perhaps the fastest growing use of barcodes is for price discovery on mobile phones. As discussed in Chapter 9, consumers can use applications, such as Red Laser, to take photos of barcodes and then query the web to determine if the item is cheaper elsewhere. Digital cameras have become almost ubiquitous on mobile phones today. I am not aware of any smartphones equipped with RFID readers, leading me to believe that barcodes will remain popular in the years to come.

RFID—The End and the Beginning of the Story

You may be wondering what did happen to RFID. As stated in a 2009 *Information Week* article, RFID did not end up "changing the world" as many predicted, but it has made slow and steady progress in many industries.[171] Consumer products manufacturers such as Kimberly Clark and Procter & Gamble are no longer the strong public advocates they were back in 2005. However, some retailers such as Marks & Spencer, Metro, Tesco and Walmart have continued to evolve their RFID programs.

Walmart's RFID efforts continue to enjoy the media spotlight. In 2007, Walmart expanded the program to include shipments to selected Sam's Club distribution centers. In 2010, Walmart announced a plan to begin tagging jeans to improve inventory management. Blue jeans are a particularly challenging merchandise category to manage. There are many different sizes, styles, and washes. Jeans are typically stacked for display in a manner that does not allow store associates to identify potential out-of-stocks. By tagging the jeans, retailers can quickly assess inventory positions by waving a RFID reader in the proximity of the items.

Walmart is not the only retailer utilizing RFID to manage inventory of apparel merchandise. In fact, there has been a surge in interest for RFID within the department store and apparel sectors in recent years. Numerous public case studies have documented the benefits found by American Apparel. The retailer has wall-mounted RFID readers on the stockroom doors to track which items are moved onto the sales floor. American Apparel has found that it can reduce staff levels by 20-30% in RFID-enabled stores by eliminating manual inventory checks. Furthermore, American Apparel found that sales rose by 14% in stores with RFID compared to those without.[172]

Perhaps, the retail industry had the right idea with RFID but was focused initially on the wrong merchandise categories. Instead of food and beverages, the industry could have realized greater ROI from tagging apparel and footwear merchandise. Nonetheless, the RFID sector has moved on and is no longer dependent upon retail for its livelihood. Only 10% of the $6 billion RFID sector is funded by the retail supply chain. The other 90% of spend represents a diverse range of industries, the largest of which is the public sector. One of the biggest users of active RFID tags is the US Department of Defense, which tracks all shipping containers outside the US with RFID. Other significant uses include private toll roads that use RFID in pre-paid, windshield-mounted passes to track usage in countries from Pakistan to Brazil. Public transportation systems, ranging from London's Oyster card to Hong Kong's Octopus card, are RFID-based. RFID tags are used extensively in passports. Malaysia was the first to tag passports, recording the travel history of entries and exits from the country. The US introduced RFID tags to new passports in 2006. The Chinese government is perhaps the biggest investor, spending $6 billion over several years, to embed RFID tags into all of its national ID cards.[173]

Even the casino industry uses RFID tags to track high-value chips, as a means of preventing counterfeiting and theft. The Bellagio casino was robbed of $1.5 million of chips in 2010. The tags in the chips were immediately invalidated by the Bellagio, making the value zero.[174] Perhaps the RFID tagging of chips as a theft deterrent, is a key reason why we have not seen *Oceans 14* released yet.

SECTION 4
Health Care

Chapter 12
Electronic Health Networks

Have you noticed that every time you visit a new doctor you are forced to fill out a small mountain of paperwork? Suppose that your primary care physician refers you to a specialist for a consultation. When you arrive at the specialist's office, you typically will spend 15 minutes in the waiting room filling out forms. There are questions about your demographics, family history, current medications, known allergies, surgery history and insurance carrier. Once you speak to the specialist, you discover they seem to know very little about your situation and medical history. The situation is not very confidence-inspiring. You might presume that the redundancy in information gathering is due to the cautious and overly inquisitive nature of physicians, but this is not the case. In today's health care system there is very limited information sharing between different physicians. The limited data sharing that does occur is usually over the phone, fax or illegible handwritten notes.

The average person's medical records are scattered across several different physicians' offices, hospitals, laboratories and radiology centers. Studies have found that pertinent patient health information is undeliverable in 81% of cases in outpatient clinics.[175] The situation is worse for certain patient groups, such as seniors on Medicare that visit an average of 6.4 different providers every year.[176]

Today's paper-based health record system not only introduces higher costs, but it also introduces unnecessary risks. Imagine a patient being admitted in an unconscious state to an emergency room after an automobile accident. The attending physician will have no information about the patient's medical history, current medications or known allergies. As a result, the physician needs to substitute educated guesses in place of objective data. The situation creates serious risks to the patient's health. At the very least, missing information could lead to suboptimal care, return visits or adverse side effects. At worst, incomplete medical records could lead to a life-threatening misdiagnosis or even death.

The best analysis of health records in the US was published in 2004 by the Center for Information Technology Leadership (CITL) study. The specific report, entitled *The Value of Healthcare Information Exchange and Interoperability*, found that $77.8 billion in annual savings would be realized by electronically connecting the various organizations in the US health care industry. In order to achieve the savings, the health care industry would need to deploy a framework for sharing Electronic Health Records (EHRs) across a National Health Information Network (NHIN).

An EHR would store a comprehensive set of information about each patient, including personal demographics; weight; current and past medications; immunization status; known allergies; radiology images; laboratory test results; past surgeries; family medical history; discharge notes; insurance carrier's name and group number; patient's co-payment responsibilities and privacy policy preferences.

EHRs have the potential to radically improve administrative efficiency, enhance the quality of care and reduce the spread of disease. For example, EHRs could reduce duplicate lab tests and radiology requests. And they could reduce the likelihood of a doctor prescribing a drug that leads to adverse reactions with other medications that are already being taken. Let's explore each of these concepts in further detail, starting with the redundant tests.

Two Lab Tests are Better than One

A friend of mine experienced some minor complications during a recent pregnancy, so her primary doctor referred her to a specialist for further consultation. Upon arrival at the specialist's office, she was told by the nurse that she needed to have a pregnancy test performed before any further analysis could be done. Her response, of course, was that the sole reason for her visit was to discuss the side-effects of her current pregnancy. The nurse acknowledged, but stated that her medical records had no documentation or proof of her status. Consequently, although she was five months pregnant and noticeably "showing," an additional lab test needed to be performed. This is one of the more ridiculous examples of how the US health care system continues to be fraught with waste and inefficiency. And although I suspect this specific scenario does not occur with a great deal of frequency, there are numerous cases in which duplicate lab tests or radiology images are ordered.

As discussed earlier, patient's medical records exist primarily on paper today in the US. Consequently, the records do not travel with patients as they visit different providers, such as specialists or emergency care locations. Often, physicians need access to lab tests and radiology images, in order to make an accurate clinical diagnosis. In the absence of a complete medical record, physicians may be unaware that a particular test has been performed. Or, if they are aware, they may not have access to the results or associated images. In such a scenario, physicians are prone to order a redundant test in order to gather the information they require.

Duplicate lab testing is more widespread than you might expect. The CITL study found that 14.3% of all lab orders were considered duplicative or unnecessary.[177] In other words, a similar test had been performed recently. With electronic records, the lab tests and radiology images become portable and available on demand to whichever physician needs the data to make a decision.

Electronic records could also help reduce other inefficiencies associated with processing lab tests and radiology orders. Controlling expenses associated with lab tests is one of those examples. Lab order forms rarely include pricing, because the costs vary, depending upon the insurance company used and the patient's benefits plan. Consequently, physicians may unintentionally order an expensive test rather than seek out less costly mechanisms to gather the necessary information. Electronic records would provide access to a patient's insurance profile and the corresponding price schedule, enabling physicians to better assess costs at the point of care.

Another root cause of inefficiency in the area of laboratory and radiology images is that most physicians' offices have to outsource these tests to third-party providers. Smaller practices lack the funding, resources and space to host the lab equipment in-house. Outsourcing of tests is a smart decision for smaller practices, but does create additional administrative overhead in the form of interactions with the third-party lab or imaging center. Paper-based lab or radiology forms must be filled out by physicians, then mailed or faxed to the lab. The lab must then re-key the order form into the administrative systems they use. Once completed, the lab results must be mailed back to the provider who then has to insert them into the patient's records. Often, when test results are not received in a timely manner, the provider will phone the lab to obtain the information verbally.

The process of scheduling, ordering and reporting on each lab test performed by a third party may seem insignificant for one individual request. However, multiplied across the hundreds of thousands of lab orders placed daily across the US, the aggregated costs are quite considerable. The process for radiology images such as x-rays, ultrasound, computed topography (CT), positron emission topography (PET) and magnetic resonance imaging (MRI) is similar. Duplicate tests are frequently ordered using paper-based processes.

Electronic transmission would eliminate all of the clerical work associated with printing, mailing and filing the paper documents. Furthermore, it would substantially reduce inbound calls to labs from physicians' offices by accelerating the transmission of results. The CITL study concluded that a total $31.8 billion in costs could be reduced by establishing full electronic connectivity between physicians and laboratories.[178] An additional $26.2 billion could be eliminated by automating interactions between physicians and radiology centers.[179]

As with the other industries we have discussed, there is a long list of B2B e-commerce standards in use throughout the health care industry. There are specialized B2B standards specifically for electronically transmitting lab test results and radiology images. For example, ELINCS is the EHR-Lab Interoperability and Connectivity Specification. It is specifically designed to transfer the results of lab tests to EHRs. Suppose you visit a third-party lab such as Quest Diagnostics to have a drug screening or cholesterol test performed. ELINCS would provide a method for Quest to send the results of your test into your EHR for future reference.

Most radiology images are stored in a format called DICOM or Digital Imaging and Communications in Medicine. The DICOM standard ensures that images created on various medical devices are technically interoperable across different equipment and hospitals. DICOM is used in radiology, cardiology, oncology, dentistry, surgery, pathology and even veterinary offices.

What Medications are You Taking?

The previous examples focused on the external communication breakdowns between different organizations. However, my experience has been that within a single hospital or medical practice there is a lack of record sharing as well. Even when you visit the same doctor consistently, you are still asked a series of repetitive questions. For example, every time I visit my primary care physician, both the nurse that checks my vitals and the physician who consults me, ask for a list of current medications.

Why doesn't the provider track the prescriptions that I am taking since they are the ones recommending the medications in the first place? The CITL study found, on average, a primary care physician knows only 70% of their patient's medications.[180] Patients may not know their complete medication list either, especially those with chronic diseases. The problem is more challenging for specialists, who typically only know 40% of the drugs used by their patients.[181] Emergency room and urgent care providers may not know any of the prescription drugs, as they are dependent upon a patient being conscious and capable of providing the list. Surely, the process of tracking prescription medications by patients could be simplified. The good news is there has been an effort underway for almost a decade to digitize the exchange of prescription data throughout the health care system.

The initiatives, commonly referred to as e-prescription or e-Rx, have taken longer than expected to deploy due to regulatory barriers. The ability to send e-prescriptions had to be approved state-by-state in each domicile's legislature. Today, all 50 states and the District of Columbia now support electronic transactions for most prescription drugs. In fact, many states have active incentive programs in place, via their Medicaid or Health Department organizations, to financially reward providers for e-prescription adoption. In addition to the state-sponsored incentives, numerous catalysts, such as the American Recovery and Reinvestment Act (ARRA), are combining to accelerate e-prescription usage at an exponential rate. There are three primary use-case scenarios for e-prescriptions today.

In the first scenario, a doctor needs to obtain information about the patient's health insurance benefits before prescribing a new medication. And in many cases, the physician needs to understand the preferred medications, or "formulary" of the patient's insurance company. Most large health insurers sign contracts with specialized firms called Pharmacy Benefits Managers (PBMs) to manage their prescription drug benefit programs. PBMs negotiate discounts with pharmacies on certain brands of medications that become the basis for the formulary. As a general rule, PBMs and insurers prefer that prescriptions are written for lower cost, generic drugs, rather than name brand pharmaceuticals, in order to reduce costs. Enabling physicians to access formularies and eligibility data before writing a prescription, can help facilitate a significant reduction in prescription drug costs.

A similar, but secondary scenario involves obtaining a patient's prescription drug history. With a patient's consent, a doctor can use e-prescription technologies to obtain a list of current and past medications. The benefits of knowing this information are numerous. Physicians can avoid harmful drug-to-drug interactions. Certain drugs should not be taken while pregnant or past a certain age. Actor Heath Ledger's death in January 2008 was found to be due to an accidental, but toxic combination of painkillers, anti-anxiety drugs and sleeping pills.[182] The exact number of deaths due to adverse drug reactions is unknown. Some estimate that 7,000 deaths per year occur, while others believe a more accurate statistic is 100,000 per year. If the latter statistic is correct, then adverse drug reactions would be the fourth leading cause of death in the US, ranking above diabetes, AIDS, pneumonia, accidents and automobile deaths.[183]

The third scenario is electronic prescription routing between a doctor and a pharmacy. Doctors have notoriously bad handwriting. It is amazing to me that there is not a higher rate of fatalities and hospitalizations due to incorrectly interpreted prescriptions. The CITL study found that 10% of handwritten prescriptions are illegible to pharmacists, resulting in a follow-up call.[184] Fortunately, not all providers use handwritten prescriptions. Some 50% of doctors phone prescriptions in.[185] While the phone calls may be less prone to error than chicken-scratch notes, the process does consume a few minutes of time for a nurse or administrative staffer.

E-Prescription Networks

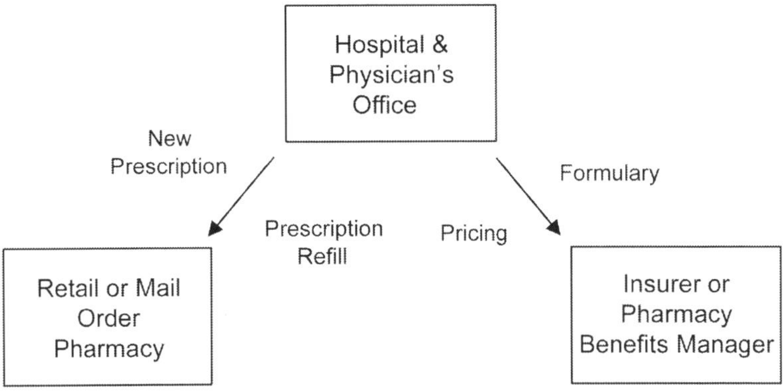

Perhaps, the biggest benefit of e-prescription technology found in the refill process. Instead of pharmacies having to fax or phone in renewal authorizations, the request can be sent from the physician or hospital's systems electronically to the pharmacy. Electronic routing eliminates the 15 minutes of a nurse's time processing a refill.[186]

E-Prescription Networks and Standards

During the dot-com era, there were two specialized e-prescription networks formed in the US. The first one represented the pharmacies and the other represented the Pharmacy Benefit Managers (PBMs). Surescripts was formed in 2001, by the National Association of Chain Drug Stores and National Community Pharmacists Association, as a privately held company. The second was RxHub, founded by PBMs—CVS Caremark, Express Scripts and Medco. Seeking to improve interoperability and create further economies of scale, the two e-prescription networks, Surescripts and RxHub, merged in 2008. The merged company, using the Surescripts name, maintains a vast network of connections to pharmacies, providers and insurers for the purpose of e-prescription routing. In addition, Surescripts provides services such as certification, education and standards development.

Every year Surescripts publishes a report of the activity on their network, serving as a gauge of the growth in adoption of e-prescription technology. The 2009-2010 report had some very interesting data about the progress being made with specialized B2B integration networks. By the end of 2009, there were 156,000 "prescribers," such as hospitals or physicians' offices, routing prescriptions electronically. The 156,000 represents 25% of the potential. By the end of 2009, Surescripts had access to 65% of US patients' prescription benefit and history information. There were only two states—North Dakota and Mississippi—in which Surescripts had access to less than 40% of the population. The greatest adoption of any segment has been with retail pharmacies. Surescripts found that 97% of chain pharmacies, such as Rite Aid, CVS and Walgreens, were connected to e-prescription networks along with six of the largest mail-order pharmacies.[187]

The B2B e-commerce standards that support e-prescriptions routed over networks, such as Surescripts, are developed by the National Council for Prescription Drug Programs (NCPDP). There are specific messages for medical history inquiries, drug formulary information, new prescriptions and refill requests. NCPDP standards and the Surescripts network can also be utilized to populate an individual's EHR. Ideally, the system would be set up to always ensure that a patient's medication information is up-to-date, thereby empowering physicians with all the relevant historical information necessary to make a decision.

ARRA—More than Just Road Signs

EHRs became a popular topic in 2008 when President Obama made advancing the US health care system a top policy item for his administration. In fact, the American Recovery and Reinvestment Act (ARRA), passed in 2009, allocated federal funds to accelerate the adoption of EHR. Most people associate the ARRA with the road signs you see on secondary highways and bridges. After sitting in a 45-minute traffic jam, I am always pleased to see a sign that states, "This Project Funded by the American Recovery and Reinvestment Act" followed by "Your Tax Dollars at Work." Or maybe it is "Putting America to Work," but you get the idea. ARRA is about more than just road signs, however. The legislation includes a significant allocation of federal funds to build a series of regional Health Information Exchanges (HIE) for the exchange of EHRs.

The ARRA allocated $59 billion for health care reform. Specifically, included with the economic stimulus package, was the Health Information

Technology for Economic and Clinical Health Act (HITECH Act). HITECH provides funding for a number of grant programs for higher education programs in Health Information Technology as well as R&D funds to invest in fortifying security and network architectures for EHR. HITECH also includes grant programs to enable states to rapidly develop HIEs within their jurisdictions. As a result, in March 2010, over $500 billion in State Grants were awarded to 56 different US states and territories. The leading beneficiaries were the most populated states—California ($38 billion), Texas ($28 billion), New York ($22 billion), Florida ($20 billion) and Illinois ($18 billion). There is also a set of financial motivators for hospitals and physicians' offices to embrace EHR. Physicians can receive up to $44,000 of incentive payments, if they can demonstrate "meaningful use" of a certified EHR. Hospitals and larger provider groups are eligible for millions of dollars in incentives.[188] There are also penalties for those that do not participate. After 2015, deductions will begin to be assessed from Medicare payments for physicians or hospitals that have not met the EHR requirements.

A diverse and broad range of constituents in the health care community will benefit from sharing or viewing EHR. The largest benefits in both patient care and administrative efficiencies can be gained by hospitals and physicians' offices. Additionally, as discussed earlier, tremendous efficiency gains can be obtained by connecting independent laboratories, radiology centers, retail pharmacies and Pharmacy Benefit Managers.

Although entities such as Medicare, Medicaid and commercial health plans do not provide patient care, connections to these "organizations" will help to enrich the data available in an EHR. In the health care system, the insurers that pay the bills are frequently the most authoritative data source for details, such as prescriptions requested, lab tests ordered and physician visits.

One of the key B2B standards for exchanging data related to patient care is called Health Level Seven (HL7). The 7 in the name is a technical reference to the Open Systems Interconnection (OSI) model which governs how most computer and data networks interact. There are seven layers in the OSI model, with the top, or seventh, being the application layer that we humans utilize the most.

HL7 supports the delivery of clinical care at locations, such as a hospital, laboratory, imaging center and outpatient surgery center. Examples of business processes supported by HL7 include, patient admissions, registrations and discharges as well as appointment scheduling requests, changes and cancellations. There are also messages to support care delivery, such as requests for laboratory, imaging or blood product orders. Unlike many of the other health care B2B standards which focus on the US, HL7 has an international influence with many countries in Western Europe, Latin America and Asia.

HIEs—Coming to a County near You

EHRs are only valuable if the data within them can be accessed by the community of physicians providing care. As a result, the industry is in the process of building specialized networks called Health Information Exchanges (HIEs) to support the data exchange requirements of EHRs. HIEs will support all EHR-related transactions, including those already conducted on e-prescription and imaging networks today. The best source of information about the development of HIEs is an annual study released by the eHealth initiative. The 2010 version of the report, entitled *"State of the Health Information Exchange in 2010,"* indicated that there were over 230 active HIEs operating in the US. Many of these HIEs have been founded recently using federal funds allocated through the HITECH program of ARRA.[189]

One of the key issues with the US HIE sector is the high degree of fragmentation. The 230 HIEs are spread across all 50 states, DC and five US territories. Only 17 HIEs are operating in multiple states. The majority are focused on providing services in a single state. There is another group which operates in smaller geographic regions than a state. For example, 11 HIEs cover a single county and 6 HIEs cover only a single city or part of a county. As a result of the abundance of local HIEs, many of the more populated states have multiple HIEs operating within their borders. Florida alone has 22, while New York (20), California (15) and North Carolina (13) are not far behind. HIEs have also been established in numerous US territories, including Guam, Puerto Rico, American Samoa, Virgin Islands and the Mariana Islands.[190]

Today's community of HIEs is a patchwork of regional, state and county-level networks with each operating independently. The HIEs do not interoperate today which means that EHRs can only be shared within the confines of the geographic regions of their home network. Interoperability is not foremost on most HIEs' minds. Simply getting two providers within a community to exchange data with one another is still a major milestone, most have yet to achieve. Only a few state-designated HIEs are exchanging data across state lines today. However, there is a vision and plan to connect the HIEs together into one larger National Health Information Network (NHIN). The NHIN would provide portability of EHRs across the entire nation, ensuring that patients receive optimal care even when traveling to other states.

HIEs will also need to interoperate with the other health care networks in existence today. Earlier in this chapter, we discussed specialized e-prescription networks, such as Surescripts, that are designed to transmit new prescriptions, refill requests, formularies and benefits eligibility information between doctors, pharmacies and PBMs. There are also specialized networks to transmit radiology images, such as MRIs, CT-scans and X-rays. In the next chapter, we will discuss health care clearinghouses that are utilized to exchange claims and payment-related transactions.

The fragmentation of the HIE sector naturally leads to concerns about the financial viability of these networks in both the long and short term. Recall the explosion in B2B e-marketplaces that occurred in the dot-com era. The current HIE sector bears a striking resemblance to the marketplaces of the dot-com era. Of course, however, the HIEs are largely funded by government grants rather than venture capitalists.

In fact, building a sustainable business model was the top concern cited by HIEs in the 2010 eHealth study. A current concern for many in the industry is the dependency of HIEs upon continued federal or customer funding to support their operations. The ARRA funds have provided the "startup capital" for many of these organizations, but that seed funding may not be enough to reach profitability.

Not all HIEs are dependent upon federal funds, however. There are over 100 HIEs developed by consortia of private sector hospitals or insurers. Nonetheless, operating 230 different HIEs around the US does not lead to a sustainable model, in my opinion. Starting with smaller exchanges organized around local communities will catalyze growth, but likely lead to an eventual consolidation of networks.

Chapter 13
Health Care Claims & Payments

One of the largest opportunities for improvement of the US health care system is in the area of claims and payment processing. Approximately $2 trillion of payments is exchanged within the US health care sector annually. However, much of the spending is wasted on administrative overhead today. A 2007 study by the management consulting firm, McKinsey & Company, found that 15% of every dollar spent on health care in the US is applied to administrative costs associated with billing, invoicing, collections and losses in the form of bad debt.[191] Financial settlement in the health care sector is horribly inefficient when compared to other segments, such as retail, which average only 2% administrative overhead for payment processing. The issue has grown so problematic that Congress has proposed legislation, which would force insurers to use at least 85% of premiums received from large employers for medical care and profits. The law would effectively cap administrative costs at 15%.

The most significant challenges in processing inefficiencies are in the $1.3 trillion exchanged between the insurers paying health care claims and the hospitals and physicians' offices providing the services. McKinsey found that providers, such as hospitals and physicians' offices, spend $100 billion on claims submissions activities. And payers, such as health insurers, take another $150 billion in total operating costs and profits.[192] The authors of the McKinsey study stated, "Some of this spending—on actuarial activities, disease management, customer service, and wellness programs, for example—is clearly beneficial, and health insurers deserve a fair return for risking capital in an insurance business. But much of this expense comes from the contracting, claims and revenue-cycle processes, which are essentially payment and transaction-settlement functions."

Part of the excessive administrative costs is due to the manual, paper intensive nature of the claims and payment process. Health care transactions, such as claims submission and referral authorizations between insurers and hospitals or physicians' offices, are only partially automated. For example, only 40 to 60% of claims are submitted electronically.[193] As with other segments, the automation is concentrated within the largest firms.

However, the root causes of inefficiency are not simply a factor of using paper instead of electronic communications. Insurers have very specific policies on claims submission and reimbursement. You are probably familiar with this from your experiences with the health care system. When disputing or filing a claim you must submit very specific documentation filled out in the correct manner before the insurer will evaluate the request. Even if you submit all the appropriate documentation, your insurance policy may only cover a percentage of the associated fees for a hospital stay or doctor's visit. The highly specialized policies of insurers lead to a high percentage of denied claims and billing disputes, both of which require significant manual intervention.

Eligibility Verifications

The challenges with administrative costs originate at the start of the claim's lifecycle with a process called eligibility verification. When a patient arrives at a hospital or physician's office, the front desk must verify an insurer will provide reimbursement for the costs to provide service. The reimbursement may come from a state-operated Medicaid plan, a federal Medicare program or a commercial health insurer, such as Kaiser Permanente, WellPoint or United Healthcare. Most patients have insurance, so the question becomes not whether they are eligible for insurance, but what percentage of the specific fees will be reimbursed. There are numerous factors that determine who holds the payment obligation, be it the insurance policy's deductible, the types of care being delivered and whether the provider is in- or out-of-network.

Ideally, eligibility verification would occur prior to the patient's appointment to ensure appropriate treatment is provided. A specialized EDI transaction exists which enables a hospital or physician's office to request confirmation of the patient's coverage. In theory, the process should work as efficiently as a credit card authorization at a hotel check-in, however, it does not. The insurer may respond to the eligibility inquiry immediately. Or, they may respond hours later after the patient has left the point of care. Imagine an emergency room or urgent care facility sending a request over the weekend or at night when the payer's eligibility verification response system is offline for maintenance.

Furthermore, most payers simply respond with a "Yes" or "No" without providing further, qualifying details. For example, a patient may be eligible for health care benefits, but may be limited to medical and not dental, vision or chiropractic care. Alternatively, a patient may be eligible for care, but only if they fund part of the bill, as the policy carries a co-payment, co-insurance or deductible.

Just as important as the real-time eligibility verification is the "adjudication" of claims that determines the division of financial responsibility between the patient and insurer. Ideally, a real-time adjudication would occur before the patient left the point of service so that fees could be collected on site. However, most hospitals and physicians' offices have limited ability to estimate a patient's financial liabilities at the point of service. Instead, these providers submit claims to insurers and then wait for the results. Any excess fees not covered by insurance must be collected directly from the consumer. Hospitals and physicians' offices send bills for post-insurance balances directly to consumers, hoping they will pay.

You have undoubtedly experienced this problem following a visit to a health care facility. A few weeks after a doctor's visit you get an Explanation-of-Benefits (EOB) statement in the mail from your insurer. In big letters the statement says, "This is not a bill," but nonetheless lists charges that were not reimbursed by the insurance company. A few weeks later you receive a bill from the physician's office for an amount different than the costs listed on the insurer's EOB. By this point over a month has gone by since your doctor's visit, and you are unlikely to remember the details of the services provided or have copies of the original receipts.

On average, physicians and hospitals only collect about 50% of the post-insurance balance. Collection rates are the worst for those without insurance that may not have sufficient funds to pay. In total $60 billion in bad debt is incurred by hospitals and physicians annually.[194]

During the Bush administration, the concept of a Consumer-Directed Health Care (CDHP) plan became popular. The idea was that if consumers had more information about the costs of health care and were accountable for a greater share of the payments, then they would make more financially responsible choices which would reduce costs. For example, a consumer might elect a generic drug over a brand-name equivalent. Alternatively, certain types of medical treatment, which are considered non-critical, might be reimbursed at lower rates. For such a model to work, however, the provider must be able to actually collect fees for these higher expenses from the consumers.

Some experts have proposed that consumers should be required to sign up for a credit line or medical bill-payment program when enrolling in insurance. Other experts have proposed that consumers provide a credit card which is pre-authorized for a percentage of treatment costs upon arrival at a physician's office or hospital.[195] The model is similar to the pre-authorization of charges that occurs with a hotel or rental car. Unfortunately, there has been no consensus on the best approach.

Eligibility verification at the beginning of a claim's lifecycle is a large source of pain for providers and payers today. Equally challenging is the process at the end of a claim's lifecycle which is the payment reconciliation. One big source of inefficiency is the paper-based nature of the process. Most payers still mail checks to providers for reimbursement. Checks introduce additional processing costs and banking fees, but the more significant cost challenge is the need to manually reconcile claims to the associated payments.

The payments sent by insurers do not always match the amounts requested in claims submissions. There are several reasons for the discrepancies. First, the payer may elect to pay only a percentage of the claim depending upon the patient's eligibility. Even when insurers do pay in full, they may consolidate multiple claims into a single payment to reduce banking fees. McKinsey estimates that $6 billion per year could be saved by eliminating much of the postage, processing and accounting activities associated with paper remittance advices and checks.[196]

HIPAA

The administrative overhead associated with health care payment processing is so cumbersome that the US federal government has enacted a series of regulations aimed at standardizing processes and reducing costs. The first key regulation passed was the 1996 Health Information Portability and Accountability Act (HIPAA). HIPAA is the most misspelled acronym in the United States. Most people assume there is some correlation between the health care regulation and the large hippopotamus creatures you see in a zoo. The correct spelling is HIPAA with two As versus HIPPA with two "Ps."

HIPAA is also infamous in the legal community. HIPAA was the first in a series of vaguely worded health care regulations issued by the US government. The result of using terms such as "reasonable and appropriate" in HIPAA and "meaningful use" in HITECH has been widespread confusion among the health care community as to how to most effectively comply with the legislation.

HIPAA consists of two parts. The first part provides protection to ensure workers can maintain or regain health insurance when changing or losing jobs. The second part, which is the most relevant to the discussion herein, sets out the administrative simplification procedures. There are four primary aspects of the HIPAA administrative rules: 1) security, 2) privacy, 3) transaction sets and 4) national provider identifier.

The security and privacy rules have been the most confusing for technology vendors. One of HIPAA's goals is to ensure that a set of 18 data elements defined as Protected Health Information (PHI) remain private between the patient and his/her health care provider. The protected fields include information that could independently, or in combination with other fields, uniquely identify an individual. Examples include: Social Security number, driver's license number, name, home address, phone number, email address and/or date of birth. The goal of PHI is to prevent incidents of identity theft and insurance fraud. Additionally, PHI is designed to prevent public exposure of sensitive information about an individual that could lead to public embarrassment, loss of employment or denial of insurance coverage. For example, if it was disclosed that a person was HIV-positive, the individual could suffer negative consequences professionally in the workforce or socially in the community.

Every year there are real-world examples of privacy violations discovered in the health care community. For example, between the years of 2005 and 2008, employees at the UCLA Health System accessed over 1,000 different patients' records inappropriately. One administrative specialist admitted to selling information from the files of Britney Spears and Farrah Fawcett to the National Enquirer. A medical school researcher served four months in prison for reading medical files of celebrities, such as Drew Barrymore, Arnold Schwarzenegger and Tom Hanks. As a result, the UCLA Health System agreed to pay $865,000 for violation of federal privacy laws. It additionally took disciplinary actions such as warning, suspending or firing more than 150 of its employees.[197]

To ensure that companies provide adequate privacy and security for patient health information, the HIPAA regulations specify a set of administrative, technical and physical safeguards that "covered entities" must comply with. Covered entities might include health insurers, hospitals and physicians' offices as well as B2B e-commerce vendors, such as HIEs and e-prescription networks. HIPAA suggests that companies deploy security technologies, such as firewalls, intrusion detection, antivirus software, biometric authentication and virtual private networks. Furthermore, HIPAA requires companies to put in place methodologies for responding to security breaches. Health care organizations must obtain the patient's consent to share information and must establish sanctions for employees who break the law.

While HIPAA is best known for its privacy and security guidelines, the regulation also created standardized EDI transaction sets utilized in claims processing across the US health care system. There are five primary EDI transactions in the health care revenue cycle management process. When a patient arrives at a hospital or physician's office, the registration staff may perform eligibility verification with the insurer to confirm the patient's coverage is current and valid. After the patient's appointment, the provider will submit a claim to the insurer requesting reimbursement for services rendered. Attachments, such as Lab Test results, are typically forwarded along with the claim. If the patient needs to see a specialist, the provider's office may also send an electronic referral authorization to the patient's insurer. And, when the insurer pays the claim, they will send an explanation of benefits or remittance advice with details about the payment.

Prior to HIPAA, a myriad of different paper and electronic documents were used for claims processing in the health care industry. One example is the set of HCFA forms. HCFA, which stands for Health Care Financing Administration, was the previous name of the Centers for Medicare and Medicaid Services. Others include UB04 and UB92. The last one reminds me of the British Reggae Band, UB40, which produced the hits "Red, Red Wine" and "Can't Help Falling in Love." The name UB40 comes from the UK government's Department of Health and Social Security's Unemployment Benefit Form 40.[198] I have never been able to ascertain the origins of the terms UB04 or UB92 in the US health care context, however.

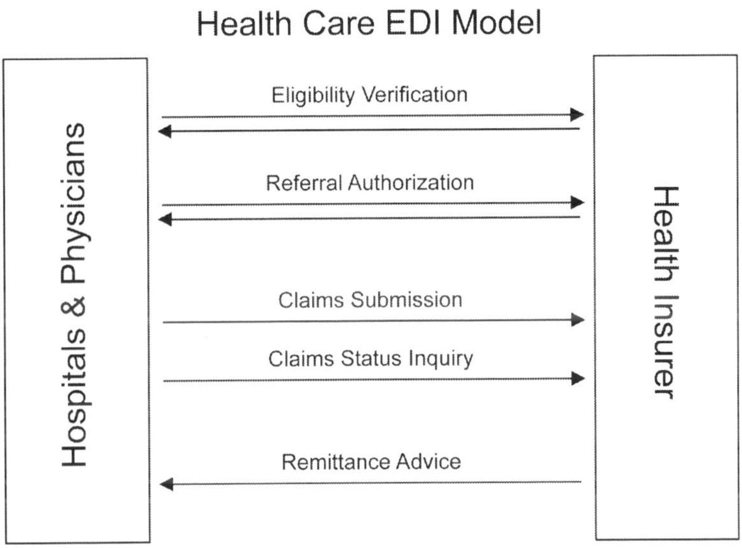

Usage of the different standards varied sometimes by the geographic region of the country or by the preference of the payer. HIPAA put an end to the multiple competing standards and highly customized payer-centric policies.

The original deadline for implementing HIPAA transactions was October 2003, but it was extended several times to accommodate smaller physicians' offices that needed more time to complete the upgrade. The upgrade to HIPAA required extensive work by the IT departments of health insurers and health care providers. It effectively created another Y2K-type of compliance effort within the health care industry.

From 4010 in 2010 to 5010 in 2012

Not long after the HIPAA deadlines passed, the health care industry embarked on another major standards upgrade of similar size and scope. The first part of the upgrade involves the use of internationally standardized codes to represent medical procedures and diagnoses in claims submissions. Today, the US uses a code system developed back in the 1970s by the World Health Organization (WHO). Needless to say, medical knowledge has advanced considerably in the past four decades. Consequently, part of the upgrade effort is migration from the older version of the International Statistical Classification of Diseases and Related Health Problems (ICD-9) to the latest version (ICD-10). ICD-10 is already in use within countries such as Canada, France, Germany and Australia.

There are over 150,000 new ICD-10 codes, as compared to less than 15,000 codes in ICD-9. As a result, ICD-10 can provide very specific and granular diagnoses for medical events. For example, there are two separate codes to diagnose whether a patient was bitten by a turtle or only struck by one. There are over 300 different animal-related codes with over 70 focused on injuries related to birds. In addition to codes specifically for injuries obtained in a chicken coop, ICD-10 also allows physicians to pinpoint events that occurred in opera houses, art galleries and squash courts.

In September 2011, there was an article on the front page of the *Wall Street Journal* questioning the need for some of the ICD-10 codes. The article stated, "Some codes could seem downright insulting: R46.1 is 'bizarre personal appearance (see code),' while R46.0 is 'very low level of personal hygiene (see code).' It's not clear how many klutzes want to notify their insurers that a doctor visit was a W22.02XA, 'walked into lamppost, initial encounter' (or, for that matter, a W22.02XD, 'walked into lamppost, subsequent encounter')."[199]

One expert interviewed asked, "Why are there codes for injuries received while sewing, ironing, playing a brass instrument, crocheting, doing handcrafts, or knitting—but not while shopping? Code V91.07XA, which involves a 'burn due to water-skis on fire,' is another mystery she ponders: 'Is it work-related?' she asks. 'Is it a trick skier jumping through hoops of fire? How does it happen?'"[200]

The second aspect of the upgrade is migration from an older version of the ANSI EDI standards (version 4010) to a newer version (5010). The deadline for the upgrade was set for January 1, 2012. As transformative as the original HIPAA transactions sets were to the industry, they did not resolve all the issues with payer to provider communications. For example, the 4010 documents cannot accommodate the ICD-10 codes which are much larger than ICD-9 codes. 4010 also does not accommodate data fields such as "Present on Admission (POA)." The POA field denotes whether a particular symptom was being exhibited when the patient arrived at the hospital. Certain insurers are discontinuing reimbursements to providers for medical conditions that were acquired during hospital stays.[201]

The scope of the 5010 changes is considerable. There are more than 850 changes between EDI versions 5010 and 4010. The new implementation guide for the claim submission transaction is 700 pages alone with a change on every single page. You may be wondering if the health care industry's time and efforts would not be better spent focusing on digitizing the 40 to 60% of transactions that remain paper-based. There has been considerable debate on this topic, but most industry experts agree that the upgrades are a necessary step towards aggressively reducing administrative processing costs for health care payments. The US Health and Human Services (HHS) agency commissioned an independent study by Gartner to determine the costs and benefits of an industry-wide upgrade to 5010. Gartner concluded that the industry could realize a net benefit between $11.6 and $33.8 billion by upgrading to the new standards.[202] While the industry-wide benefits are compelling, the return on investment to a small physician's office with limited technology expertise may be less obvious.

I find the most interesting aspect of these upgrades is the ability of the industry to work collectively towards a single deadline date nationwide. Such a uniform migration would never occur in the other industries that we have discussed. The choice to upgrade is not based upon a sense of altruism by the health care community, however. The true driving force behind the upgrades to ICD-10 and 5010 are the government payers that represent more than 50% of claims reimbursements in the US. Both Medicare and Medicaid have established deadlines after which they will accept electronic transactions in the 5010 format only.

HIPAA Clearinghouses

In the 1990s, a group of health care claims "clearinghouses" were established by technology vendors to solve the health care efficiency problems related to administration of claims and payments. Much like EDI VANs, B2B e-marketplaces, e-prescription networks and HIEs, these technology vendors act as intermediaries that provide connectivity between large communities of customers and suppliers. In this case, the suppliers are hospitals, physician group practices, laboratories, radiology centers or long-term care facilities. The customers are private health insurers, Medicare and Medicaid that pay the bills.

In the days prior to standardized HIPAA transactions, clearinghouses helped to mask the differences in local codes and document formats being used by the various insurers around the country. A hospital could submit a claim to a clearinghouse that would scrub the data and reformat the transaction into the format expected by the insurer. The reverse process would occur with transactions flowing from the insurer to the hospital or physician's office. However, during the period of 2003-2005, as HIPAA implementations were coming to completion, many in the industry predicted the demise of these clearinghouses.

The widespread availability of Internet connections enabled providers and payers to connect directly to one another via FTP without the use of a clearinghouse or intermediary. Furthermore, the HIPAA transaction sets were highly standardized, removing most of the need for the transformation of codes and documents to meet payer-specific requirements. Consequently, many industry insiders predicted that the revenues generated from HIPAA clearinghouses would rapidly decline as customers found more efficient means for connectivity. However, much like the EDI VANs in the retail sector, clearinghouses managed to survive the threat of Internet substitutes. In fact, the competition from direct Internet connections drove a consolidation within the vendor community. These mergers created a handful of stronger, more financially stable clearinghouses, which have grown considerably in recent years.

Emdeon—The New New Thing

On August 11, 2009, one of the leading health care clearinghouse vendors, Emdeon, held an Initial Public Offering (IPO) on the New York Stock Exchange (NYSE), which generated $365 million in capital. Back in 2003, at the time of the first HIPAA deadlines, Emdeon referred to itself as WebMD. The company enjoyed the leading position in the HIPAA clearinghouse sector. By the time of its IPO, Emdeon had not only changed its name, but also expanded its value proposition. It no longer positioned itself as an EDI network or even a HIPAA clearinghouse, but rather as a leading provider of *"revenue and payment cycle management solutions for health care payers and providers."*

Emdeon is the largest player in the Health Care Revenue Cycle Management segment that has effectively replaced the HIPAA clearinghouse sector. In fact, it is fair to say that Emdeon is the 800 pound gorilla in the space. Emdeon states that its network *"has connections to more payers, providers and vendors than any other healthcare business in the marketplace."* To fully appreciate the reach and commanding position of Emdeon, consider the following statement from its August 2009 S-1 registration filing with the US Securities and Exchange Commission, "We have developed our network of payers and providers over 25 years and connect to virtually all private and government payers, claim-submitting providers and pharmacies, making it extremely difficult, expensive and time-consuming for competitors to replicate our market position."[203]

Emdeon's network connects to 340,000 health care providers: 81,000 dentists, 55,000 pharmacies, 5,000 hospitals, and 1,200 government or commercial payers (e.g., Medicare, Medicaid, HMOs, and PPOs). During 2010, one out of every two commercial health care claims delivered electronically in the US was processed by Emdeon. In total, Emdeon processed almost six billion health-care related transactions in 2010.[204]

Emdeon's roots can be traced to the dot-com startup, Healtheon, invented by Netscape and Silicon Graphics co-founder Jim Clark in 1996. Having been involved in numerous legal entanglements with Microsoft at Netscape, Clark was seeking a green field opportunity to invest in a new space that his archrival could not penetrate. Michael Lewis's *The New New Thing* described the thoroughly underwhelming process by which Clark dreamed up the original idea. An excerpt from the book reads as follows:

"In late 1995 Clark was diagnosed with a rare blood disease, hemochromatosis. Essentially, his blood produced more iron than his body needed.

The disease required Clark to visit the hospital once every few weeks...The blizzard of forms and the bureaucracy was more than any new billionaire could be expected to tolerate. It got him thinking of a solution. By early 1996 Americans were spending $1.5 trillion a year on their health care and about a third of that was pure waste. Much of the waste could be avoided by simply eliminating the paperwork."[205]

The plan for Healtheon started with a four corner diagram that Clark drew on a piece of paper. In the four corners he wrote the words: Payers, Providers, Consumers and Doctors. The diagram later evolved into a more advanced diagram with Healtheon at the center of 11 different circles which became known as "The Chart of Many Bubbles." Each circle represented one of the many players in the health care space, such as Labs, PBMs, pharmacies and employers. Another way of explaining Clark's vision was succinctly summarized by Lewis as,

"To his way of thinking there were health care professionals who clearly served a purpose. They were called doctors. And there were people who clearly needed health care. They were called patients. Everyone else in between—the hundreds of billions in paperwork and bullshit—could go."

"We want to empower the doctors and the patients and get all the other assholes out of the way" Jim Clark said. "Except for us. One asshole in the middle."[206]

A formal business plan for Healtheon was never published. Most of *The New New Thing* chronicles the rather haphazard manner in which the startup was launched. Healtheon attempted an IPO in July 1998. However, unfavorable stock market conditions and a critical article published in the *Wall Street Journal* forced the company to defer its public listing. But, in February 1999 when the company did IPO, Healtheon's shares rocketed up 400% on the first day of trading. The stock peaked at $120 later in 1999 when a merger with WebMD was announced.[207] Ironically, Clark's nemesis, Microsoft, was one of WebMD's original investors.

Fast forwarding a few years, WebMD became a subsidiary of a holding company called HLTH. A new name, Emdeon, was created for the business services division in 2005. The name, drew a link to the present and the future (the "MD"), while calling upon the company's past (the "eon"). Starting in 2006, HLTH began to sell off stakes in Emdeon to private-equity firms. As an independent, privately owned organization, Emdeon pursued an aggressive series of acquisitions. All of these acquisitions prepared the company for a very successful IPO.[208]

Emdeon was one of the first companies to go public when the capital markets were still rebounding from the global financial crisis in 2009. I consider the success of the offering to be a strong testimony to investor confidence in the value of B2B e-commerce solutions. In fact, in 2010 Emdeon surpassed $1 billion in sales, a feat that no other B2B e-commerce network has yet to achieve.

At the time this book was published, Emdeon had just gone private again. The company received a takeover bid from the private equity firm, the Blackstone Group, in 2011.

Chapter 14
Pandemics and Medicare Fraud

On March 19, 1997, FBI agents raided the hospitals and offices of Columbia/HCA in El Paso, Texas. The health care provider was accused of providing illegal kickbacks to outside physicians and committing massive Medicare fraud. Scrutiny of Columbia/HCA's business practices had been published throughout 1996 and 1997 in *The New York Times*.[209]

Columbia/HCA was started in 1987 by the CEO, Rick Scott, and a partner. The company grew rapidly to more than 350 hospitals in just 10 years.[210] By 1997 Columbia/HCA had almost $20 billion in annual revenue. It was the largest for-profit hospital chain in the US, and the country's ninth-largest employer.[211] In fact, one year *Fortune* magazine declared Columbia/HCA the most admired health care company in America.[212]

The troubles for Columbia/HCA began when an accountant from a Montana hospital, James Alderson, was asked by a supervisor to start keeping two sets of cost report books. The first, which would be sent to Medicare, would have inflated expenses. The second set of books would track the actual legitimate expenses. Alderson refused and was fired several days later.[213] He filed a whistle-blower suit in 1993. In the coming years another thirty employees came forward to join Alderson to help form the Justice Department's case against Columbia/HCA.[214]

Columbia/HCA had made a regular practice of systematically overcharging the government for Medicare claims. It exaggerated the illnesses of its patients to receive larger reimbursements. It billed for unnecessary lab tests. It struck illegal deals with home care agencies and filed false data about use of hospital space.[215] The company did have a concern about getting caught.

Consequently, it held up to $1 billion in reserves in case Medicare complained about the falsified claims. However, the reserves were shifted to profits after a certain length of time, contributing to 25 to 30% of Columbia/HCA's profits during the peak period of the fraud.[216]

Ultimately the hospital group pleaded guilty to 14 felonies. It paid over $1.7 billion in civil law suits, including $500 million to the two key whistle-blowers.[217] After finally settling with the US government and civil law suits in 2003, Columbia/HCA appointed new leadership, and then changed its name to Hospital Corporation of America. A few years later, in 2006, Kohlberg Kravis Roberts and Bain Capital acquired HCA for $31.6 billion.[218] The private equity firms focused on transforming the troubled hospital group over a period of five years. And in March 2011, HCA rejoined the ranks of public companies with a listing on the NYSE. The company raised $3.8 billion which was the largest private-equity backed IPO ever on a US stock exchange.[219]

Medicare fraud remains a significant problem today, fifteen years after the Columbia/HCA scandal. Certain areas of the country are more prone to Medicare fraud than others. For example, just two individual counties in Florida accounted for $400 million in fraudulent Medicare claims. In 2008, Miami-Dade County billed Medicare six times more for home health services than Los Angeles County, where the Medicare population is three times larger.[220] Ironically, Rick Scott, the former CEO of Columbia/HCA, is now the governor of Florida. However, the systematic fraud long predates his election.

In 2005, over 70% of all Medicare claims for HIV/AIDS infusions nationwide were billed from Miami-Dade County.[221] HIV/AIDS infusion injections that can cost a few thousand dollars each are primary targets for Medicare fraud. Fraudsters recruit sick patients to receive injections they believe to be HIV injections. However, the shots are really filled with saline or another liquid. Medicare is then billed for the cost of the HIV medication.

Durable medical equipment such as wheelchairs and oxygen tents, are another target for fraud. Fraudsters charge Medicare for the wheelchair, but never deliver it. A 2007 investigation by federal authorities, found that over half of all durable medical equipment suppliers were not in compliance with Medicare rules.[222] Medicare fraud has become more attractive to some organized crime groups than drug smuggling. Medicare fraud offers more money with a lower chance of being caught. Those caught will be prosecuted as white collar criminals as opposed to drug dealers that suffer more severe penalties.[223]

Medicare's Most Wanted

Improper payments represented almost 10% of the $500 billion spent on Medicare in 2010.[224] Most Medicare claims submitted by providers are paid automatically. The system was designed to pay claims quickly and smoothly, not to root out false claims. As a result, the system remains susceptible to fraudulent billing. Fraudulent providers bill Medicare for unnecessary procedures, tests or equipment. "Upcoding," which is the practice of inflating bills for a more expensive procedure, is also popular. In many cases, the patients are in on the scam in exchange for a kickback.

Overall health care fraud, waste and abuse are expected to rise as high as $330 billion by 2013 across both public and private sector insurers.[225] The topic of private insurer fraud has not been as publicized in the media, but the same criminals that are abusing Medicare and Medicaid, are also exploiting insurers, such as Cigna, United Health Care and Blue Cross/Blue Shield organizations. The average private health insurer has 800 cases of inappropriate payments per year. Insurers maintain anti-fraud investigative units with annual budgets of more than $1.9 billion and teams of nine full-time staff members.[226]

As the size of investigative task forces has increased, so has the frequency and size of the arrests. For example, in February 2011, a Medicare Fraud Strike Force, led by Health and Human Services along with FBI and US attorneys from the Department of Justice, arrested 111 different people from nine metro areas on Medicare fraud. Through a process of 40 different schemes, the group is accused of defrauding the government of $225 million.[227]

The level of fraud in the US health care system is viewed by most to be simply unacceptable. Public outrage has increased in recent years, as much of the expense is being funded by US taxpayers, who are already frustrated with the growing US federal budget deficit. The good news is that radical improvements are possible. The health care industry can learn by example from the financial sector, which tightly manages and monitors fraud. The US credit card industry processes more than $2 trillion in retail spending annually, which is approximately the same size as the health care industry. However, credit card fraud is only a fraction of 1%.

One of the challenges in identifying fraud, particularly for private insurers, is the ability to analyze trends across a statistically significant sample of data. Private insurers only have access to the claims submitted to them. As a result, a scam artist could use the same technique a few times with different insurers without much notice being taken. Credit card companies have an advantage in that they have significantly higher volumes of transactions channeled across their network. Consequently, card networks can deploy sophisticated fraud monitoring solutions to perform pattern recognition and data analysis. If only the US health care system had a concentrated network of transactions that could be analyzed for fraud patterns.

But we do. Of course, I am referring to the HIPAA EDI clearinghouses discussed in Chapter 13. Clearinghouses provide the most transaction-intensive data hubs, and offer a rich set of statistically significant data for analysis. In recent years, vendors, such as Emdeon, have begun to deploy predictive analytics capabilities on their clearinghouses to monitor for patterns of illegitimate claims. Analyzing transaction patterns in HIPAA clearinghouse networks could allow us to identify instances of fraud. For example, when Prime Healthcare Services submits Medicare claims indicating that 16% of their patients in the Mount Shasta and Mojave Desert area are experiencing malnutrition, a special investigative unit could be deployed.[228] When a Portland, Oregon neurosurgeon submits a claim for his seventh spinal surgery on a single patient in two years, the claim could be "red-flagged" for further investigation.[229] When patients that have previously deceased seem to be brought back to life for further medical work, the fraud detection software on the clearinghouse could automatically deny payment and alert federal authorities. Unfortunately, the last example was not an exaggeration. There were $27.3 million in Medicaid payments for services performed after death in 2006.[230]

Comparing Effectiveness, Comparing Prices

Combating fraud is not the only value-added service that can be provided by clearinghouses. The vast database of historical claims can be leveraged to compare and contrast the effectiveness of different treatment programs. Traditionally, medical research was designed to evaluate the effectiveness of a single treatment approach at a time. A new model called "comparative effectiveness," which has become popular in recent years, evaluates two or more different treatment approaches simultaneously. For example, a comparative effectiveness study could be performed on patients with knee problems to examine the effectiveness of surgeries versus physical therapy and prescription drugs. A Congressional Budget Office study found that "patients in the highest-spending regions of the country receive 60% more health services than those in the lowest-spending regions, yet this additional care is not associated with improved outcomes."[231] Proponents of comparative effectiveness research argue that the health care system should reduce spend on additional services that do not yield better results. Such an approach could be another strategy for reducing health care costs.

As a result of ARRA, over $1.1 billion was allocated to expand effectiveness research at the National Institutes of Health (NIH) and Agency for Healthcare Research and Quality (AHRQ).[232] Comparative effectiveness research can be performed through clinical trials where patients enroll as healthy volunteers into a small pilot study that examines the efficacy of different treatment options. An alternative, less expensive option for comparing effectiveness is through historical comparison of insurance claims. By analyzing the series of claims before and after treatment of a particular symptom, the effectiveness of different approaches can be determined. Consider the potential of a vendor such as Emdeon which has in excess of 25 terabytes of historical claim and reimbursement data. The use of HIPAA clearinghouses to monitor for fraud or to perform comparative effectiveness studies is another example of the network effect we discussed in Chapter 6. The more companies that join the network, the larger the available data set becomes.

Another noteworthy clearinghouse is a company called Ingenix with revenues roughly twice the size of Emdeon. Ingenix generates $2.3 billion in revenues annually, which is impressive for a technology vendor.[233] However, Ingenix's revenues represent only a small percentage of the $87 billion collected by its parent organization, United Health Group. Although Ingenix does have larger overall revenues, EDI only represents a small percentage of the total. The company processes 400 million transactions per year, as compared to the four billion processed by Emdeon.[234]

The relationship between United Healthcare and Ingenix has come under scrutiny in recent years because of potential conflicts of interest. In addition to EDI, Ingenix also offers a data service which provides the market price for common medical services. The Ingenix database is used by insurers to research how much a particular type of medical service would cost when given a combination of specific physicians and geographic locations. Can you guess what the source of this data might be? Among other inputs, the pricing data provided comes from the 400 million EDI transactions Ingenix processes annually.

Ingenix has been accused of essentially manipulating the data to favor insurers, such as United Healthcare. In 2008, New York Attorney General, Andrew Cuomo, conducted an investigation which revealed that rates listed by Ingenix were much lower than the actual cost of medical expenses. In other words, Ingenix was encouraging insurers to reimburse hospitals and physicians at lower prices than they should have. United Healthcare settled in 2009, offering $350 million to customers for medical providers. It also agreed to provide $50 million to fund a new independent database to determine reimbursement rates.[235]

Tracking the Next Pandemic

In recent years, a series of influenza outbreaks have terrified the world for months at a time, as fears of a global pandemic became widespread. The most recent pandemic was the H1N1 influenza virus, informally called the "swine flu." The outbreak started in Veracruz, Mexico in April 2009.[236] Most of nearby Mexico City was closed in an effort to contain the virus. However, it spread throughout the world until it reached official pandemic state. There was widespread panic, with the media devoting front page coverage to H1N1 daily, for almost a month. The pandemic began to slow down seven months after the first cases were publicized. A year later, in August 2010, the World Health Organization (WHO) officially ended the pandemic threat. It received only a brief mention in the major newspapers.

Prior to H1N1, there was a worldwide scare over the avian influenza (bird flu) which was detected in Vietnam in the year 2004. The virus spread throughout different parts of the world in 2005. Scientists began to predict a global influenza pandemic was emerging. However, the disease proved not to transmit as easily between humans, which significantly limited its impact.

A few years earlier, in 2002, the Severe Acute Respiratory Syndrome (SARS) broke out in southern China. It took a few months for the world to recognize the new potential pandemic. However, once identified, the threat was a focus of swift action by the WHO that proved to slow transmission. The SARS outbreak was contained, although the disease has not been fully eradicated, and could potentially return.

SARS and the bird flu were not the first pandemics to emerge from Southern China and Hong Kong. Back in the 1950s, the Asian flu originated in mainland China, quickly spreading throughout the world and causing approximately two million deaths.[237] In the late 1960s, another virus was detected in Hong Kong. The virus quickly spread to Singapore, Vietnam, India, the Philippines, Australia and Europe. US troops from the Vietnam War carried it into California and other states. Ultimately, the Hong Kong Flu pandemic killed one million people worldwide in the years 1968 and 1969.[238]

Both Europe and the US have been spared from the majority of deaths caused by these recent pandemics. However, public health authorities are highly focused on identifying these outbreaks as soon as they occur in order to minimize the spread of infection. One of the techniques utilized for disease tracking is reporting from hospitals and physicians' offices. US state laws require providers and laboratories to report cases of certain diseases to local and state public health departments. Nationally "notifiable" diseases are forwarded by the state agencies onto the Centers for Disease Control and Prevention (CDC).

Public health reporting is fraught with challenges. Connections between the state health departments and the CDC are electronic and highly automated. However, the "first mile" between the providers and the local and state agencies is highly manual. Providers typically utilize the phone, fax, hard copy forms or primitive web portals to communicate with public health agencies. To complicate matters, the 50 US states maintain more than 100 different systems to collect data. Each of these 100 systems has a different user interface or file transfer protocol to accept data. For larger hospital groups operating in multiple regions, the need to interact with multiple state agencies can be quite challenging.[239]

Studies indicate, that despite the regulations, the most closely monitored "notifiable" diseases are under-reported in the US. Various studies conducted between 1970 and 1999 showed that only 79% of all Sexually Transmitted Diseases (STDs), tuberculosis and AIDS cases were reported to public health agencies. Reporting rates for other diseases were much lower at 49%.[240] There are several reasons for the under-reporting. Some are procedural or economic. For example, the process depends upon overworked and understaffed personnel taking the time to consistently file the reports. However, there is no question that the primitive communications methods used to collect provider data is a factor as well.

A better methodology for reporting on "notifiable" diseases would be to eliminate the dependency on human action altogether. The process could be completely automated by connecting health care providers' systems, containing the patient data, to Public Health and Safety tracking systems. One option would be to connect the tens of thousands of medical practices to the hundreds of different public health systems. But, such an endeavor could prove quite an ambitious integration project, taking decades for full adoption and costing tens of millions of dollars. A less complex and costly alternative would leverage HIEs and EHRs. These technologies would significantly simplify the tracking of public health epidemics without the need to establish individual connections between various state agencies and each different medical provider.

In the event of a pandemic or bioterrorist event, public health officials could easily access EHR data such as physicians' notes, patient demographics and medical history that has been de-identified. Without the dependency upon manual data entry, the speed of information flow could be accelerated and the quality of information collected could be improved. In fact, triggers could be set up to automatically identify trends in data sets that might not be otherwise noticed, helping to provide an early warning system for potential disease outbreaks.

Administrative costs to support public health reporting would be reduced considerably. The average cost to send a report manually is $14, as compared to only $0.03 electronically. CITL estimated that the use of electronic data flow from providers and laboratories to public health agencies would reduce administrative costs by $195M annually.[241] CITL did not quantify the potential economic savings from early identification of pandemics and bioterrorist events, but there is no question that these could be in the billions of dollars.

Tracking Flu Trends on Google

One of the best leading sources of data on flu outbreaks today is Google. The search engine leader launched an application called Google Flu Trends in November 2008. Officially, Flu Trends is called a "syndromic surveillance system," which is a form of "infoveillance." It analyzes end-user search patterns in an attempt to map flu outbreaks geographically. Google states, "We have found a close relationship between how many people search for flu-related topics and how many people actually have flu symptoms. Of course, not every person who searches for 'flu' is actually sick, but a pattern emerges when all the flu-related search queries are added together."[242]

Flu-related topics might include symptoms such as fever, fatigue and headache. The search terms could also include products such as cold medicine, tissues and orange juice. Google has found a very high correlation between its flu models and the actual statistics reported by the European and US Centers for Disease Control. There is one key difference. Google's data is several days, if not weeks, ahead of the public health authorities. The difference is no surprise to me. Google is analyzing search patterns in real time, while the public agencies are analyzing historical data from clinical providers.

US Public Health authorities have envisioned building a similar system to Google's Flu Trends, called the National Electronic Disease Surveillance System (NEDSS). The NEDSS would collect data from a number of relevant sources outside of the health care system to gain earlier insights into emerging threats. Examples might include 911 call analysis, veterinary clinic activity, OTC pharmacy sales and school absentee records. The NEDSS could also leverage search engine results and retail sales of facial tissue and orange juice.[243] Such practices have been deployed by the US Department of Defense and the Utah Department of Health during the Salt Lake City Olympics in 2002. The key challenge with building an NEDSS is the integration of all state and local agencies, educational institutions and retail chains electronically. The NHIN would provide a start, but the non-health care community would have to be connected as well, using B2B e-commerce technologies.

Such Internet-based surveillance techniques are already in practice within some countries. In fact, the World Health Organization (WHO) first learned of the SARS outbreak that occurred in China during 2002 via an Internet surveillance system. Canada's Global Public Health Intelligence Network, an electronic warning system, picked up reports of a flu outbreak in China through Internet media monitoring. The reports were sent to the WHO immediately.[244]

SECTION 5

Financial Services

Chapter 15
SWIFT and Bank Communications

In June of 2006, *The New York Times* published a front-page story about a secret US government program designed to monitor international banking transactions for evidence of terrorist activities. The program, known as the TFTP or Terrorist Finance Tracking Program, was initiated by the Bush Administration shortly after the September 11th attacks. The objective of the program was to identify and cutoff the international sources of financing that terrorist cells in the US are dependent upon to conduct their operations. The 9-11 Commission investigations found that nine of the hijackers responsible for September 11th funneled money from Europe and the Middle East to SunTrust bank accounts in Florida.[245]

To develop the story, *The New York Times'* journalists, Eric Lichtblau and James Risen, interviewed over 20 government officials about the classified program to gather further details. The story was so controversial that it was almost not published. The Bush Administration requested *The New York Times* not disclose the program fearing it would jeopardize TFTP's effectiveness. Bill Keller, *The Times* executive editor, stated, "We have listened closely to the administration's arguments for withholding this information, and given them the most serious and respectful consideration. We remain convinced that the administration's extraordinary access to this vast repository of international financial data, however carefully targeted use of it may be, is a matter of public interest."[246]

The concerns about national security quickly shifted to public outcry about data privacy concerns after the article was published. In fact, there have been several attempts by members of European Parliament to formally discontinue US access to data involving European citizens. But, before we explore the data privacy issues in further detail, you may be wondering what the relationship between TFTP and B2B e-Commerce is? The source of the data for the US TFTP program are the international finance transactions transmitted over the B2B e-commerce network operated by SWIFT.

SWIFT stands for the Society for Worldwide Interbank Financial Telecommunication and is a specialized type of B2B e-commerce network that connects all the major financial institutions around the globe. SWIFT enables financial institutions to exchange information related to payments, securities, foreign exchange and letters of credit transactions. SWIFT is not a bank. SWIFT does not process payments, exchange currencies, nor facilitate securities trades. Instead, SWIFT is an information network that allows its customers, primarily financial institutions, to send instructions about what bank account balances are, which payments to execute, and how to settle securities trades. SWIFT does not refer to itself as a B2B e-commerce network. But I classify them as one, due to the fact that their primary business is the exchange of standardized messages between companies.

Although SWIFT supports a wide variety of transaction types, the network's strong suit has always been activities related to cross-border, high-value payments. Consequently, SWIFT possesses a rich source of international financial transaction data that would be of great interest to US government agencies seeking to track terrorist money flows. That is exactly the nature of the relationship that has existed between the US TFTP and SWIFT since a few weeks after the September 11th attacks. The US government claims, that by mining data from SWIFT transactions, it has been able to identify thousands of terrorist-related funding activities, leading to several high profile arrests. Of particular interest to the US, are transactions originating in the United Arab Emirates or Saudi Arabia, destined for the accounts of US businesses and individuals with known terrorist affiliations. For example, SWIFT data provided a link that helped to locate Riduan Isamuddin, known as the Osama Bin Laden of Southeast Asia. Isamuddin was believed to be responsible for a 2002 bombing of a Bali resort in Thailand.[247]

Critics of TFTP were shocked to find that the program had been in operation for nearly five years before being disclosed to the public. Perhaps, more interesting is that the program became effectively permanent without any Congressional approval or formal authorization. TFTP's access to SWIFT data was justified under the International Emergency Powers Act that gives the President authority to "investigate, regulate, or prohibit" foreign transactions in responding to "an unusual and extraordinary threat." The Act enabled government agencies to access financial data without seeking court-approved warrants or subpoenas.[248]

Criticism within the European Union

Shortly after the publication of *The New York Times* article, SWIFT came under high levels of scrutiny by both the European Union and Belgian governments. Note that SWIFT is headquartered outside of Brussels. The primary concern was the ability of the US government to access European citizens' financial data. SWIFT was originally accused of breaking the EU's data protection laws. It is unclear whether any EU Parliament Members or European Commission members were aware of the TFTP program prior to *The New York Times* story. However, SWIFT has disclosed that its 25-member Board of Directors as well as many of the Central Banks that leverage its services, were notified.

SWIFT offered a strong response to Parliamentary criticisms of its actions, stating, "SWIFT is subject to lawful subpoenas in the United States because it has substantial business and operations there, including data storage."[249] In its defense, SWIFT cites the controls and audits put into place to ensure restricted use of the data.

"SWIFT negotiated with the US over the scope and oversight of the subpoenas to protect the confidentiality of its members' data and obtained extraordinary protections and assurances as to the purpose, confidentiality, oversight, and control of limited sets of data produced under the subpoenas. These protections ensure that only a limited set of data is accessed."[250]

In 2003, SWIFT threatened to suspend data sharing efforts with the US due to concerns regarding the scope and use of the data. A meeting between SWIFT executives and US officials, including Alan Greenspan, solidified a longer term agreement.[251] A key outcome of the negotiation was that an outside auditing firm would be used to verify that data searches are focused on terrorist-related activities as opposed to tax fraud, drug trafficking, or other illegal activities.

In November 2009, a nine-month interim agreement was reached that would allow the US to continue mining selective SWIFT records for terrorist activities.[252] But, in February 2010, the European Parliament rejected the deal due to concerns about inadequate data privacy protection for European citizens.[253] EU Parliament Members have called for additional stipulations in the data sharing agreement. The EU wanted reciprocal access to data about the activities of US citizens, if the EU chose to create a similar terrorist finance tracking program. The EU also wanted stricter limitations on data usage, such as maximum retention periods of five years and embargoes on sharing the data with third-party governments. There was also discussion about the need to offer remedies to EU citizens seeking restitution from the US government, if data was misused, and the ability to terminate the agreement upon evidence of privacy violations.

In November of 2008, *The New York Times* published a cable, obtained by WikiLeaks, of a transmission from the US embassy in Berlin. The cable states that Chancellor, Angela Merkel, was "very, very angry—angrier than he had ever seen her" with the outcome of a recent parliamentary vote which opposed expansion of the TFTP program. The cable states, "Merkel is particularly irritated with German MEPs from her Christian Democratic Union (CDU) and sister Christian Social Union (CSU) parties, most of whom reportedly voted against the agreement despite previously indicating they would support it." Merkel "expressed concerns to Beust that Washington will view the EP veto as a sign that Europe does not take the terrorist threat seriously. Merkel also worried about the ramifications (presumably within Europe and for transatlantic relations) that might follow were a terrorist attack to occur that could have been prevented had Swift data been exchanged."[254]

The situation got even more interesting during the global financial crisis of 2008-2009. SWIFT is not a public company, rather it is a co-operative society, governed under Belgian law. SWIFT is owned by its customers, the large financial institutions that use the service including Citigroup, HSBC, RBS, Deutsche Bank, BNP Paribas, Commerzbank, JPMorganChase and Bank of America. During the financial crisis, several of these large financial institutions, that were deemed "too big to fail," were nationalized by the US and various European government organizations. In February of 2009, the US government took a 36% stake in Citigroup. A few months earlier, Her Majesty's Treasury began to acquire stakes in the Royal Bank of Scotland group, which eventually grew to an 84% controlling interest. The British government also took stakes in HBOS and Lloyds TSB. The Dutch government took an equity interest in Fortis. Ironically while tensions were escalating around government access to the SWIFT data, these same government entities were obtaining a minority equity stake in SWIFT itself. Nonetheless, there were never any publicized examples of the US or UK governments using their positions in these banks to influence data sharing policies.

While the European Parliament and US government have been negotiating agreements, SWIFT has been busy reorganizing its operations to mitigate the risk of EU citizen data privacy breeches. Historically, SWIFT has operated two data centers—one in the US and the other in the EU. For business continuity purposes all transactions and data were mirrored into both centers. Consequently, all data related to European transactions was stored both in the Belgian data center and US data center that operates in US jurisdiction. SWIFT has recently brought a third data center online in Switzerland.[255] The third center will allow SWIFT to logically segregate data, while maintaining business continuity. Transactions that occur within the EU will be replicated to the Swiss and Belgian centers, but not the US. Such an approach should mitigate the risk of the US seeking access to intra-EU transactions. However, transactions that involve money transfers between the EU and the US may continue to be hosted in the US center.

What TFTP Can Teach Us About B2B

There are a few aspects of the SWIFT TFTP story that are particularly significant. The issue of US government access to data stored in information networks, or "the cloud," is a growing area of concern for non-US companies. Many European, Canadian, and Asian corporations have expressed concerns that any data stored in the US, or data center operated by a US service provider, can be easily accessed by the US government under the powers granted by the PATRIOT Act. For example, in early 2011, selected data from the WikiLeaks

Twitter account was subpoenaed by the US government.[256] Non-US firms fear that their own sensitive corporate or consumer data, hosted in US data centers, could be subpoenaed as well. The American Embassy cable published by WikiLeaks stated that, "Paranoia runs deep especially about US intelligence agencies. We were astonished to learn how quickly rumors (spread) about alleged US economic espionage."[257]

The issue of government access to corporate data records, however, is not limited to US. Every country has national security measures that allow monitoring of telecommunications and Internet Service Providers for criminal or terrorist behavior. You may recall that in 2010. Research-In-Motion (RIM), the creators of Blackberry smartphones, had several regulatory entanglements in the Middle East and India.[258] Local governments threatened to ban RIM's devices from the country, unless they guaranteed that the handset manufacturer would provide access to data stored in its offshore data centers. Nonetheless, the US remains the target of most corporate concerns. Since the American government data requests are usually prominently featured in the global media and major motion pictures, the US continues to suffer from a public perception problem.

The result of these data privacy concerns is that many companies have not elected to outsource their business applications to cloud-based service providers, such as Google, Amazon.com and Salesforce.com. Keeping data firewalled in corporate data centers does not enable companies to avoid government data requests. However, these companies believe that a third party, such as RIM or Twitter, is less likely to invest significant legal resources to oppose a government data request. I should point out that not everyone agrees with the notion that data in the cloud is inherently more susceptible to theft, exposure, or government access. Critics state that data privacy is merely an excuse used by xenophobic groups seeking to promote local employment.

You may have been wondering why the US government needs to obtain data from a European-based organization such as SWIFT. Why doesn't the US government just go to the major financial institutions based in New York to request access to the same data? The first question would be which institutions to ask. While SunTrust may have been used in the September 11th attacks, one of thousands of other financial institutions in the US could be the recipient of funds for the next operation. I am certain there are regular requests to individual institutions. However, there is a strong argument for monitoring the much larger volume of data flowing through a B2B network, than the smaller quantity of information housed in the applications of individual institutions. Even the largest of the banks, only has a relatively small sampling of data about international funds transfers. Furthermore, the data is company-centric, meaning that it may have a disproportionate concentration of certain types of customers within a particular industry or geographic region. A network, by contrast, represents the convergence of a much more diverse community of participants. A network has a much larger sample size of data that is typically more statistically significant. While the primary value of a network is to connect communities of business partners to enable the frictionless exchange of information, even further value can be obtained by warehousing the data to perform analytics upon it. This is another example of the network effect discussed in Chapter 6.

More about SWIFT

SWIFT was formed back in 1973, when 239 banks from 15 different countries joined together to form the co-operative. The objective of this new consortium was to create a private worldwide network for data processing and communications between financial institutions. SWIFT was also tasked with developing a common set of standards for inter-bank communication. In 1973, the Internet was still in the early stages of development, with only a few dozen educational institutions connected to the original ARPANET. The primary means of automated communication between banks was the Telex. The SWIFT network did not go live until 1977, when Albert, Prince of Belgium, sent the first message. Shortly after the launch, transaction volumes began to explode. Volumes grew to over 10 million in less than 12 months. By 1983, the network had reached 1,000 members. More importantly, SWIFT had achieved a profitable operating model.[259]

Over the past four decades, SWIFT has been the de facto solution for high value, cross-border payments due to its extremely high levels of availability and security. The SWIFT network regularly operates with five nines of availability or 99.999% uptime. Visitors to one of SWIFT's three data centers will tell you that the security controls applied for entering the building are greater than those of Fort Knox.

You may be wondering why the banking community chose to develop their own network, rather than contracting with one of the large telecommunications providers to build it. At the time, the financial institutions believed that the telecom carriers were not up to the task. Not only were telecom providers perceived to be expensive, but they also lacked meaningful penalties for service level agreements, and the necessary network intrusion technologies to prevent fraud. In effect, SWIFT utilizes four networking partners to provide the communications links between its customers and its data centers: AT&T, Colt, BT Infonet and Orange Business Services.[260] However, SWIFT retains operational control over the network design and day-to-day operations.

Today, SWIFT is among the largest and most successful B2B e-commerce networks in the world. In 2010, the co-operative generated €537 million in revenues.[261] Over 9,000 banks, securities firms and non-financial corporations are now connected from over 200 countries. Without question, SWIFT has the broadest reach of any B2B network. In fact, they often joke about whether there are more countries connected to SWIFT than participate in the World Cup. SWIFT exchanges almost 4 billion messages annually, approximately 50% of which are payment related. Securities messages represent the majority of the remainder. Foreign exchange transactions and trade finance documents are only a small fraction of the overall transaction volume.

As mentioned previously, SWIFT does not clear payments, settle stock trades, nor exchange foreign currencies. Instead, SWIFT enables financial institutions to share the information about payments, securities, and foreign exchange transactions. SWIFT's historical value proposition has been to enable banks, operating in different countries, to collaborate with one another to support the international needs of their customers. SWIFT's function is a very necessary one, as only a few of the very large financial institutions maintain significant operations outside of their home countries. Despite their local footprint, most of these banks still need to service customers with multi-national needs. For example, a midsize bank in Germany may have local manufacturing customers in Cologne that export parts to the Americas, Asia, and other parts of Europe. The German manufacturer will need to collect payments in local currencies from its various customers around the world. The German parts company may also need to pay suppliers that operate in different countries around the world. To facilitate these transactions, the German bank will set up a series of correspondent relationships with foreign banks operating in different countries. When the German parts supplier needs to make a payment in Argentina, Egypt, or Thailand, its local bank will send a payment instruction through the SWIFT network to the corresponding banking partners requesting the local funds transfer.

SWIFT Should Go Public

As I mentioned before, SWIFT is a private cooperative that is currently owned by its member banks. But, it is interesting to ponder what SWIFT would be worth as a publicly traded company. SWIFT's commercial offerings generated over €420 million in recurring revenues in 2010 from its reach into the banking and securities processing functions of every major financial institution in the world.

The idea is not as far-fetched as you might think. Numerous other mutually owned service providers in the financial industry have pursued similar initiatives. Most of the major credit card networks and stock market exchanges were originally formed by a consortium of large banks. Over the past 20 years, most of these organizations have demutualized and transformed into publicly traded companies. The Helsinki, Copenhagen and Australian Stock Exchanges were among the first to demutualize and IPO back in the late 1990s. The Chicago Mercantile Exchange, Hong Kong Exchange and Deutsche Borse quickly followed between 2000 and 2001. A second wave of IPOs started around 2004, with the Osaka Securities Exchange, Chicago Board of Trade, International Securities Exchange and NYMEX. Even the famous New York Stock Exchange (NYSE) and NASDAQ went public in 2006. Far more lucrative for the banks, however, was the demutualization and IPOs of MasterCard in 2006 and Visa in 2008.

The mean IPO value of these demutualized exchanges and card networks at the time of IPO was 4.1 times revenues and 14.0 times EBITDA (Earnings before Interest, Taxes, Depreciation, and Amortization). Assuming a comparable valuation, SWIFT could generate more than €2 billion through an IPO. Despite the valuation that could be obtained from such an equity sale, it is unlikely that SWIFT will go public any time in the near future. Although its owners collectively would benefit from the proceeds, no individual financial institution would receive a significant amount of cash from such an offering. SWIFT's equity is divided among several thousand banks. I suspect that even the largest member owners, such as HSBC and Citigroup, likely have less than a 5% equity stake.

Chapter 16
SEPA and Electronic Payments

In the movie, *Catch Me if You Can*, Leonardo DiCaprio plays the character Frank Abagnale, who became famous as a teenager in the 1960s for impersonating others and check fraud. Abagnale passed $2.5 million of fake checks in 26 countries over the course of five years. Pan Am estimated that while impersonating a pilot Abagnale flew over 1 million miles on over 250 flights free of cost. He billed all his food and lodging during these trips to the airlines as well. Later Abagnale impersonated a pediatrician in Georgia for nearly a year performing primarily supervisory duties of interns, which allowed him to avoid the need to actually practice medicine. Abagnale also posed as a lawyer for eight months although he primarily performed administrative duties rather than actual case work. Perhaps most impressive is that he managed to pass the Louisiana state bar exam after three attempts.[262]

One of Abagnale's famous tricks was to print his account number on a blank deposit slip and add it to the stack of real bank slips at a local branch. Most customers did not notice the pre-printed account number resulting in the deposits written on those slips being entered to his account rather than that of the legitimate customers.[263] Another trick that Abagnale used in the movie was to exploit the fragmentation of the US check clearing system. Most checks are cleared through the US Federal Reserve System. The Federal Reserve performs check clearing in 12 different geographic regions in the US. Some regions are fairly wide, such as #12 in the western US that includes Alaska, Hawaii, California, Nevada, Washington, Oregon, Idaho, Utah, and Arizona. Others, such as region #2 consisting primarily of the state of New York and northern New Jersey, are fairly small. Checks are routed for clearing in different regions based upon the routing numbers printed on them. Yes, the numbers on the bottom of the check do mean something. Abagnale learned that if he cashed a check in New York City from a bank in California, it would take longer to process. The check has to travel through the clearing system from region #2 in New York to region #12 in the Western US. Abagnale exploited this latency in the clearing system knowing it would take longer for the banks to discover that his accounts were overdrawn.

Many corporations try to exploit the check clearing system in the US as well. Corporate payers are not seeking to defraud anyone or manipulate the system, but they do want to hold on to their cash as long as possible. Suppose that a retailer owes one of its suppliers $50,000 for invoiced merchandise it received. The retailer could opt to initiate an electronic payment that would be processed in one to two days. Or the retailer could issue a wire transfer which would occur in a matter of minutes. Another option would be to issue a check. With the paper clearing process the payment could take anywhere between two and 14 days to be processed. The check travels through the mail to the supplier's location. The supplier must then take the check to the bank, which must forward it on to the closest Fed check clearing center for settlement. The actual processing time duration will be determined by the distance between the buyer and supplier as well as the transportation time between a supplier's bank and the clearing center. The entire process could easily drag on for over a week. Meanwhile, the retailer is able to hold onto their $50,000 for a few days longer. If the retailer is short on cash, the extended processing period provides a significant cash flow benefit. The retailer will have collected additional money from consumers at its stores while the check is "floating" through the mail and clearing process.

In practicality, most suppliers have gotten wise to these float techniques used by their customers. One of the financial metrics that public companies have to report to their shareholders is Days Sales Outstanding (DSOs). The difference in a few DSOs can have a significant impact on a company's cash flow and borrowing needs. As a result, CFOs are very focused on mechanisms to accelerate receivables collection by reducing float.

Suppliers utilize specialized facilities called lockboxes to collect and process check payments. All but the largest corporations typically outsource these lockboxes to banks or other third parties. Within a lockbox is specialized equipment that can automatically scan, sort, and package checks upon receipt. The "PO Box" that you often see when mailing in your mortgage, insurance, or credit card bill is typically a lockbox location operated by a third party. The supplier requests that a buyer submit payment to the lockbox location closest to the supplier's operations. The geographic proximity cuts down on the length of time the check is in the mail. To reduce clearing cycles, lockbox operators locate their facilities in short driving distance of Federal Reserve or private check clearing centers. Checks received into the lockbox can be quickly scanned, validated, and routed for clearing. Reducing the distances between the various parties involved in the overall process can reduce float by several days.

The hassle of dealing with checks became quite simpler when the US passed the Check 21 legislation. Check 21 allowed corporations and banks to convert paper checks into electronic payment transactions without the permission of the consumer. The process is formally known as truncation. Check 21 allows a check received at a lockbox to be made into an electronic copy, or image, of the check. The check data can then be used to create an electronic transaction. If you live in the US you may have noticed around 2005 that checks you wrote were no longer being returned with your monthly statement. Instead a cryptic phrase such as "ACH conversion" was listed on the statement along with a photocopy of the check.

The idea behind Check 21 was to create efficiencies for suppliers collecting payments without forcing any change to the customer's business process. Customers could continue to pay with checks, however, the supplier had a legal means to accelerate processing by converting the paper to electronic.

US B2B Payments

While converting checks into electronic format partially digitizes the payment flow, the overall process would be more efficient if it were fully electronic. However, convincing corporations to switch from paper to electronic payments has proven to be considerably challenging. As recently as 2005, the typical US-based corporation processed 80% of payments using checks. You might think that there would be an obvious cost savings for switching from checks to electronic payments. Wire transfers and ACH payments, which are the primary electronic payment options, are both faster and less expensive.

ACH payments are typically used for lower value payments, which are less time sensitive. ACH systems are operated by the central banks of most countries. An ACH system will transfer funds between two financial institutions in one to two days for a relatively small fee. Although you may not be aware of it, your financial activities depend upon ACH payments. If you use online bill payment for your mortgage, insurance, phone, or utility bill then your bank is performing an ACH payment on your behalf. If you are paid your salary via direct deposit, then you are the recipient of an ACH payment from your employer. ACH payments have been around since the mid-1970s. The US Air Force was the first to distribute payrolls electronically through direct deposit in 1974. The US Treasury followed quickly using direct deposit for all Social Security payments in 1976.[264]

The other primary B2B payment mechanism is the wire transfer. Wires are typically used for higher value payments over $10,000. Wire transfers, or as the bank industry calls them, real time gross settlement (RTGS), occur quickly in a matter of minutes. Central banks in most countries facilitate the actual exchange of funds through wire transfer services. Some private operators also offer wire transfers to support international payments, for example.

Three B2B Payment Models

Checks	Automated Clearinghouse	Wire Transfer
Paper-based	Electronic	Electronic
Processed in 2-14 days	Processed in 1-2 days	Processed in minutes
Low value payments	Low value payments	High value payments

One of the primary reasons corporations continued to pay by check was the perceived float that existed from paper-based clearing systems. However, float was not the only reason that US corporations continued to pay by check. There was a considerable level of investment required to migrate to electronic payments. Ideally, payments would be approved by accounting personnel then sent electronically to a bank for execution. Technology is required to send instructions directly from a corporate accounting system to a financial institution. However, many of the popular accounting packages for small businesses did not have robust e-banking capabilities until recently. Today all of the major ERP and accounting software vendors have built-in technology that allows corporations to generate e-payments. As a result, since 2005 there considerable progress has been made converting a large percentage of checks from American corporations into electronic payments.

B2B Payments in Europe

The situation in Europe differs significantly from the US. Most of the European nations migrated to electronic payments long before the US. However, the overall payment landscape in Europe has historically been very fragmented. Different processes, prices, technologies, and regulations for making payments existed in each country.

Consumers and corporations who purchased the payment services as well as the financial institutions who deliver the services all suffered from the limitations of the country-specific model. First, consumers paid different prices for the same banking services depending on their country of residence. Italians and Germans might pay ten times what a Dutch or French citizen was charged for basic retail banking services. Second, geographic limitations constrain service offerings. Many of the banking services consumers purchase were limited to the home country in which the financial institution was based. For example, when a Belgian citizen travels to another country, such as Austria, his debit card from the Belgian bank would most likely not allow him to withdraw funds from a local ATM.

Corporations suffered many similar challenges to consumers. The fees assessed by banks for payables and receivables services varied widely based upon country. A multi-national corporation making a €1000 payment to a supplier might pay €0.75 in Italy; €0.25 in Spain, and €0.05 in France.[265] In addition to the variation in fees, the timing, regulations, and processes for making payments varied by country as well. Historically, there was one consistency in payments across all European nations: cross-border transactions were expensive regardless of the country of initiation. For example, historically the example of the €1000 payment would have cost €20 if it were to be made from a payer using a German account to a payee using a foreign bank.

Single European Payments Area

In the 1990s, the European Union began an initiative to harmonize and simplify payments across the 15 countries that have embraced the Euro as the national currency. The program, known as the Single Euro Payments Area (SEPA), was designed to establish a common set of regulations, processes, standards, and technologies for making payments across the Eurozone. Consumers and corporations would enjoy consistent pricing and service levels irrespective of their country of citizenship and the location of their bank account. Surcharges for cross-border transactions within the Eurozone effectively would be eliminated. As a result, citizens and corporations are able to make payments in any Eurozone country as easily and cost-effectively as they can in their home nation.

SEPA offered numerous benefits to consumers, corporations, and financial institutions. The efficiencies gained through SEPA were expected to lead to a 1% increase in GDP for the EU.[266] However, the productivity improvements would not come for free. The gains were to be achieved at the expense of revenue losses for the banks. Specifically, financial institutions would need to reduce the payment processing fees they charged for transfers of money between accounts. It was originally forecasted that SEPA would reduce bank payment revenues by 30 to 60% or a total of €13 to €29 billion across the industry.[267] One of the greatest areas of impact would be cross-border payment fees that would be reduced from between €16 to €24 per transaction to under €0.50 per transaction.

Why are banks willing to participate in SEPA if they stand to lose so much money? While SEPA requires banks to sacrifice short-term payment fee revenue, it does offer the promise of much larger long-term revenue and profitability gains. In today's model, financial institutions must manage their payment products and systems differently in each country. Therefore, it is challenging for financial institutions to gain economies of scale. Regulations and requirements for operating a bank vary by country. As a result, only the largest financial institutions can afford the startup costs to establish operations in multiple countries. With SEPA the barriers for financial institutions to expand into new markets would be reduced considerably. As a result, banks could expand their geographic footprint to capture a larger share of the overall Eurozone market with its 15 million corporations and its 300 million citizens. Furthermore, banks could offer a unified product set across the various countries gaining significant economies of scale in back office operations.

SEPA is, of course, just one part of a broader plan to harmonize the financial systems throughout the EU. In January of 1999, the EU launched the Euro as a currency for a selected group of its member states. The Euro was first introduced only in electronic form for use in fund transfers or travelers checks. In 2002, the Euro fully replaced currencies such as the French Franc, German Deutsche Mark, Italian Lira, Spanish Peseta, and Dutch Guilder. Unification of the currencies in Europe is just part of a broader plan to harmonize the financial systems across the Union. Europe seeks to create a single economic market across its various countries. Much as the US operates as a single market across its 50 states, the EU seeks to reduce obstacles to cross-border commerce. The ideal end state is that a European company will be able to do business in any other EU country as easily as it does business within its home country. As a result, the EU has established similar initiatives to harmonize not only its currency and payments, but also tax policy, securities clearing, financial reporting, and electronic invoicing.

Similar harmonization programs are being attempted in other regions. For example, the Middle Eastern nations of Saudi Arabia, Bahrain, Kuwait, Oman, Qatar, and the UAE have already started efforts to unify their economies. This group, known as the Gulf Cooperation Council, also seeks to establish a common currency similar to the Euro.

SEPA was introduced to the European banking sector in multiple phases through the introduction of two major transactions. The first was the "Credit Transfer," which allows customers to "push" funds electronically to their suppliers. The second was the "Direct Debit," which allows a supplier to withdraw funds from its customer's account using a "pull" model. Direct Debit is popular in the B2C segment. For example, high volume billers such as insurance companies, telecom providers, and electrical utilities request that consumers enroll in an automated payment system that allows for debiting of their accounts on the date of the monthly billing cycle. Adoption of SEPA has been slower than expected. By the middle of 2011 only 20% of all credit transfers in the EU were being processed with the SEPA Credit Transfer[268] and less than 1% of all debit transfers were being processed with SEPA Direct Debit.[269]

The key subject of debate in recent years has been the need for an end-date for SEPA. In other words, when will the legacy, country-specific payment processing systems be turned off? The politics surrounding SEPA became particularly interesting during the global credit crisis of 2008-2009. EU leaders were challenged with a number of issues. Sovereign debt challenges began to emerge in countries such as Portugal, Ireland, Italy, Greece, and Spain (PIIGS). Several of these countries had to formally request a bailout package from the EU in order to avoid insolvency. Some of these distressed nations were home to the banks that would be most impacted by the pricing harmonization expected to result from SEPA. What would be the impact of removing billions of dollars in transaction fees during a period of crisis in the financial sector?

Another expected outcome of SEPA was consolidation of the European banking sector. Seeking local presence in a broader set of markets, banks would merge in hopes of developing a Pan-European footprint. The driver for consolidation would be the need to achieve economies of scale in payment processing. However, the entire industry was rethinking the risks associated with having the majority of the banking system concentrated in the hands of a few firms. The failure of Bear Stearns and Lehman Brothers nearly collapsed the world's financial system. Numerous other banks in Western Europe and the US deemed "too big to fail" were given government bailout packages to ensure long-term solvency. EU officials began to deliberate whether further consolidation of European banks was in the best interests of the industry.

SEPA was not the only initiative being reconsidered. As the sovereign debt crisis continued to grow in 2011, EU leaders began to question the use of a common currency. At the time of publication the future of the Euro remains uncertain.

Standardizing Electronic Banking

One of the necessary foundations for a successful SEPA framework is the need for standardization of electronic banking technologies. A common language is needed to communicate wire transfer and ACH payments between financial institutions and the centralized clearing systems. The challenge in migrating to such a universal standard is that historically, each country operated its own ACH system. There was the CEC in Belgium, SIT in France, RPS in Germany, BI COMP in Italy, CSS in the Netherlands, SNCE in Spain and BACS in the UK. Not only did each country have different clearing systems but each country adopted different B2B standards to communicate payment instructions as well. The CIRI1128 standard was used for domestic payments in Belgium. The CFONB160 was used in France. The DTAUS was used in Germany. The ClieOp03 was used in the Netherlands. The ELIXIR-O was used in Poland. The CSB19 was used in Spain. And the DTA was used in Switzerland.

Europe is not unique in its multiplicity of standards. Several major electronic banking standards exist within the single country of the United States. First, the US National Automated Clearinghouse Association (NACHA) created a specific set of standards for payments and electronic funds transfers. NACHA formats are the actual messages that the banks and Federal Reserve use for payment processing. A second group called the Bank Administration Institute (BAI) was formed to develop specialized B2B standards for banks to deliver account statements to corporate customers with cash balance information.

In addition to the country-specific banking standards in Europe and North America, other "global" standards were developed by various trade groups. For example, the US-based American National Standards Institute (ANSI), which does not specialize in banking, created a group of EDI standards for payment transactions. These EDI messages provide corporate clients with an alternative to the NACHA formats for payment instructions and BAI for statements. Similar to ANSI in the US, the UN created a group of EDIFACT messages, which provide an alternative to country-specific payment formats in Europe. SWIFT also has a set of message standards for electronic banking. The SWIFT MT standards include payment messages such as MT 101 and MT 103 and account statement reporting messages such as MT 940 and MT 942.

In practice, corporations in the US and Europe use a mix of these different country-specific and global standards depending on their size and the preferences of their bank. Some companies ignore these standards altogether and simply send a large file with payment instructions from their accounting system. Consequently, files from SAP, Oracle, and QuickBooks applications are among the fastest growing standards used within the banking system.

ISO 20022—In Search of Payments Harmony

The existence of many different banking standards creates challenges for all participants as information sharing is not consistent across geographic regions. As in many other industries, a consortium has formed with the goal of harmonizing electronic banking standards. The harmonization would be useful even without SEPA, but has gained a new sense of importance and urgency with the looming SEPA deadlines.

The outcome of the efforts has been a new standard called ISO 20022 XML. ISO is designed to replace the many different country-specific, bank-proprietary, and vendor-developed payment file formats in use throughout the world today. ISO 20022 is officially known as UNIFI (UNIversal Financial Industry message scheme). The early focus of ISO 20022 was centered upon payments. However, the standard has ambitions which extend far beyond that domain. The scope of ISO 20022 is all financial messages including payments, foreign exchange, international trade, and securities transactions. And the standard is beginning to gain widespread adoption as organizations have started to embrace it. ISO 20022 will be the foundational standard for SEPA's clearing and settlement systems. Versions of the ISO 20022 messages were created for Credit Transfers, Direct Debits and other types of SEPA payments.[270]

Advocates of ISO 20022 XML believe it will harmonize the world of banking standards. However, it is unlikely that it will occur any time in the near future. Most corporations and financial institutions are heavily invested in legacy standards from SWIFT to country-specific formats. The business case to perform an upgrade to newer XML standards will be challenging to make unless a major system upgrade is occurring. Although ISO 20022 XML will be adopted by some of the largest corporations and financial institutions. I am confident that in the year 2020 standards such as BAI, NACHA, EDIFACT, ANSI and SWIFT MT will continue to be widely used.

Chapter 17
Securities Trading and FIX Networks

At 2:45 p.m. on May 6, 2010, the Dow Jones Industrial Average plunged 900 points within the period of just a few minutes. It was the biggest one-day point decline on an intraday basis within Dow Jones history. For a few minutes over $1 trillion in market value disappeared. Stocks of blue chip companies such as Procter & Gamble and Accenture began to trade for as low as a penny and as high as $100,000.[271]

There were numerous theories as to the root cause of the so called "flash crash." Some believed that the precipitous decline in the market was the result of a trading error. For example, a trader may have accidentally placed a large sell order for Procter & Gamble stock that sent prices spiraling downward. Others believed a technical glitch on the New York Stock Exchange (NYSE) and other trading exchanges had contributed to the crash.

Industry insiders had more sophisticated conspiracy theories, blaming a group of high-frequency traders. In high-frequency trading, extremely fast computer programs analyze market data to identify trading opportunities that may open up for a fraction of a second. These firms buy securities, then turn around to sell them a few seconds, minutes or hours later. Although these trades individually might only yield a penny per trade, the high volumes can generate considerable profits. High-frequency trading has become very popular in the US during recent years. In fact, 70% of equity trades during the year 2010 originated from high-frequency strategies.[272]

To cause the flash crash, some hypothesized that high-frequency traders sent a series of non-executable orders to exchanges that overloaded and crashed systems. A non-executable order refers to a trade that is priced outside of the current "bid" and "ask" range. For example, one trader might offer to sell Accenture stock at $100,000 per share or to buy Procter & Gamble for $0.01 per share. These "stub quotes," used by high-frequency traders, are utilized to test response times from exchanges and to detect early price trends.

Months later an investigation by the US Securities and Exchange Commission (SEC) and the Chicago Futures Trading Commission determined that the source of the flash crash was not directly triggered by a high-frequency trader, but rather just a large trade placed by a mutual fund. The fund, named Waddell & Reed attempted to sell 75,000 E-Mini contracts for a total value of $4.1 billion.[273] Those of you not familiar with the stock market might be thinking that an E-Mini is an electronic battery powered version of those little Mini cars you see on the highway. However, that is not correct. Instead, the E-Mini is the world's most popular "equity index futures contract." In other words, the E-Mini is a security which represents the market's perceived future value of the Standard & Poor's (S&P) 500 index. Traders buy and sell the E-Mini based upon their view of how they anticipate the S&P will perform in the near future.

The root cause of the flash crash was the sale of the large position in the E-Mini, which drove the prices in the futures market down rapidly. The computers of high-frequency traders then began to aggressively sell E-Mini positions as well, as they were programmed to do. A "hot potato" effect emerged in which the computers began selling positions to one another continuously, leading to a downward spiral. During the period between 2:45:13 p.m. and 2:45:27 p.m. of May 6th high-frequency traders had exchanged over 27,000 contracts accounting for 49% of the trading volume.[274] But shortly thereafter, the computer systems began to scale back trading and withdraw from the markets. As these high-volume computerized traders disappeared from the market there became a scarcity of buyers and sellers. Non-executable orders for $0.01 or $100,000 were the only bids and offers remaining, which resulted in the extremely odd stock prices for P&G and Accenture.

Although the market value reappeared within minutes the psychological effect on many retail investors was longer lasting. Just as the world appeared to be heading out of the recession in 2010, the flash crash gave individual investors yet another reason to lack confidence in the stock market.

There are lots of articles on the Internet explaining the pros and cons of high-frequency trading as well as the root causes of the flash crash. The issues I want to explore in this chapter, however, are the key technologies which have enabled stock markets to operate at this extreme pace electronically. Historically, stocks were traded on a physical exchange with people managing the process. Today, computers are not only facilitating the trading, but also making the buy and sell decisions. B2B e-commerce technologies have played a large role in helping computerize the activities throughout the lifecycle of a trade.

Electronic Trading

The concept of electronic trading became popular back in the 1990s. Numerous retail e-trading sites emerged to support retail investors during the dot-com era. Examples included E*Trade, Ameritrade and Charles Schwab. Online trading eliminated the need for investors to have to phone trades into brokers. Orders could be placed online instead. Traders gained access to a wealth of real-time data about stock prices and market performance. The autonomy and empowerment of online trading served to inspire a new generation of day traders. These individual investors sat behind their desks trying to capitalize on the inflationary prices of the dot-com era.

The majority of stock market trades are not actually initiated by individual investors, but rather by institutional investors such as mutual funds, hedge funds, pension funds or university endowment programs. Pension funds often hire professional money managers to make investment decisions on their behalf. A mutual fund might manage the assets of a $1 billion growth fund owned by 10,000 individual retail investors. Insurance companies are also large institutional investors. An insurer might manage a $5 billion portfolio of assets that it uses to pay out death benefits for individual life insurance policies.

Electronic trading for institutional investors started long before the concept emerged on web-sites. Some stock markets have always been fully electronic—such as the NASDAQ—which started as a digital bulletin board in 1971. The company that owns the New York Stock Exchange, NYSE Euronext, also has an electronic trading platform called Arca that was formerly known Archipelago. The New York Stock Exchange that you see on TV continues to operate its trading floor on 11 Wall Street. Although NYSE has started to go digital, there are still numerous human beings on the pit of the exchange which buy and sell shares of NYSE listed stocks.

The move to electronic trading simplified the lives of institutional investors considerably. A money manager could now initiate trades directly from their computer rather than having to phone a broker. Not only did electronic order routing save time, but it reduced errors as well. For complex trades, sending the instructions from computer to computer reduces the risk that the order will be incorrectly received and executed. Furthermore, once the trade was executed a confirmation could be transmitted electronically back to the investor notifying them of the status of the trade.

In the past twenty years, the volume of electronic trading has increased exponentially. All the major mutual funds, pension funds, hedge funds and institutional investors route trades to brokers electronically. In most cases, portfolio managers at these institutions are initiating the process. However, in other cases the computers are programmed to make decisions about what to trade. These computer-driven algorithmic trading techniques may or may not include the high-frequency trading strategies referenced above.

High-frequency trading was first introduced by a Long Island hedge fund named Renaissance Technologies.[275] The use of high-frequency trading grew significantly during the period of 2005 to 2009. Although high-frequency traders represent significant volume in the market, only 2% of the 20,000 firms which actively trade, use such an approach.[276] High-frequency trading is not necessarily bad for the average investor. By increasing the volume of stock trades, it has created economies of scale for exchanges and brokerages. These higher volumes lead to lower commissions and trade processing fees. Additionally, high-frequency trading contributes to increasing what is called "liquidity" in the markets. In other words, if you or I go to sell a popular stock, the chances are good that a high-frequency trader will buy that security in an attempt to exploit a temporary opportunity within the market. You are not being taken advantage of. In fact, if these high-volume traders were not in the market, you may have waited several minutes to find someone else willing to trade. And your order may not have been executed at the price you were seeking.

The stock market has become so electronic that there are more computers talking to other computers than there are people interacting with people. In the past decade more and more of the trading lifecycle is being orchestrated by B2B e-commerce technologies. The scrolling tickers of stock prices, market indices and news events you see on news programs are powered by a form of B2B technologies. The instructions for orders routed between institutional investors and their brokers are encapsulated in B2B messages. Trade confirmations are another type of B2B transaction.

An Example Trade

Let's walk through an example of a stock trade to illustrate how B2B e-commerce technologies form the critical foundation to the process. Suppose that a large institutional investor, such as Putnam, Fidelity or American Funds, is interested in taking a position in Amazon.com, because they believe the online retailer is well poised for future growth with its e-book reader and cloud computing product lines. The investor wants to buy a block of 20,000 shares of Amazon.com initially to add to three different mutual funds that it operates.

The institutional investor (or buyer) monitors the stock price and trading activity via "market data feeds" from companies such as Reuters and Bloomberg. The market data feeds might be distributed in an XML schema called Market Data Definition Language or MDDL. When the investor is ready to buy the Amazon stock, the money manager will create the order for the block of shares in a software application called an order management system (OMS). The OMS then will create a specialized type of B2B transaction called a FIX message which indicates the security to be traded; whether it is to be bought or sold and the type of order. In this case, the order is for 20,000 shares of Amazon.com. The FIX message is routed over a specialized FIX network operated by a technology vendor called NYFIX to a broker.

Large institutional investors usually rely on specialized brokers such as Goldman Sachs, Morgan Stanley or Merrill Lynch (now owned by Bank of America) to perform trades on their behalf. Depending upon where the stock is traded, the broker might place the order on the New York, Tokyo or London Stock Exchanges or the NASDAQ. If the stock is not traded on an exchange, as some happen not to be, then the broker will contact another broker who "makes a market" in the stock. In our case, Amazon.com happens to be traded on the NASDAQ. So, the broker can route a FIX message with the block order details to the NASDAQ for execution. Once the trade is completed, the broker will send a Notice of Execution back to the institutional investor.

Of course, I have only told the story from the perspective of the buyer. There is also a sell-side to the trade. Someone had to be willing to sell the block of 20,000 Amazon.com shares. In fact, the trade may have consisted of several smaller purchases from different sellers. A similar set of message exchanges occur on the sell-side of this Amazon trade, but I will omit them from this discussion for brevity's sake.

The Unlimited FIX Protocol

Like many of the other B2B e-commerce standards we have discussed thus far, FIX has an interesting history. FIX is an acronym which stands for Financial Information Exchange. It was developed in 1992 as a means for Fidelity Investments to communicate electronically with Salomon Brothers.[277] In this case Fidelity, being an institutional investor, would request Salomon's brokerage services to perform buys and sells of securities on its behalf. FIX remains the de facto standard for these processes today.

The primary users of FIX messages are broker/dealers such as UBS, Morgan Stanley and Goldman Sachs that receive electronic trade execution instructions from their large clients, such as mutual funds, hedge funds or endowments. Trade execution messages are the most popular transaction type, but FIX also supports related processes such as price quotations; indications of interest; and trade confirmations. Both the types of securities and business processes supported by FIX have been gradually expanding over the past decade. FIX is most popular in stock trading today, but it is also used for bonds, foreign exchange and derivatives such as options and swaps. According to the FIX Protocol Limited site, "No one knows with certainty how many people use FIX or how much of the global volume of securities transactions is effected via the FIX Protocol. What is certain is that virtually every major stock exchange and investment bank uses FIX for electronic trading, as do the world's largest mutual funds and money managers and thousands of smaller investment firms."[278]

A report by the research firm, Tower Group, estimated that 75% of all "buy-side" firms, such as institutional investors, utilize FIX as do 75% of all exchanges, such as NYSE and NASDAQ. Over 80% of all sell-side firms, such as brokers, utilize FIX.[279]

FIX has continued to evolve since its inception. There is now a FIX 5.0 version which is XML-based. Additionally, there is a new set of messages specifically for high-speed algorithmic trading called FIX Algorithmic Trading Definition Language (FIXatdl).

FIX Networks

Several specialized FIX networks exist to route these messages back and forth between brokers, institutional investors and other participants in the trading process. FIX networks have a variety of different owners ranging from stock exchanges to telecom carriers.

A few of the FIX networks are operated by technology vendors. The two biggest software vendors with FIX networks are Investment Technology Group (ITG) and Sungard. Sungard is a powerhouse in the software industry, although not quite as large or well known as Microsoft, Oracle and SAP. With $5 billion in revenues, Sungard ranks in the Fortune 400. Sungard was originally part of SUNOCO. Yes, the same company that sells you gas for your car. Sungard has a number of businesses, but it is best known for its disaster recovery services and financial software applications. The company developed a FIX network which it refers to as the Sungard Transaction Network to act as an extension of its securities trading software applications.

FIX networks are also owned by media and information services conglomerates. Both Thomson and Reuters each developed separate FIX services independently. The networks were combined when the two companies merged in April 2008. Thomson grew up as a publishing and media business while Reuters is best known for its stock market data and news services. The FIX services of the combined company are now branded as the Tradeweb Routing Network. Thomson Reuters claims that its FIX network originates 12 to 15% of the NYSE and NASDAQ executed order volume.[280] The inclusion of FIX-based trading services in the Thomson Reuters portfolio is very logical when you consider that they distribute much of the market data (news and price quotations) used to make trading decisions.

Several of the FIX networks are owned by telecommunications companies. Savvis, which was recently acquired by CenturyTel, is one example.

Savvis offers Financial Transaction Service (FTS) as part of its broader suite of data networking services for Financial Institutions. BT Radianz, the IT Services division of UK-based British Telecom, also operates a FIX network. Radianz is a leading provider of FIX network and other secure networking services for financial institutions. Interestingly, Radianz originally was part of Reuters before being acquired by BT.

Another example of a FIX network is the company NYFIX, which was acquired by the owner of the New York Stock Exchange, NYSE Euronext, in August of 2009. NYFIX was integrated with the NYSE Technologies division, which offers a wide assortment of services ranging from data center co-location to market data feeds for securities quotes. The acquisition was interesting because NYFIX was the last major independent FIX network in the sector. There are a few regional players such as Meta-Bit in Japan, UULINK in France and Marco Polo in emerging markets, but most of the FIX networks have been acquired and assimilated into larger corporations.

Much like the other sectors we have explored, there is no clear pattern to the acquisition of B2B e-commerce vendors by larger companies. NYFIX was acquired by a stock market exchange. Thomson Reuters is an information services company. Savvis and BT Radianz are both telecommunications vendors. Others are owned by technology companies such as Sungard.

Each of the combinations offers a different mix of product and market synergies. Most IT organizations already have relationships with telecom carriers and IT vendors, such as Savvis, BT or Sungard. Being able to purchase FIX services from these vendors along with other communications and technology products offers convenience. There are lots of interesting possibilities for owners of FIX networks to develop new value added services for their customers. For example, FIX networks can enable investors to trade outside of the traditional financial exchanges.

Electronic Communications Networks

Suppose you are seeking to accumulate a large position in a stock. Instead of just purchasing 20,000 shares of Amazon.com you want to accumulate two million. If you go to the NASDAQ with an order for 2 million shares there may not be a sufficient number of sellers in the market to fill the order immediately. You may have to buy shares in lots of 50,000 over a period of a few hours or a few days to accumulate two million. During the buying process the natural laws of supply and demand will begin to take effect. The price of the Amazon.com stock will rise as there is more demand than there is available supply. Furthermore, by distributing your trades across a longer time period you are exposing your accumulation strategy to others in the market. NASDAQ broadcasts all stocks being bought and sold and the quantities to anyone who subscribes to their data feed. Sensing that someone is accumulating Amazon.com, owners of the stock may try to drive the price of the shares higher, forcing you to pay a premium for the position.

But what if there were a way that you could accumulate 2 million shares without exposing your strategy to the market? What if there were a way to quietly match your buy orders with Amazon.com shareholders that wanted to sell without the trades being broadcast to the general public? In recent years, electronic communication networks (ECNs) have evolved which allow investors to buy and sell shares outside of the centralized stock markets such as NASDAQ and NYSE. An ECN will take a buy-side order and automatically match it to a sell-side order. These alternative trading systems, such as ECNs, are sometimes called "dark pools" because the general public has no visibility into trading that occurs there. Dark pools do not share their trades with any public data feeds unless legally required to do so; and when legally required, they will delay publication as long as is allowable. Consequently, ECNs are very popular with large institutional investors that prefer the secretive nature of these venues. Beyond lowering the visibility around trades, ECNs offer additional benefits such as off-hours trading and lower processing fees for clients.

Some FIX networks have been able to achieve such high volumes of orders that the operators can begin to offer their own trade execution services. In other words, the FIX network can act as an ECN by identifying opportunities to match buyers and sellers of securities without having to route the orders to traditional marketplaces such as NASDAQ and NYSE. Several of the leading FIX networks offer ECN or alternative trading services today.

ECN services enable FIX vendors to offer a higher level of value to their customers. FIX-based ECN services are a great example of how B2B e-commerce providers can evolve beyond technology infrastructure into business applications. E-commerce hubs can quickly reach a point of critical mass at which such high volumes of information are being exchanged that network patterns can become a source of intelligence and opportunity. Securities professionals refer to the concept as liquidity. The greater the number of participants in a securities B2B network, the greater the liquidity. FIX-based ECNs are just one of many examples of the B2B network effect, a concept we discussed in Chapter 6.

Chapter 18
STP and Securities Clearing

In the spring of 1968, the stock exchange system in the United States was on the brink of disaster. The potential catastrophe was not the result of a nationwide mortgage meltdown such as the one which precipitated the crisis of 2008. Instead, the challenges were brought on by the rapidly growing volume of trades. The average daily volume on the New York Stock Exchange had tripled in just the three years between 1965 and 1968.[281]

One of the key factors behind the rapid rise in trading volumes was a shift in the dynamics of the capital markets. Up until the late 1960s, the majority of trades were conducted on behalf of "retail investors" which are individuals like you or me. Of course, many of these investors were likely high net worth individuals with a great deal more money than I have to invest. In the late 1960s, a powerful group of institutional investors such as pension funds, mutual funds and insurance companies began to dominate trading activity. Institutional investors remain the highest volume traders today, although new types of organizations, such as hedge funds, have emerged in the markets.

When a surge in trading volume from institutional investors occurred during the late 1960s a number of problems began to arise in the back offices of these firms. Unlike today where most stock records are managed electronically, shares of stocks in the late 1960s had paper certificates associated with them. To settle a trade, the selling broker needed to hand-carry the paper certificate to the buyer's custodian in order to receive payment. A custodian is a third party appointed to safeguard and keep records of the asset for an investment manager. Whenever a professional investor is charged with managing the assets of an external client there is potential for fraud. Think Bernie Madoff! The use of a custodian significantly reduces the risk of such scenarios.

The rise of institutional investor trading led to an exponential increase in paperwork processing for clearing and settlement. The process quickly became unwieldy. Imagine hundreds of couriers riding bicycles through the streets of Manhattan carrying stock certificates between different firms. Stocks were piled up on the desks and filing cabinets. They were mailed to the wrong owners. In some cases the certificates were lost or stolen. However, at the time, the regulatory framework required such a manual, paper-based process. It was illegal to settle a trade without taking possession of the corresponding certificate.

When trade volumes surged, the back-office operations of the brokerage firms and custodians were not able to keep up with the delivery of certificates. Settlement of trades began to fail because the paper stock certificates were not delivered in time. In April of 1968, the average value of shares not delivered within a four-day period after a trade was $2.7 billion.[282] Government regulators responded by imposing a rule which stated that any broker that could not deliver securities within 30 days of the due date would be forced to buy stock in the open market to complete a delivery. Stock prices could rise or fall considerably in a 30-day period creating considerable risk for those brokers which did not comply. Nonetheless, the problem continued to grow. By December 1968 the value of unsettled trades reached $4.13 billion.[283]

A cascading effect began to form from the failed settlements. Not only were the trades not settled, but dividends were being issued to the wrong investors. Many public companies distribute a percentage of their earnings to shareholders in the form of quarterly dividends. Who receives the dividends depends upon whose name is listed as the owner of the shares. If the shareholder records are not kept up to date, then new buyers of shares may not receive dividends for stock they recently purchased. The dividends instead would be routed to the former owners, who had recently sold the stock.

From T minus 1 to T plus 1

Up until the late 1960s, there had not been much focus on the clearing, settlement and recordkeeping functions associated with stock trading. Few had cared about these mundane "back-office" processes. The focus of attention was with the brokers and investment managers that were involved with the buys and sells.

In response to the growing paperwork crisis, the New York Stock Exchange, American Stock Exchange and National Association of Securities Dealers cut back trading hours to enable back-office workers to catch up on trade clearing and settlement activity. In January 1968, the time of market closing was pushed up from 3:30 p.m. to 2:00 p.m. for a period of six weeks.[284] By June of 1968, the situation had not improved and exchanges decided another reduction to trading hours was required. The three exchanges decided to suspend all trading on Wednesdays during the month of June. Ironically, all these challenges were occurring one year before the first human landed on the moon. While the US had mastered the technology necessary to win the Space Race, the major stock markets were being crippled under the weight of excessive paperwork. The temporary, one day per week, closings were continued until January 1969 when the exchanges changed the approach again. Starting in 1969 the markets resumed trading five days a week, but for a shorter period —10:00 a.m. to 2:00 p.m.[285]

There was some relief for back-office operations in 1969 and 1970 as the economy moved into a recession and trading volumes declined. However, these two years saw a high number of liquidations and mergers of brokerage firms. Nearly one sixth of the US brokerage firms went out of business. Thousands of people lost their jobs, careers and fortunes. Certainly the reduction in brokerage revenues associated with lower trading volume was a factor in the decline. However, many insiders cite the paperwork crisis in the back office as the hidden root cause for the failures.

The securities industry looked to computer technology as a method for handling higher volumes of trades. One of the strategies to reduce the paperwork issue was the immobilization of stock certificates. Instead of transporting paper certificates between different custodians and brokers, a centralized depository would be created to keep the records electronically. Trades would be made via bookkeeping entries instead of physical paper exchanges. The New York Stock Exchange was the first to move to the new model with its Central Certificate Service in 1968. Five million dollars was invested in the project with the goal of eliminating the brokerage firm's work to inspect, count and store certificates.[286]

A few years later, in 1973, the Depository Trust Corporation (DTC) was formed to be the depository for stock certificates. Over the years, DTC merged with other entities to expand its scope. DTC grew to become not only a depository but the primary vehicle for clearing and settlement of securities. The company was renamed the Depository Trust & Clearing Corporation (DTCC). It remains the primary depository for the US capital markets. Today, the DTCC holds the records for 3.5 million securities issues worth $34 trillion.[287] DTCC also settles most of the securities trades that occur in the US and some international markets. It is part of the US Federal Reserve system and regulated by the US Securities and Exchange Commission.

In the decades following the 1960s, the dematerialization of stock certificates and the growing computerization of many routine post-trade activities, enabled back-office groups to keep pace with growing trade volumes. In 1995, the US stock market made a major leap forward. The standard timeframe for settlement of trades was reduced from five days down to three. However, the industry aspired for a better approach. While better than five days, the three day settlement period still created a great deal of inefficiency and risk for buyers and sellers within the market.

The Securities Industry Association (SIA) estimated that in the late 1990s, approximately $1.8 trillion worth of trades remained outstanding and unsettled globally every day.[288] One significant impact of the longer settlement period was that $1.8 trillion worth of investment capital was being tied up unnecessarily. If the market were operating perfectly, trades would settle on the same day they were executed. As a result, the $1.8 trillion could be potentially re-introduced to the marketplace.

The other significant impact of the three-day settlement was the introduction of settlement risk to buyers and sellers. Settlement risk occurs when one party to a trade fails to deliver the cash or securities required for settlement. Suppose that the seller of our 20,000 shares of Amazon.com became insolvent in the time between execution and settlement of the trade. If the valuation of Amazon had increased in the next few days, then the investment manager may be forced to buy the shares at a higher price. One common cause for settlement risk is the failure of a major player in the market. In the stock market crashes of 1987 and 2008 there was risk that major brokerages could collapse. In fact, both Bear Stearns and Lehman Brothers did collapse during 2008, but with the former receiving a takeover bid from JPMorganChase.

In the late 1990s, the US securities industry had joined together to propose migration to a one-day settlement. The initiative was known as "T+1"? referring to trade date plus one day. The SIA paid Accenture and the Capital Markets Company (Capco) to develop a business case analysis of the benefits of T+1. The study indicated that risk could be reduced by 67% by migrating from a T+3 to a T+1 model.[289]

The securities industry set a target date of June 2004 for its transition to T+1. However, a number of obstacles would need to be overcome to reach the milestone. To appreciate the magnitude of the challenge requires an understanding of the process for clearing and settling trades after they have been executed. Let's continue to follow the trade lifecycle with the Amazon.com example discussed in Chapter 17.

After the Trade

People love to complain about the fees they pay their stock brokers for handling trades on their behalf. In the past decade, millions of investors have opened up discount online brokerages accounts to reduce the commissions being paid to brokers. However, not all of the fees paid to stock brokers go towards a down payment on their new Mercedes convertible. A good percentage of the fees are required to fund the back-office operations associated with clearing and settling a trade.

After a trade is executed, a number of activities need to occur prior to settlement. First, the trade needs to be allocated among different accounts. For example, the block of 20,000 shares of Amazon.com was not purchased for a single mutual fund, but rather to be split between the three different funds. Let's say 10,000 shares are allocated to a general "Large Cap" fund. Another 5,000 shares are allocated to a specialized fund for individuals retiring in the year 2025. The final 5,000 shares are placed into a fund specializing in Internet companies. Prior to settlement, the investment manager needs to determine the allocation of trades into the various accounts then communicate the information to the broker and the custodian.

Securities Clearing & Settlement

Trade Executed

Allocation

Commissions & Taxes

Settlement Instructions

Settlement

The second process that needs to happen is the "net money calculation." Stock brokers charge commissions for their trades. Commission structures are negotiated between brokers and investment managers as part of an overall contract. However, the commission for any one particular trade might vary depending upon the type of security traded (stock, bond), trade location (domestic, cross-border) and volume traded (low, high). In addition to commissions, taxes need to be assessed. For certain transactions the government may withhold taxes at the time of settlement. For other transactions, the investor may be responsible for reporting gains and losses during their annual tax filings. The specific commissions and taxes associated with each trade need to be determined in advance in order to pay the broker and tax authorities at the time of settlement.

The third activity that needs to occur is to provide settlement instructions. The investment manager must tell the custodian how they want to exchange any money associated with the trade. If 20,000 shares of Amazon.com were purchased at $50 each, then the investment manager must present $1 million at the time of settlement. Institutional investors typically rely on custodians to perform the settlement on their behalf. As previously mentioned, the custodian acts as the safe-keeper and record-keeper for the institutional investors securities. The investment manager will need to provide the specific bank account from which the custodian can draw the funds for settlement. Many of the large custodians are banks such as Citigroup, JPMorganChase, HSBC or BNP Paribas. As a result, the funds being used to settle the trade may be held in a bank account with the custodian.

With the trade allocation, net money calculation and settlement instructions completed, the settlement process can then occur. Actual settlement occurs with the DTCC. The custodian delivers the $1 million to the DTCC electronically and the DTCC makes a bookkeeping entry reflecting the change in ownership of the 20,000 shares of Amazon.com stock. The custodian will track within its books which of the three different mutual funds own which quantity of Amazon.com shares.

Post-Trade Challenges

In the late 1990s, the post-trade clearing and settlement process was not highly automated, which was one of the primary reasons why the industry operated on a T+3 basis. Much of the information exchanged between investment managers, brokers and custodians occurred via fax or the phone. Automated data exchanges did occur between the larger firms; however, these were often nightly batch processes rather than real-time data exchanges. A migration to T+1 would require investment managers to allocate trades and provide settlement instructions within just a few hours after the trade occurred. Furthermore, custodians and brokers would need to be able to accept automated data feeds from the investment managers in real-time.

For "buys," investment managers would need to arrange for funding within one day of the trade. In the late 1990s, many investment managers would mail checks to custodians to fund the settlement. To accomplish one-day settlement, T+1 Electronic Funds Transfer (EFT) would need to be utilized rather than checks. As we discussed in Chapter 16 EFT transactions such as wire transfers and automated clearinghouse payments were more cost effective than checks, but required business process changes for the investment managers.

And cross-border trades would create additional challenges. Consider a US Large Cap mutual fund that maintains a 25% weighting in international securities. Such a fund will need to regularly purchase securities in Asia, Europe and Latin America. What settlement period would be appropriate for these trades? If the US moved to T+1, but the European and Asian exchanges remained at T+3 or T+2 a series of alternative settlement procedures would need to be negotiated.

Perhaps, the most challenging aspect of migrating towards T+1 was the smaller window of time available to correct errors. Studies in the late 1990s suggested that up to 60% of trades required repair or manual intervention prior to settlement. With T+1 an army of back-office personnel would be required to respond to the high volume of exception processing.

The industry believed that the only way to reach a T+1 settlement model would be through significant automation of the trade lifecycle. The industry focused its automation investment around a concept known as "Straight Through Processing" or STP. Alan Greenspan, Chairman of the US Federal Reserve commented at the time that, "The clearance and settlement process for US equities and other corporate securities is still a sequential and repetitive process that involves significant manual intervention... achievement of straight through processing will significantly reduce costs of settlement, including the growing costs of resolving errors in the documentation and processing of trades... Finally, the achievement of STP will remove many, if not all, the obstacles to realization of what should be the ultimate goal—settlement on T+0."[290]

STP is the capability of a financial institution to process trade execution, clearance, payment, settlement, custody, reporting and accounting activities without the need for human intervention. STP rates were unacceptably low in the late 1990s. Institutional investment managers had an average of 60% STP for US stock trades while brokerages were more efficient at 87%.[291]

In addition to the T+1 initiative to reduce settlement timeframes in the US, another major initiative was to further automate cross-border trades. Cross-border STP trade rates were much lower than those for domestic activities. However, cross-border trades introduced a number of complexities that increased the likelihood of a settlement failure. Settlement procedures and systems are different for each country. In the late 1990s, Europe alone had 30 different centralized depositories similar to the US DTCC. Cross-border trades involved foreign currency exchanges and international payment transactions. Furthermore, each country had different settlement timeframes, unique tax policies and local reporting requirements.

Further compounding the challenge was the fact that cross-border trades in the late 1990s were growing at a rate of 40% annually. The industry would not be able to absorb increased volumes of trades without either charging higher prices to fund exception processing or decreasing the rate of failed trades. Failed settlements resulted in fees and penalties to the responsible party, not to mention the risk of suspension from marketplaces. Every dollar spent on back-office processing and operations effectively was money taken from the investments of pension funds, endowments, life insurers and retail investors making the trades.

The Global Straight Through Processing Association

In 1997 a new organization was formed to solve the cross-border trade settlement process. Called the Global Straight Through Processing Association (GSTPA), the organization was backed by over 100 different securities firms worldwide. The major brokers, including DLJ, UBS, Citigroup, Merrill Lynch, Goldman Sachs and Morgan Stanley, were each members of GTSPA, as were the large global custodians, such as Chase Manhattan Bank, Credit Suisse, Deutsche Bank, State Street and the Bank of New York. Investment managers including AXA and Fidelity Investments joined GSTPA as well.[292]

The goals of GSTPA were to accelerate the flow of cross-border trade information and reduce the number of failed cross-border trades. GSTPA was not designed to perform settlement. The individual depositories such as DTCC in the US would continue to perform these functions. GSTPA's purpose was to simplify information exchange. GSTPA was referred to as an industry utility, but its purpose and nature is very similar to the B2B e-marketplaces, FIX Networks, EDI VANs and HIPAA clearinghouses, discussed in earlier chapters.

GSTPA's design included a few innovative ideas which were expected to greatly simplify information flows. First, GSTPA would act as a hub for information flows between the investment manager, broker and custodian. GSTPA promised to eliminate the spaghetti-like maze of connections that existed between different brokers, custodians and investment managers. In the new model, a party could communicate information once to the GSTPA hub that would then distribute it on to all interested parties. It was also believed that by removing the bilateral, sequential flow of information, custodians could get access to information faster, enabling a shorter settlement period.

Information Flows in Securities Clearing & Settlement

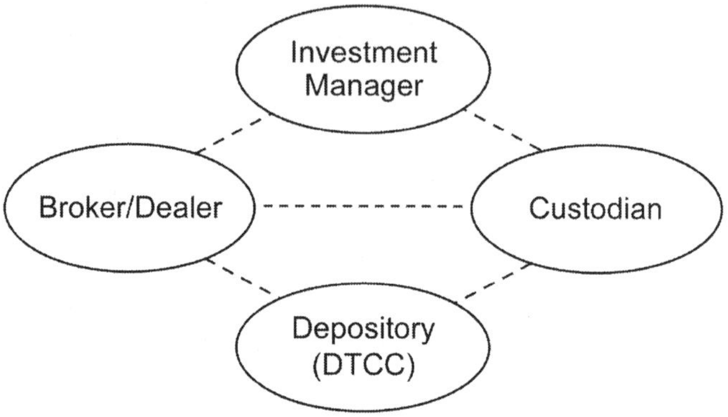

In addition, GSTPA would provide matching services. One of the key reasons for settlement failure was inconsistencies in data. As a result, GSTPA would "match" the trade allocation, net monies and settlement instructions to ensure that the investment manager, broker and custodian were completely synchronized prior to settlement.

The vision for GSTPA's was to enable T+1 and global STP for domestic and cross-border trades. By enabling real-time information flows using industry standards, exception rates and failed trades would decline substantially. Needless to say GSTPA's vision was quite ambitious. In fact, there are many parallels between GSTPA and the B2B e-marketplaces discussed in Chapter 2. And the two shared a very similar fate.

The STP Wars

The vision for GSTPA was evolving quickly in the late 1990s. Founded in 1997, GSTPA's membership quickly grew to 100 firms. The organization had raised $90 million in funding as of mid-2000, which was double its original target amount.[293] However, the plan began to unravel when one of GSTPA's major supporters withdrew from the consortium in early 2000.

The DTCC's technology division which was a favorite to win the bid to build out the GSTPA TFM platform asked to be suspended from the consortium citing potential conflicts of interest. As it turned out DTCC had opted instead to form a joint venture with Thomson to create a competitor to GSTPA. Both

DTCC and Thomson had built applications which automated post-trade functions such as electronic trade confirmations and allocations. If the GSTPA were successful, it would cannibalize the revenues from Thomson and DTCC's existing services. Furthermore, DTCC had ambitions of growing beyond its base in the US to become a global provider of settlement and information services.

The joint venture between DTCC and Thomson, known as Omgeo, was viewed to have a natural advantage against GSTPA. First, the product lines from the respective organizations that were transferred to the venture had a total of 15,000 investment managers already using the service. Together the organizations controlled 80 to 90% of the electronic trade confirmation market.[294] Omgeo also had a large database of settlement instructions. Clients could continue to use the post-trade services Omgeo offered just as before the venture was formed. There was no need to throw away existing platforms and technology investments. Omgeo offered a gradual migration to full STP as compared to GSTPA which was described as a "big bang" model.[295]

For several years, the two dual strategies of Omgeo and GSTPA were pursued in parallel. However, many were concerned with the inevitable duplication of effort between the two. Critics viewed the existence of both Omgeo and GSTPA as failure of the industry to agree upon a single approach to STP. However, experts believed that both utilities would be able to co-exist in the market provided that some level of interoperability could be obtained. It was theorized that the US clients would use Omgeo due to their pre-existing relationship with its owners and that European clients would opt for the newer GSTPA service.[296]

Omgeo was not the only competitor to GSTPA. Recognizing the massive opportunity to create value through STP, a number of firms including Accenture, Bloomberg, State Street and several FIX networks entered the market. All of these ventures were competing for the attention of the investment managers. As the customers in the securities trading ecosystem, investment managers had the most influence over which utilities would be successful. A few years earlier, Fidelity Investments had driven significant adoption of FIX technologies among brokers by requiring it as a pre-requisite to doing business. Once an investment manager chose Omgeo or GSTPA they would require their brokers and custodians to leverage the same utility. Since custodians and brokers service a diverse group of investment managers that might choose different platforms, it was likely that each firm would have to interface with both Omgeo and GSTPA.

GSTPA proceeded on schedule for several years. A commercialized version of the TFM finally was delivered to market in 2002. However, shortly after the "go live" the shareholders decided to suspend operations. The CEO of GSTPA, Jurgen Marziniak, stated that the utility did not receive the minimum number of transactions necessary to fund its operations. Following the announcement Marziniak was "disappointed and embarrassed." In perhaps the ultimate expression of the "build it and they will come" attitude that dominated the era, GSTPA's CEO said, "We built a very beautiful machine, a nice car that nobody wants to buy."[297]

GSTPA was not the only initiative to fail. The US securities industry also backed off the T+1 mandate for 2004. There were numerous explanations for GSTPA's failure. Some cited the weak economy that followed the dot-com collapse. Others cited the September 11th terrorist attacks as distracting the industry. Insiders criticized GSTPA for focusing too much on building great technology and not enough on building a compelling business model.

In a post-mortem article from 2003, a Senior Vice President from the Bank of New York, stated, "Once the project started, there were personality issues and a lot of individual self-interest on a number of parties getting into politics. It just became a flawed project that was doomed to fail. It is unfortunate that the industry had to spend $100 million in hard cash."[298]

Despite all the criticisms of the business model, no one had negative opinions of the technology developed. A Swiss law firm was retained by GSTPA to auction off its assets and distribute the cash among remaining employees and owners. There was widespread speculation that Omgeo or Sungard would purchase the TFM for $20 million.[299] However, a buyer never emerged.

It is easy to point the finger at Omgeo as the root cause for GSTPA's failure. Why did Thomson and DTCC not agree to the venture in 1997, preventing the need to create GSTPA altogether? Critics state that DTCC and Thomson placed their own self-interest above that of the industry in forming its joint venture. But isn't corporate self-interest the spirit that drives every enterprise in the capitalist model?

Perhaps, what really caused the collapse of GSTPA was the reluctance of its member-owners to leverage the utility once built. The custodians, brokers and investment managers that had provided the funding and direction were reluctant to make investments to integrate with GSTPA's TFM, or to pay the ongoing transaction fees necessary to fund the operation.

SECTION 6
Government

Chapter 19
International Trade Gateways

In October 2008, I flew to Singapore to present at the annual SCMLogistics World Asia conference on the topic of Consumer-Driven Supply Chains. It was a long and painful flight. There are direct flights from New York City to Singapore. But living in Washington, DC, I decided to split up the trip by connecting in Tokyo. After a 14-hour flight I arrived in Tokyo's Narita Airport around 2:00 p.m. local time, which was the middle of the night in DC. I had to clear security for a second time. I then had an hour or so before catching my connecting flight. As my luck would have it, the connecting flight was delayed by about three hours, which left me sitting in the airport lounge for four hours struggling to stay awake. The flight from Narita to Singapore was another eight hours. Along the way I was a bit concerned about my next mode of transportation upon arrival. My flight to Singapore was originally scheduled to arrive at midnight. The two-hour delay would push the arrival time back to 2:00 a.m. It was my first trip to Singapore. I was not sure if taxis would queue at the airport so late at night. In most airports you would be waiting a considerable time for a taxi that late at night.

When I arrived in Singapore, however, I was pleasantly surprised to find the airport fully operational. After a short walk from the plane I easily navigated my way to the immigration desk, which was fully staffed with five officers despite the late hour. I waited no more than three minutes before being admitted through immigration. The next stop was baggage claim. Again, I was surprised to find my suitcase was already on the rotating belt when I walked up. This was just 10 minutes after disembarking from the plane. Outside there was a taxi queue at least twenty deep, one of which transported me quickly into the city to my hotel.

If you have visited Singapore you are probably not surprised at all by my story. Singapore's Changi Airport is legendary for its customer service and operational efficiency. In fact, Changi has won over 360 awards since it opened in 1981.[300] The airport authority has a development policy of proactively building new capacity years ahead of demand to avoid congestion and service issues. For example, Changi recently spent $60 million Singapore dollars to be able to accommodate the introduction of the Airbus A380 jumbo jet.[301]

Changi is not only efficient at transporting passengers, but it excels at cargo freight as well. It is among the 10 busiest airports in the world along with Hong Kong's Chek Lap Kok, Shanghai's Pudong, Seoul's Incheon and FedEx's Memphis hub. Singapore is frequently a transfer point for air cargo being routed between East and West Asia. Re-exports comprise approximately 40% of Singapore's sales to other countries.[302]

Local cargo is heavily electronics-oriented due to the high concentration of semiconductor fabricators and contract manufacturing facilities in Singapore and neighboring Malaysia. All of the major cargo transporters including Asiana, Cathay Pacific, China Airlines, FedEx, Korean Air, Lufthansa, KLM, Singapore, TNT and UPS have landing slots at Changi.

Singapore's sea ports are highly efficient as well. Singapore's leadership in transportation infrastructure did not happen by chance. Instead, it is the result of a deliberate focus by the government to be a leading international trade hub in Asia. International trade competitiveness is particularly important to developing nations for a few reasons. Acting as a regional hub for trade will create demand for local sea ports and airports which creates jobs. In addition, fees are assessed on goods traveling through a hub, creating revenue for local governments.

More important, however, is the relationship between trade efficiency and foreign direct investment. When a multinational company such as Intel is evaluating whether to build a new semiconductor fabrication site in Malaysia, Vietnam, the Philippines or Southern China, it will compare a variety of factors such as local labor skills, government tax incentives and local regulation complexity. It will also evaluate the transportation networks in and out of the sites. No company wants to have inventory tied up in its supply chain unnecessarily due to traffic congestion on roads, inadequately sized ports or poorly operated air hubs. Furthermore, no company wants inbound shipments of materials or outbound shipments of finished goods delayed due to inefficient government trade policies.

The World Bank performs an annual ranking of all the countries in the world to identify which are the easiest to do business in. If you are developing nation seeking to be the home of the next manufacturing plant that Nike, Foxconn or Toyota invests in, then you want to rank high on this World Bank list. One of the key factors evaluated is cross-border trade policies. In its description of the ranking, World Bank states, "Excessive document requirements, burdensome customs procedures, inefficient port operations and inadequate infrastructure all lead to extra costs and delays for exporters and importers, stifling trade potential."

One of the keys to Singapore's successful development as an international trade hub was the strategic decision to become an early investor in B2B e-commerce technologies during the 1980s. In the mid-1980s, trade processes were highly inefficient in Singapore and most other countries around the world. Third-party studies had found that the cost of processing trade documentation comprised 4 to 7% of the value of the goods being shipped. Traders were required to prepare multiple copies of import and export declaration forms. The forms had to be physically delivered to government agencies for processing. These agencies were overwhelmed with paperwork. As a result, processing and approval times ranged from four hours to two days.[303]

Your International Customs Experience

Why do companies have to submit so many documents for each incoming and outgoing shipment? If you have traveled internationally, then you may have undertaken a similar document submission process at the airport. Each country requires the submission of immigration and customs paperwork. The documents may be a simple one-sided form that is handed to you by a flight attendant on the airline. Other countries may require more specialized visas in order to travel. If you are accompanied by a pet in your travels, the dog or cat may have been quarantined before being admitted into the country.

Suppose you were taking a business trip from New York to Shanghai.

US citizens traveling to China have to request a visa prior to embarking on the trip. To get a visa you will need to submit an application form to one of the Chinese embassy or consulates located in the US. Along with the application you may need to submit additional supporting documentation. US citizens must present a letter from the company in China requesting your visit and a passport-sized photograph. There is a nominal $130 fee for the visa, which takes two to three days to process. The visa will be physically appended to your passport. China's process may sound cumbersome, but I have found the processing to be highly efficient as compared to other countries such as Brazil which take over a month to grant a visa to US citizens.

When you return from Shanghai back to the US, your documents may be inspected prior to departure. You will need to present your passport and airline boarding pass to Chinese emigration officials. Upon arrival in the US, you will need to fill out a US Customs and Border Protection form that asks you a series of questions about your trip.[304] The form asks you to list the countries you visited, the items you purchased while abroad, the number of people traveling with you, and the flight number of the airline you took. The form will ask you whether you are returning with any plants or vegetables, meats or animal products, disease agents or cell cultures. These questions seem bizarre to most people who wonder why proximity to a farm or livestock is such a great concern. The answer is that meats, fruits, vegetables and plants on these farms may have pests or diseases which are a threat to US food crops or livestock. Highly contagious diseases could cause severe economic damage to the US agriculture industry, but more important, shortages in global food supplies for crops such as wheat. The US customs form also inquires about snails. I've never understood why snails are called out specifically.

The form also asks whether you are carrying over $10,000 in US or equivalent foreign currencies. There is no tax or duty paid if you say "Yes." However, if you do not report these currencies, then you may be subjected to fines for violations of the US Currency and Foreign Transaction Reporting Act. Each country has enacted a set of regulations which govern the transfer of items across international borders. Some of the laws have existed for so long that most people don't know the purpose of the regulations, nor does anyone bother to ask.

International Documentation for Cargo Freight

Governments have similar regulations in place for cargo imports and exports. A full explanation of these regulations would require an entire book, so I will offer only a summary of the reasons why government agencies need such extensive documentation for cargo freight.

First, there may be economic sanctions imposed on specific countries for the purposes of trying to isolate it economically. For example, there are various economic sanctions in place against Iran, North Korea and Cuba. As a result, all shipments in and out of a country may need to be inspected to ensure that no violations of the sanctions are occurring.

Second, there may be import quotas which set a physical limit on the quantity of a specific good that can be imported to a country. Quotas are designed to maintain a fair balance of trade between two specific countries. However, most economists argue that quotas are not in the best interests of the imposing country. The World Trade Organization has been focused on liberalizing global trade in recent decades. As a result import quotas have become less common.

Third, there may be a tariff or tax levied on certain types of imports or exports. It is usually instituted with a goal of protectionism. For example, in 2003 the US imposed an 8 to 30% tariff on steel as a protectionist measure. The US was concerned that foreign companies were "dumping" cheap steel in the American market creating an unfair playing field for domestic manufacturers. More than 30 steel makers had declared bankruptcy in the years leading up to the tariff.[305]

Fourth, there may be excises on certain goods. Excises are similar to duties, except that they are generally levied for domestic transactions, as opposed to being instituted for imported goods. Excises typically are applied as a deterrent to discourage individuals from pursuing potentially inappropriate behavior. For example, excise taxes are popular for alcohol, tobacco and gambling.

Fifth, a growing number of supply chain security regulations have been enacted by countries around the world. The US initiated a much higher standard for import security following the September 11th terrorist attacks. Many other European and Asian countries have adopted similar procedures. Shipping manifests must be submitted several days before the cargo leaves its port of departure. More extensive data about the shipment contents and its owners are being requested as well.

The requirements for international trade documentation are so complex that most companies enlist the help of a third party to ensure goods flow smoothly across borders. Paying a specialized customs broker can help to avoid delays or seizure of merchandise. Customs brokers prepare the documentation, calculate taxes, duties and excises, and facilitate the communication between their customer and the government authorities. These brokers have specialized expertise in tariff schedules and import regulations. A broker might specialize in a particular type of trade category such as apparel, technology or food products.

Another type of specialized company that can assist with international trade is called a freight forwarder. These forwarders will arrange for cargo movements across borders. Sometimes forwarders also perform the duties of a custom broker, such as submitting documentation and calculating taxes, duties and excises. Most of the large logistics companies offer freight forwarding services. FedEx, UPS and DHL each can provide these functions. There are also thousands of smaller freight forwarders which specialize in particular categories of trade or regions of the world. Companies which do not actually carry goods or own transportation assets such as planes, ships, trucks or rail cars are referred to as third-party logistics providers or 3PLs.

Singapore's TradeNet

To become a global leader in international trade, the Singapore government needed to ensure that it could enforce sanctions, quotas, tariffs and excises, but do so quickly and efficiently. The ability to process import and export transactions faster and cheaper than other Asian ports could provide Singapore with a competitive advantage in global trade. Yeo Seng Teck, head of Singapore's Trade Development Board in the 1980s, puts the situation in perspective, "Singapore is a small country. We have no natural resources. Our population is stabilized. We know we cannot compete by just bringing in new labor. If we are to be successful, we must improve our competitiveness in every way and especially in external trade, which is our largest business sector. This means cutting costs."[306]

One of the catalysts to Singapore's investment in B2B e-commerce was a recession that started in 1985. To stimulate growth the Singapore government decided to develop a more aggressive strategy for national economic development. Investment in technology to grow external trade was decided to be one of the top priorities. As a result, a national initiative called TradeNet was launched in 1986 to re-engineer the trade documentation process. The use of new technologies such as EDI was viewed as a key success factor for the project. Over 20 different technology firms bid for the rights to develop the TradeNet application. The top three candidates were McDonnell Douglas Information Systems, IBM and GE's Information Services division. IBM was announced as the winner in December 1987. To build TradeNet, IBM leveraged its Information Exchange EDI system that was developed by a group of engineers in Tampa, Florida.[307]

A few months later a for-profit company was created to be the official operator of the TradeNet application. The new company, named Singapore Network Services (SNS), was owned primarily by Singapore's Trade Development Board (TDB). As the majority shareholder TDB had a 55% equity stake. Singapore Telecoms, the Port of Singapore and the operator of Changi International Airport (the Civil Aviation Authority of Singapore) each had a 15% share of the new company as well.[308]

One of the greatest challenges with the project was to re-engineer the procedures of the many different government agencies involved with international trade. Automating the current workflow of highly duplicative documents being routed independently to different agencies would not yield the levels of efficiency required for competitiveness. The challenge was more political than technological. Nonetheless, after a relatively short period of analysis, Singapore successfully consolidated the information previously captured in over 20 different forms onto one computer screen.[309]

TradeNet Goes Live

The first TradeNet transaction was initiated on January 1, 1989, by Merchants Air Cargo. User adoption grew quickly as word spread about the faster turnaround times available through TradeNet. The trade process, which had previously required standing in line and hand-carrying paper documents around the city, now could be completed electronically in 10 minutes. Documents could be submitted 24 hours a day to TradeNet, which tripled the eight-hour operating schedule previously maintained by the government offices.[310]

TradeNet was considered the most advanced trade system of its kind, not only in Asia, but around the world. A few years after the system went live, Harvard Business School wrote a case study on TradeNet, declaring it as the world's first nationwide Electronic Data Interchange system. IBM estimated that TradeNet saved Singapore around $1 billion per year. Upon completion of the project, Yeo Seng Teck the head of TDB stated, "TradeNet facilitates trade. It makes it easier to do business in Singapore. That draws foreign investment to our economy and makes us competitive internationally."[311]

Today TradeNet links to more than 30 controlling agencies in the Singapore government with the local community of freight forwarders, air cargo agents, shipping agents and traders. Ninety-five percent of trade permits are processed in less than one minute. The fees assessed for electronic documents are only five Singapore dollars as compared to the ten to twenty dollars required previously. Overall TradeNet processes nine million permits annually.[312]

Although TradeNet remains operational, a next generation platform called TradeXchange was launched in October 2007 with even greater ambitions.[313] The company operating TradeNet, SNS, was renamed Crimson Logic. Crimson has continued to develop systems not only to support Singapore's e-government initiatives, but it has also developed TradeNet equivalents in several other countries, such as Ghana, Panama, Madagascar and Saudi Arabia.[314]

The strategy of investing in transportation efficiency with projects such as TradeNet has clearly paid off for Singapore. The World Bank named Singapore to be the easiest country in the world to do business in both in 2010 and 2011.[315] Singapore also enjoys the top ranking in the category of trading across borders. Its time to export is an average of five days as compared to 22.7 for the entire East Asia and Pacific region.[316] Its cost to export and import is roughly 50% of its neighbors throughout Asia.[317] Singapore has also re-engineered the business processes for global trade so that only four documents —the bill of lading, commercial invoice, customs declaration and packing list —are required. The average across developed countries is eleven documents for import and export procedures.

Hong Kong—Hub for International Trade

Despite its remarkable progress, Singapore still faces significant competition for cargo volumes, particularly with other ports in the South Asia region. Hong Kong is one of Singapore's key competitors for international trade. Hong Kong claims to have the busiest airport in the world, processing higher cargo volumes than Changi. The Chep Lap Kok airport, which opened in 1998, is located on reclaimed land on one of the outer islands in the Hong Kong Special Administrative Region. Hong Kong's sea ports are highly competitive as well. For the period between 1987 and 2004, Hong Kong ranked as the world's busiest container port 15 times.[318] It competes for that honor with other mega-ports such as New York, Rotterdam, Shanghai and Singapore.

Hong Kong's leadership in international trade is no coincidence. Much like Singapore, Hong Kong's government has invested aggressively to maintain a leadership position in the international trade sector. In fact, Hong Kong and Singapore actively compete on a country level for leadership in the logistics sector. Hong Kong's world leading transportation hub has been a key factor in enabling the growth of the manufacturing industry in nearby Southern China. Many of the goods manufactured in Shenzhen or Guangzhou are routed through Hong Kong en route to their final destination.

Much like Singapore, Hong Kong made strategic investments in technology to accelerate trade processing. In fact, Hong Kong actually started its international trade project earlier than Singapore, but fell behind due to disputes over financing the initiative. In 1983, Hong Kong first began exploring the use of EDI to support its local trade activities.[319]

For three years—between 1984 and 1987—no progress was made due to a debate over whether the project should be funded by public or private sources. The situation changed; however, when news of Singapore's TradeNet program began to circulate. Hong Kong leaders were concerned that the new EDI system would provide Singapore with a competitive advantage. Singapore was not the only country investing in an EDI platform for international trade. Similar initiatives were being pursued in Europe and North America. Another concern of the Hong Kong leaders was that their largest trade partners would soon be requesting international trade documentation to be exchanged via EDI.[320]

Financial challenges stalled the development process. However, eventually the Hong Kong government infused additional capital which led to a successful launch of TradeLink services in the late 1990s.

In 2000, TradeLink reached profitability. The community of businesses using TradeLink grew to 50,000, making it the largest electronic trading network in the world. In 2005, TradeLink became publicly traded on the Hong Kong Stock Exchange. The company earned over $200 million Hong Kong dollars in 2010 (approximately $25 million US). TradeLink's agreement to continue offering services has been extended by the government until 2016.[321]

Chapter 20
Supply Chain Security

On Christmas Day 2009, a 23-year old Nigerian man named Umar Farouk Abdulmutallab boarded an international passenger flight from Schiphol Airport in Amsterdam to Detroit's Wayne County Airport in Michigan. Abdulmutallab had checked into Northwest Airlines Flight 253 with only carry-on luggage for the flight. He had purchased the ticket with $2,831 in cash a few weeks earlier. Approximately twenty minutes before the plane landed he quietly ignited a small explosive device in his seat that failed to detonate properly. Passengers, smelling an odor and hearing firecracker noises, noticed the attack. The fire was extinguished by flight attendants while a Dutch film director named Jasper Schuringa tackled and overpowered Abdulmutallab.[322]

The botched terrorist attack targeted one of the largest US cities on the biggest holiday of the year. A few days later the Al-Qaeda cells operating in the Arabian Peninsula claimed responsibility for the attack. While detained by US authorities, Abdulmutallab claimed that he had obtained the device in Yemen. He had also received instructions and orders on how to detonate it when the plane was over US soil. However, the plane was physically in Canadian airspace when the detonation attempt occurred.[323]

Although suicide bombing attempts have become the most popular form of terrorism in recent years, hijacking of airlines has been the primary threat to commercial aviation since the 1930s. Hijacking became popular during the 1950s and grew rapidly in the 1960s. The worst year was 1969 when a total of 82 hijackings occurred. No hijackings caused as much loss of life or economic damage as those which occurred during the September 11th attacks.

In the wake of the attacks on the World Trade Center and Pentagon, the US has implemented far more rigorous airline security procedures. The Transportation Security Administration (TSA) was created under the new Department of Homeland Security. The TSA has deployed more and more sophisticated security technology throughout many airports in the US. The agency is now using millimeter wave scanners, explosive detection systems, and threat image protection software. There is even a "Cast-Ray" system deployed to screen passengers with casts, braces, and heavy bandages. Perhaps the most controversial technology introduced is the full-body scanner. These intrusive devices enable the TSA to look for hidden objects without requiring anyone to remove their clothes. One technology that has been deployed successfully without any complaints or inconvenience to travelers is EDI.

Secure Flight Powered by EDI

In August of 2009, the TSA implemented its new "Secure Flight" program. Secure Flight is one of the many Homeland Security recommendations put forth by the 9/11 Commission. The program calls for airline operators to transfer responsibility for watch list monitoring and passenger screening to the US federal government, specifically TSA. Through government ownership, the risk of security breaches can be minimized and a higher level of consistency can be enforced across airlines. The first phase of the program focused on screening of only US domestic flights. The program was quickly expanded to include international flights.[324]

The process starts by airline operators, such as Delta, United, and American, submitting EDI messages for each scheduled flight that include the names of all passengers as well as their date of birth, gender, and full itinerary. TSA performs a matching process against its "No Fly List," that contains approximately 2500 known terrorists restricted from boarding any commercial aircraft in or out of the US.[325] A secondary security screening selection process is then performed to identify passengers who require additional inspections. While the criteria for this selectee list are not published, a few known triggers exist such as one-way tickets and tickets purchased in cash or on the day of travel.[326]

The data is exchanged between airline operators and government agencies using two new EDI messages called PAXLST and CUSRES. These two documents were specifically designed by the UN/EDIFACT group for passenger screening by border control authorities. Selected nations' government agencies, such as the US Department of Homeland Security, have extended or customized the documents to satisfy country-specific regulatory requirements.

PAXLST is a message created by an airline containing detailed information about the passengers and crew members before they board the plane. It is required to be submitted to TSA for advanced approval prior to passenger boarding. PAXLST includes a number of data elements for each flight such as origin, destination, time of departure, and scheduled time of arrival. Extensive detail on each individual passenger includes full name, gender, date-of-birth, citizenship, home address, and email address. PAXLST can include passport data like country of issuance, expiration date, and document number. If a travel agency was used then PAXLST should include the name of the specific agent who ticketed the reservation. Even flight-time data such as the passenger's seat assignment and baggage tag are included. Perhaps most interesting is that the payment details are listed in PAXLST. For the credit or debit card used for the reservation, the cardholder's name and account number are included along with the total charges, the currency, and date of booking.[327]

CUSRES is the message returned from a border control authority to the airline that either acknowledges the receipt of a PAXLST or, if appropriate, provides actions to be taken. CUSRES includes reference data about specific flights and passengers. It also provides instructions for additional inspection or the need to deny boarding approval. The screening processes must be completed before an aircraft is given clearance for departure. The next time you are waiting to board an airplane at your departure gate you can take comfort knowing that B2B e-commerce technology is working to keep you safe.

Cargo Threats

On October 27, 2010, two packages were dropped off by a woman at the FedEx and UPS offices in Sana'a Yemen for delivery to Chicago, Illinois, on November 1st. The packages each contained a collection of souvenirs, clothing, compact discs, books, and most importantly a HP LaserJet P2055 desktop printer. Contained within the printer cartridge was a sophisticated bomb filled with explosives. The packages were addressed to two fictitious individuals at local Jewish institutions outside of Chicago. The Saudi Arabian government received intelligence of the potential bomb threat that it relayed to German and American authorities.[328]

The first package traveled from Yemen to Dubai (United Arab Emirates) then onto Cologne, Germany, followed by the East Midlands Airport in Leicestershire. From the UK it was scheduled to fly to Philadelphia and onto Chicago. However, British authorities confiscated the package and defused the bomb prior to detonation. The second package traveled from Yemen to Qatar then onto Dubai. From there it was confiscated prior to being transferred to another flight destined for Newark airport.[329]

Authorities believed that the planes were the targets rather than the Jewish institutions in Chicago listed on the mailing address. Three weeks later the Al-Qaeda Arabian Peninsula group published a detailed account of what it called "Operation Hemorrhage" in the English-language magazine Inspire. Al-Qaeda's intention was to disrupt global air cargo systems, causing widespread economic damage around the world.[330]

Prior to the Yemen cargo bombs plot, most of the media attention surrounding airline security was focused on mitigating risks associated with passengers. In addition to the Christmas 2009 bomb plot there was the infamous shoe bomber, Richard Reid, who attempted to blow up an American Airlines flight just a few months after September 11th. Although the media had been focused on passenger threats, the TSA had performed considerable work to secure air cargo on US flights. Starting in November 2008, all narrow bodied, single aisle passenger aircraft such as A320s and Boeing 757s had to be inspected prior to loading the plane. The program was gradually expanded to include wide-bodied aircraft as well. As of August 2010 all cargo originating in the US being transported on passenger aircraft required an inspection.[331]

Inspecting all US air freight is no small task. Over 50,000 tons of air cargo is shipped daily with 25% transported on passenger planes. Most of these goods are palletized and shrink-wrapped to avoid potential damages during flight. These packaging configurations have to be broken apart to perform an adequate inspection. As a result, the TSA developed the Certified Cargo Screening Program that manufacturers, freight forwarders, and third-party logistics providers use to perform screening at their own warehouses before the goods are packaged for air travel.[332]

Air cargo threats will always receive high levels of visibility from the general public. However, goods transported via air cargo represent only a small percentage of the overall supply chain. The bigger challenge for the US government is not actually air cargo threats, but protecting ocean ports from potential acts of terrorism. The US has 300 different sea and river ports that process 20% of the world's maritime trade volume.[333] Cargo containers, the large rectangular steel boxes that you see transported on trucks, trains, and steamships, are viewed as the largest vulnerability. There are over 12 million cargo containers worldwide. An individual steamship could carry as many as 3000 individual containers stacked high on top of each other. The greatest challenge with inspecting these containers is that Homeland Security officials cannot visually see within the boxes to identify the contents. The sheer volume of containers makes it impossible to physically inspect each one. Even with today's Homeland Security procedures, fewer than 10% of the containers imported to the US are physically inspected.[334]

The worst possible terrorist incident would be a weapon of mass destruction smuggled into the US, but a relatively simple attack on an actual port could also have significant economic impacts. Terrorists could detonate an explosion at a major US seaport or hijack a container ship docked there. Either event would be enough to warrant a temporary shutdown of the port which would significantly disrupt trade.

In 2002 when the International Longshore and Warehouse Union went on strike almost 30 US ports were closed for 10 days. The shutdown is estimated to have cost the US economy over $1 billion per day.[335] Why so much? West Coast ports are the critical entry point for inbound ocean containers arriving from China, India, Malaysia, Vietnam, and other Asian exporters. Together the 29 ports in the states of California, Oregon, and Washington represent $1.3 trillion in annual domestic business impacts, which is equivalent to the GDP of the entire country of Mexico.[336]

The Sea of Regulations

Following the September 11th terrorist attacks the US thoroughly investigated port security. Funding grew from $259 million in 2001 to over

$1.6 billion in 2005.[337] The government agencies responsible for port security were reorganized under the Department of Homeland Security. The US Coast Guard and Customs and Border Patrol (CBP) are primarily responsible for port security. The Coast Guard boards and inspects ships approaching US waters. The CBP inspects the cargo once it arrives at the US ports.

A series of regulations and voluntary programs were introduced by Congress and CBP to improve sea port security. One of the first programs to be launched after September 11th was the Customs-Trade Partnership Against Terrorism (C-TPAT) in November 2001. C-TPAT is a voluntary program led by US CBP. It targets private companies that want to agree to increased supply chains measures in exchange for faster customs processing. Examples of participants include high volume importers of goods such as retailers, wholesalers, and manufacturers. C-TPAT also includes transportation and logistics providers. Companies must sign an agreement that commits them to the program's security guidelines. Those that engage are eligible to receive reduced port inspections at port of arrival. For the goods inspected, participants are promised expedited processing and front of line inspections.[338]

One of the more innovative approaches introduced in January 2002 was the CSI program. Not to be confused with the popular TV series, CSI stands for Container Security Initiative. As the name implies, CSI addresses the threat from inbound ocean containers. Rather than waiting to inspect potentially threatening cargo after it arrives in the US, CSI enables officials to pre-screen the contents before leaving the point of departure. Pre-screening allows CBP to identify high risk containers based on advanced access to information about the importer, exporter, and contents. The program started with the top 20 ports that represent two thirds of inbound container volume, but any port that meets certain volume and procedural requirements can join. The US offers reciprocal access to customs officials from its foreign trade partners. Consequently, countries such as Japan and Canada can now pre-screen US exports destined for their countries as well.[339]

Perhaps the most significant US regulation was the SAFE Port Act introduced in 2006. SAFE introduced new security measures and also unified and codified some of the existing programs such as CSI. One of the key programs introduced with SAFE was the Secure Freight Initiative. Physically inspecting the contents of an 8 foot by 8 foot by 20 foot ocean container can be time consuming. As a result, the US implemented "non-intrusive inspection" technology so that screening can be performed without unloading the contents of a container. For example, an X-ray or gamma ray machine can be used to check for radiation levels or chemicals that might indicate the presence of explosives. Think of these inspections as full body scanning for containers. Secure Freight also extended these radiographic inspections to foreign ports starting in April 2007.[340]

10+2 = 13

A second program introduced under SAFE was the Importer Security Filing (ISF), commonly known as 10+2. The 10 and the 2 refer to the number of data elements that the importers and transportation carriers must submit for each cargo container shipped into the US. Importers must transmit 10 data elements electronically at least 24 hours prior to the loading of cargo onto a US-bound vessel. The 10 data elements include the buyer's name and address, seller's name and address, container stuffing location, and the country of origin.[341]

Two additional elements are required from the transportation carrier. The first data element is the vessel stow plan that outlines the physical location of cargo on the ship. The second is the containment status for each container that is listed as either empty or full. The carrier data must be electronically filed even earlier, at least 48 hours in advance. There is actually a thirteenth data field that is included with each filing, which is the Master Bill of Lading number.

While gathering the thirteen pieces of data outlined above might sound like a relatively easy task, it poses challenges for many importers and transportation carriers. In many cases, the information proves difficult to gather one to two days before the steamship leaves its point of origin. However, carriers and importers have no choice as they could face potential departure delays or financial penalties if they fail to submit. The 10+2 program went into effect in January 2009 with a phase-in period that lasted until January 2010. Penalties are now being levied to violators. As you may have already guessed, B2B e-commerce technology (or specifically B2G) is used by the importers and transportation carriers to transmit the twelve data elements to the US CBP.

Another one of the SAFE legislation programs leveraged B2B e-commerce technology was called the Global Trade Exchange (GTX). The idea of GTX was to collect data about shipments from various participants in the supply chain including exporters, importers, forwarders, consolidators, terminal operators, transportation carriers, and foreign customs agencies. Data would be captured at each milestone in the supply chain—export from the foreign port, goods in transit, arrival in the US, and receipt by the importer.[342]

The GTX was essentially a massive data warehouse to collect B2B e-commerce documents for all imports into the US. The idea was that all of the information throughout the lifecycle of a container shipment would be aggregated into a central database. Historically, the data was fragmented. Certain data was available only to various private sector entities or to a specific government agency. Such a robust data set would be highly valuable for the CBP to develop risk assessments for incoming cargo. Although there were proposals from several government contractors like Northrop Grumman to build the GTX, the data warehouse was never implemented.[343]

Gambling with Supply Chain Security

Perhaps the most interesting and bizarre part of the SAFE Act were the articles that prohibited Internet gambling. I'm not sure what the connection between container security and online poker is, but clearly someone in Congress relates the two. Fortunately for all of us, fantasy football leagues were not listed among the restricted activities.

As you can imagine, businesses importing or exporting high volumes of goods across borders can find compliance with these various regulations quite challenging. The programs discussed above such as C-TPAT, CSI, GTX, and 10+2 are primarily focused on ocean freight in the US. There are various other programs for rail and ground freight crossing US borders that I will not cover here. There are also different programs within each individual country around the world. All of these are critically dependent upon B2B e-commerce programs. Hopefully you will sleep a little more soundly tonight knowing that EDI is actively providing protection from terrorist threats.

Chapter 21
Electronic Invoicing

In the fall of 2008, a 35-year-old British man named Craig Johnson was sentenced to 12 years in prison for committing tax fraud.[344] Johnson had lived what the BBC referred to as a "Pop Star" lifestyle. He owned two helicopters, an Aston Martin, two Bentleys, Rolex watches, and various diamonds.[345] Johnson also owned a 22-acre mansion in Staffordshire, a county in the West Midlands region of England, complete with a swimming pool, spa, and gym.[346] The mansion is the birthplace of a Napoleonic War hero and was valued at £3 million. Johnson was part of a criminal organization that defrauded the UK government of almost £140 million in tax revenues.[347] Johnson and his co-conspirators designed a "carousel fraud" scheme that enabled them to profit from loopholes in the EU's Value Added Tax (VAT) system. Johnson's role in the fraud was to launder the proceeds of the money by purchasing property, race horses, and sport cars.[348] The EU's VAT system is designed to collect tax revenues at each step of the supply chain based upon the "value added" during the process between purchasing an input and selling an output. For example, suppose a computer distributor purchases a PC from an original equipment manufacturer for €800. It then purchases additional memory and software for a total of €200. The distributor installs additional memory and software to the machine then resells it to a corporate end-user for €1500. The distributor must pay VAT on the difference between the purchase prices for the inputs and the sales prices for the outputs. In this example the difference is €500 (€1500 minus the sum of €800 and €200). With a 20% VAT rate the tax owed by the distributor would be 20% of €500 or €100. In practice the distributor would actually submit a VAT payment of €200 first for its purchase, and following the sale of the computer, the distributor would apply for a refund of €300, netting a difference of €100.

VAT is a form of indirect taxation that is used to fund a significant percentage of the public sector programs throughout Europe. The companies which buy and sell goods act effectively as a tax collector on behalf of the government. VAT systems are used not only in Europe but throughout most of the world.

There are several opportunities within the VAT system to defraud the government. For example, a fraudulent company could charge one of its customers VAT, but then never turn over the tax proceeds to the government. Another example would be if a fraudulent company requests a refund from the government for taxes that it claimed to pay, but never actually did.

The recent scams in the UK have involved imports and resale of high value products such as computer chips and mobile phones. For example, suppose a UK company called ABC Electronics purchases a large quantity of mobile phones from a manufacturer in the Czech Republic for £1 million. ABC then sells the phones to another UK distributor called DEF Electronics for £1.1 million. UK VAT laws require that ABC collect 20% taxes on the sales transaction. As a result, ABC would prepare an invoice to DEF for the £1.1 million base price plus 20% VAT for a total of £1.32 million. In theory, ABC is required to transfer the 20% VAT royalty it collects, £220,000, to Her Majesty's Revenue and Customs (HMRC). However, instead the owners of ABC electronics simply disappear with the £220,000, keeping it as pure profit on the transaction. This is an example of "missing trader" fraud. In our example ABC Electronics becomes the missing trader in the transaction.

The type of carousel fraud that Craig Johnson and his co-conspirators practiced was slightly more complex. In carousel fraud a number of companies collaborate to defraud the government and taxpayers. Suppose that DEF Electronics and a third company GHI Electronics were co-conspirators in the scam along with ABC Electronics. ABC imports the mobile phones from the supplier in Czech. ABC then sells the phones to DEF that in turn sells them to GHI. At each step along the way, invoices are created with the appropriate VAT charges. Finally, GHI exports the phones by selling to another distributor, JKL, in Dubai. In accordance with VAT principles, GHI then requests a credit from the UK HMRC for the VAT it paid to DEF for the purchase of the phones.

Once the tax rebate is collected all three businesses—GHI, DEF, and ABC—can vanish along with the funds.

A few months later the same batch of mobile phones is re-imported from Dubai back to the UK in another series of fraudulent transactions. The same inventory can be moved through the tax collection system numerous times much like a carousel goes around and around. In the more elaborate frauds there may never be any mobile phones at all. The goods exchanged and the companies involved may have only existed on paper.

The companies that buy and sell the goods are not always co-conspirators. A computer component distributor named Bond House Systems was levied £13.2 million in fines by the UK HMRC for missing trader fraud. Although Bond House was a legitimate business, it had purchased components sold by a missing trader upstream in the supply chain. The £13.2 million liability would have rendered Bond House insolvent immediately. Bond House appealed to the European Courts of Justice and HMRC's claim against the distributor was revoked. Nonetheless, the example does raise interesting questions about who is accountable for ensuring the legitimacy of transactions in the supply chain.

There has been an explosion in VAT related fraud in the past decade. Independent estimates suggest that the EU is losing between €60 and €100 billion per annum across all member states due to these types of tax frauds. In an interview with the Guardian one anonymous fraudster stated, "We have a straw in every VAT pot in Europe, and we're going to keep sucking money out until they're empty. The scale of this thing is much bigger than most governments either realize or are admitting."[349]

The basis for most VAT systems is a specialized type of invoice that is transmitted from supplier to buyer. The VAT invoice is considered the legal basis for the tax calculation and reporting. In cases of carousel or missing trader fraud, invoice documents provide a critical audit trail for investigators to research crimes. Since the seller generates the invoice, it is relatively easy for a criminal to create a fake invoice or to forge a legitimate invoice that misrepresents the actual terms of trade.

There are numerous investigations by tax and other government authorities into invoice fraud every year. For example, Dominique Strauss-Kahn (DSK), the former head of the International Monetary Fund, was indicted for fabricating an invoice and falsifying dates on it. At the time, Strauss-Kahn was the Minister of Finance in France. The scandal involved a series of questionable payments made by a French mutual insurance company called MNEF. A payment of 600,000 French Francs was made to DSK that did not seem to reflect any services being rendered. Using sophisticated technology the French police were able to prove that the paper on one of the invoices paid to Strauss-Kahn was manufactured at a date later than the invoice date.[350]

With the advent of B2B e-commerce many companies have been eliminating paper invoices in favor of electronic documents. One of the central concerns with electronic invoices is the opportunity for tax evasion or other types of fraud. If a paper invoice can be easily falsified surely an electronic invoice would be even easier to fabricate. If the invoices DSK had submitted to MNEF were electronic, would the government authorities have been able to perform the same type of sophisticated forensic analysis?

Fiscal Dematerialization in the EU

With VAT fraud on the rise many European nations have been aggressively implementing new controls to reduce the opportunity for tax evasion. One of the regulations recently introduced by the EU provided guidelines on how electronic invoices could replace paper documents as the legal basis for taxation. The EU regulations require that buyers and sellers of goods are able to prove the authenticity and integrity of any electronic invoice used for VAT purposes. The EU has issued a series of directives related to e-invoicing. The first directive was in 2001. Several amendments have followed since then.

The EU directives specify that companies must be able to demonstrate that an invoice sent from a seller to a buyer is authentic and was not altered in transit. Digital signatures are generally considered one of the best technologies to prevent forgery or tampering in electronic commerce. The directives also required that buyers and sellers be able to present electronic invoices to the tax authorities conducting an audit. Most electronic invoices are packaged into EDI and XML transactions that cannot be easily deciphered by a tax auditor. As a result, there is a need to create a "human-readable" version of the e-invoice. For example, a seller might create a PDF document with the invoice fields laid out in the same sequence as a typical paper document. Tax authorities also need to be able to perform forensic analysis of an invoice to ensure the integrity of its contents have been maintained. How else would the French police prove that DSK had falsified an electronic version of an invoice to MNEF? As a result, companies must keep the original EDI or XML file that was exchanged, the digital signature credentials, and perhaps even the log files associated with the transaction in order to comply with the directive. Such documentation must be kept on file for a period of three to ten years to satisfy any future tax audit scenarios.

The guidance provided in the EU invoicing directives is reasonable when one considers the amount of money being collected from VAT associated with the process. It is also worth noting that the EU directives do not require the use of e-invoicing. Private sector organizations can continue to use paper invoices as long as their customers accept them.

The EU directives provided a legal framework that enabled companies to eliminate paper invoices in favor of a fully electronic model. However, the regulations became burdensome when the individual countries enacted the practices into law. Each member state of the EU took a slightly different view on the guidance provided from the directive. The outcome of the country-level legislation was that a different set of e-invoicing regulations were enacted for each different member state. Some countries such as the UK, Sweden, Finland, and the Netherlands took a flexible approach allowing a variety of approaches to e-invoicing. Other countries including Germany, France, and Spain had a more restrictive adaptation of the directive requiring extensive archiving periods and security measures be implemented. For multi-national corporations operating in multiple countries in Europe the regulations are quite complex and burdensome.

E-Invoicing Outside of Europe

Europe is not the only region with a legal framework for e-invoicing. Tax authorities in countries around the world have introduced a wide range of recommendations and regulations governing e-invoicing. Some countries including Japan, India, China, Thailand, Egypt, and the Ukraine have not permitted e-invoicing historically. Other countries like the US, Australia, Singapore, and Hong Kong have fairly liberal views on e-invoicing with no specific legal directives in place. Between these two extremes are a number of markets permit e-invoicing subject to adherence with government specified guidelines.

Perhaps the most prescriptive e-invoicing regulations exist in Latin American countries including Mexico, Brazil, and Chile. Brazil provides one of the most interesting case studies. Before a Brazilian supplier can ship goods it must notify the government and request advance approval of the commercial transaction. An XML file containing the relevant tax details for the commercial transaction is forwarded by the supplier to the local state treasury department. The state treasury performs some basic validations on the XML file then returns an authorization of use to the seller. The state treasury also forwards the relevant tax data to a centralized federal database.[351] Tax inspectors in the origin and destination state now have advance notification of each commercial transaction. This allows tax inspectors to pre-screen shipments that may be suspected of criminal or fraudulent activity for close monitoring.

Two electronic documents must be created for each shipment. The first document is an NF-e or electronic invoice. The second document is a CT-e or electronic waybill. Once the local state treasury department has provided advanced approval for a shipment, the supplier must print a copy of both documents. These auxiliary paper documents must accompany the physical shipment of goods. The auxiliary NF-e and CT-e allow inspectors at state borders to quickly identify the contents of the shipment and verify consistency with the data previously transmitted to the government. The seller must also send a copy of the NF-e and CT-e to his customer. The customer must verify the validity of the electronic documents with his local treasury department.[352]

Why is the Brazilian government so particular about the way that invoices are exchanged between buyers and sellers of goods? The answer has to do with the tax system. Brazil is now the world's seventh largest economy and the largest in Latin America. In 2003, Brazil was identified as one of four BRIC countries expected to lead economic growth in the 21st century. However, one of the biggest challenges for Brazil is its "informal economy." The term informal economy refers to various commercial activities that occur outside of the regulations and formal rules by which most businesses operate. In this case, we are not referring so much to illegal activities like prostitution or drug trafficking, but grey market activities, such as violating employment laws or intellectual property rights.

A McKinsey Global Institute study in 2006 found that Brazil's informal economy accounts for 40% of its gross national income.[353] The relative size of Brazil's grey market is far larger than other emerging markets such as India and China. Certain industries like retail struggle with grey market activities more than others. It is estimated that 60% of Brazil's retail sales are generated from informal enterprises, many of which are street vendors.[354]

Many Brazilian companies choose to ignore the product quality and safety regulations that the government has imposed. Others infringe upon the copyrights of others by selling counterfeit versions of pharmaceuticals and entertainment products to consumers. Many employers do not pay the full social security obligations. Other employers do not report certain workers on staff in an effort to avoid paying minimum wages.

Perhaps the most significant problem within the informal economy is tax evasion. Many of Brazil's small and midsize businesses do not pay corporate income or Value Added Taxes (VAT). The challenges are somewhat self-inflicted as Brazil has some of the highest tax rates in the world. It also has one of the most complex tax codes. In the World Bank's annual Ease of Doing Business study for 2011, Brazil ranked 152 out of 183 countries.[355] Brazilian companies spend 13 times more than other countries preparing, filing, and paying social security contributions, corporate income and VAT.[356] The overall complexity of Brazil's tax system leads many businesses to choose to operate outside of the law.

The large informal economy not only impacts tax revenue collections, but also threatens to limit Brazil's long term growth. Brazil's informal players enjoy a considerable cost advantage over legitimate businesses. By avoiding taxes, ignoring regulations, and paying lower wages, informal companies can gain cost and speed advantages. As a result, the grey market represents a larger share of Brazil's overall economy than it should. Informal companies do not invest in employee training, manufacturing equipment, or computer technology. In fact, grey market players have a disincentive to grow. The bigger their enterprises become the more they will attract the attention of the local government. The result is lower productivity rates in Brazil's economy. A McKinsey study showed that Brazil could grow 1.5% faster if it shifted a greater percentage of its economy to legitimate businesses.[357]

NF-e and CT-e are part of a larger tax modernization project undertaken by the Brazilian government. By forcing e-invoicing instead of paper, the tax authorities can reduce the opportunity for fraud. Suppose a manufacturer of food products is shipping goods to a supermarket in another state. The manufacturer is selling $100,000 worth of product. But instead of reporting the $100,000 on the VAT invoice, the amount is lowered to $10,000 in order to reduce tax exposure. Such fraudulent behavior is challenging to track in a paper-based system. Using NF-e and CT-e government authorities can target suspicious commercial transactions for physical inspection at state borders. In the long term such a model promises to increase tax collections but also to deter informal activities.

In addition to Brazil, several other countries within Latin America, including Mexico, Chile, and Argentina, have enacted e-invoicing regulations. The tax authorities in each country have taken a different approach. But the goal of the various different legal frameworks is consistent across all the countries to reduce tax evasion and grey market activities.

The process described will be mandatory for companies buying and selling goods in Brazil. Once the system is fully implemented there will be no valid paper equivalent. In Europe the e-invoicing model is not mandatory, but rather customer driven. If a customer like a large government agency mandates e-invoicing, then suppliers must participate or suffer penalties for non-compliance. Throughout Latin America and Europe most of the e-invoicing programs are driven by a stick rather than a carrot. Adopt e-invoicing technology or you will be fined or penalized. Taiwan, however, has introduced a carrot-based incentive that encourages adoption through rewards rather than penalties.

E-Invoicing Can Help You Win the Lottery

To encourage reduction of fraud in B2B transactions, the Taiwanese government created an incentive program for retail purchases. Taiwanese consumers are automatically entered to win a lottery prize when they request official copies of receipts from retailers from whom they make purchases. Each of these receipts has a government issued invoice number that forms the basis of a bimonthly lottery. On the 25th day of every other month a handful of lucky lottery winners are awarded prizes based upon the eight digits of the government invoice ID. The first prize of over US $60,000 is awarded to customers with receipts exactly matching the eight digits selected.[358]

Taiwan's lottery system has been used for 60 years. In 1950 the Taiwanese government was struggling to raise tax revenues. Many of the commercial transactions occurring between businesses and consumers were not properly reported to the government. The government introduced a lottery system to promote more formal accounting for corporate revenues and to encourage consumers to obtain receipts for their purchases. Each receipt has a government issued invoice number that allows for better tracking of corporate revenues thereby minimizing the opportunity for tax evasion.[359]

Taiwan's system has been radically successful. In the year 1951 following the introduction of the lottery system tax receipts grew by 75%.[360] Taiwan supports both the business-to-consumer (B2C) e-invoicing program as described and business-to-business (B2B) transactions. The B2B e-invoice program introduced in 2006 has also been successful with over 50 million invoices exchanged electronically today.[361]

There are billions of dollars in savings to be gained through e-invoicing, not only from greater tax collections, but also through processing efficiencies. It is estimated that over €200 billion can be saved from e-invoicing throughout Europe alone.[362]

Benefits of e-Invoicing

Switching from a paper to an electronic process for invoicing can yield savings of 60 to 80% within a relatively short period of 18 months.[363] The most obvious benefit is the digital receipt of the invoice from the supplier. Invoices received in paper format must be sorted, routed, opened, and reviewed. The data must then be re-keyed into an accounts payable (AP) system. Even invoices received as a PDF attachment to an email need to be saved, printed, and re-keyed into the AP system. There is an inevitable likelihood of human error whenever manual data entry occurs. With invoicing data, the simple transposition of two numbers or the misplacement of a decimal point could have significant financial impact to a company.

Before an invoice can be paid the information must be validated by the

AP department or the original buyer in the purchasing department. For example, the arithmetic on the invoice must be checked to ensure that there were no multiplication or addition errors that would favorably benefit the supplier. One of the more complex validations performed is the matching between an invoice and the associated documents related to the purchase. The pricing and payment terms on an invoice should match those originally negotiated in the master contract with the supplier. Additionally, the product descriptions, line-item quantities, and per-unit pricing on the invoice must match the corresponding fields on the original purchase order and warehouse receiving records. Such comparisons performed by accounting clerks are time-consuming and error prone. E-invoicing applications can reduce costs by automatically performing the matching to contracts, purchase orders, and receiving records.

Perhaps the most costly aspect of invoice processing for buyers is not the capture or validation of the data, but staffing call centers to answer phone calls from suppliers. After submitting an invoice a supplier will typically contact the buyer to confirm receipt of the invoice. A few weeks later the supplier may follow up again to inquire about invoice approval and the actual payment date. Significant time and expense are incurred responding to calls from suppliers and researching the status of payment. Most e-invoicing applications will offer a portal in which suppliers can check the status of approval processing and payment.

The Battle to Send You a Bill

In most countries throughout Europe, the use of e-invoicing is just in its early stages. Experts estimate that fewer than 10% of the 30 billion invoices exchanged in Europe are electronic today.[364] The demand for electronic invoices among government organizations and corporations has not gone unnoticed by the vendor community.

As of March 2011 there were 500 different e-invoicing service providers in Europe alone.[365] There has been a mad rush to enter the e-invoicing sector by everyone from telecom providers and postal operators to commercial banks and credit card companies. Some providers are pure-play startups that focus exclusively on e-invoicing. For example, there is OB10 based in the UK, b-process of France, SixPayNet of Switzerland, Pagero of Sweden, Tradeshift of

Denmark, and Maventa of Finland.

Many of the B2B e-commerce vendors discussed earlier in this book offer e-invoicing services. For example, Ariba and Basware have expanded beyond e-procurement into the financial settlement aspects of a transaction. ERP vendors such as SAP and Oracle created electronic invoicing capabilities within their accounts payable modules. SAP also acquired a company called Crossgate, which is a leading e-invoicing provider in Latin America and Europe.[366]

EDI network providers such as Sterling Commerce and GXS have offered EDI-based e-invoicing services for over 30 years, but now also support the specific regulations of the EU. Former B2B e-marketplaces including Liaison Technologies, E2open, and SupplyOn are players as well.

Telecommunications providers and postal operators also have entered into the e-invoicing market. In some cases the companies entered via joint ventures. The e-invoicing provider Certipost is a joint venture of the La Poste, the Belgian postal service, and Belgacom, the country's largest telecommunications provider. DHL, which is owned by Deutsche Post; Swisscom, the major Swiss telco; Post Finance, the Swiss Post; and Verizon Business each offer e-invoicing services as well.

Systems integrators within Europe such as TietoEnator, Atos Origin, and LogicaCMG have e-invoicing offerings. Iron Mountain, a provider of off-site tape backup and records storage, announced it was going to hire 500 people for its e-invoicing product shortly before selling its other digital businesses.[367]

Perhaps the most interesting new entrants into the e-invoicing sector are the financial institutions. In November 2004, Mellon Bank acquired SourceNet, a specialized provider of accounts payable outsourcing.[368] In July 2006, US Bank acquired an electronic invoice presentment and payment (EIPP) application from a division of the large trucking company Schneider National.[369] A few months later in early 2007, JPMorgan Chase acquired another EIPP vendor called Xign.[370]

Not all of the commercial banks have performed acquisitions to gain e-invoicing capabilities. Many financial institutions have chosen to partner with technology vendors rather than acquire them. Today, almost every major commercial bank in North America and Western Europe including Deutsche Bank, HSBC, Citigroup, RBS, Banco Santander, and Bank of America has an e-invoicing service. In some cases the offerings are specifically focused on e-invoicing. In other cases the banks are offering a comprehensive package that includes invoicing, payments and foreign exchange. One example of a comprehensive offering was Supply Chain 360 that the US super-regional bank BB&T launched in 2007.[371]

The credit card companies are pursuing the e-invoicing sector as well. In December 2006, American Express acquired an EIPP vendor called Harbor Payments.[372] American Express rebranded the services as its Source-to-Settle (S2S) suite which it sells to corporate clients. In 2009 US Bank spun off its PowerTrack offering into a joint venture with Visa. The new company, called Syncada, specializes in e-invoicing and e-payments.[373] Even PayPal launched an e-invoicing service as it attempts to expand beyond B2C into B2B.[374]

All of these companies are competing in what I refer to as "The Battle to Send You a Bill." The record levels of investment being channeled into the e-invoicing sector are a bit ironic when you consider that no one likes to receive a bill. What is your reaction to your monthly credit card statement, personal property tax assessment, or electricity bill? Are you excited when you open your mailbox to find these bills? Perhaps, if your statement reflects a lower balance than you expected, but how frequently does that occur?

Businesses have the same opinion of invoices received from suppliers. No one wants to receive or, for that matter, pay a bill. Companies want to hold onto their cash as long as possible. In recent years companies have been slowly extending payment terms beyond 30 and 45 days to 60 or 90 days. Companies will find any excuse they can to avoid paying a bill. Accounts payable clerks will deliberately hide from vendors. Some will avoid answering the phone and not return messages. Other companies have a strategy of intentionally paying invoices late when they run short on cash. Unlike in the consumer markets, suppliers will rarely charge late fees on B2B invoices. When companies do pay bills they go to great lengths to assess penalties, deductions, and other debits to reduce the amount owed.

Considering the general corporate aversion to paying suppliers it is quite ironic that so many companies are competing for the right to be the one that transmits an invoice electronically. Why then are so many commercial banks, postal operators, technology vendors, and telecom providers investing in e-invoicing? First, the segment has been growing rapidly, at over 50% per year even during the recessionary period between 2008 and 2010. Any fast growing sector with high levels of inefficiency such as e-invoicing will attract venture-backed startups and established IT firms.

However, some of the service providers, specifically the commercial banks and credit card companies, have a broader ambition. If a bank can position itself in the middle of a retailer or manufacturer's invoice and payment flows, then it becomes relatively easy to layer additional value added services like "supply chain finance" into the account.

Supply chain finance is a process in which a bank will offer a supplier early payment on an invoice in exchange for a small processing fee. Although supply chain finance sounds complex, the process is actually quite simple. As the buyer receives and approves invoices, it will notify its bank of the intent to pay in the near future. For example, a buyer may have $5 million of invoices from 50 suppliers that it intends to pay within the next 45 to 60 days. The bank can then approach each of the suppliers with an option for immediate payment. Those suppliers which opt in will get the cash immediately. Of course, the bank deducts a process fee to reflect its administrative and processing fees. Meanwhile, the buyer is able to hold onto their cash until the invoice matures in 45 to 60 days at which point the bank collects the payment.

In the supply chain scenario everyone wins. The buyer is able to retain cash longer with extended payment terms. The supplier can obtain cash for receivables quickly. The bank provides a valuable service to its customers and obtains a small processing fee for its efforts. And these small fees can add up quickly for banks generating millions of dollars in fees per year in some cases.

The Hidden Force behind E-Invoicing

The existence of so many e-invoicing providers is not a bad thing during the rapid growth phase of an emerging market. The 500 vendors in the market have been a key force in building awareness and driving adoption of these technologies. Onboarding of buyers and suppliers will be accelerated with a large community of vendors. Perhaps the best result of a large number of vendors is that the pace of innovation will quickly increase. As each service provider attempts to differentiate itself from the competition, a feature-war will emerge providing more value to the customer community.

Beyond the vendors there have been a number of drivers in recent years that have led to the surge in e-invoicing investments. The regulatory frameworks introduced within Europe were certainly a key enabler to growth. The macroeconomic recession led many private sector companies to seek out opportunities to reduce costs. Eliminating unnecessary back-office expenses was a high priority for large corporations during the years 2008 to 2010.

Another key growth driver for e-invoicing has been government mandates. The tax authorities in countries like Brazil and Mexico require the use of e-invoices. Additionally, the procurement departments within government organizations are promoting e-invoicing and paperless trade. Numerous public sector organizations in Europe including the governments of Sweden, Norway, Spain, and Denmark have announced compulsory e-invoicing programs within their countries. As a result, all government suppliers must invest in e-invoicing technologies to perform billing. Public sector organizations providing health care, educational or defense services purchase goods from a broad range of vendors. In effect, government mandates have seeded a large percentage of the private sector with e-invoicing technologies. E-invoicing is just one dimension of a broader strategy many government organizations are pursuing with B2B e-commerce. The next chapter focuses on the broader strategy of e-procurement initiatives within governments.

Chapter 22
PEPPOL and E-Procurement

On May 5, 2010, over 100,000 people took to the streets of Athens, Greece, to protest new austerity measures recently imposed by government officials. At the time, Greece was at the center of a financial crisis that threatened the economic stability of the entire European Union (EU). Although the EU and International Monetary Fund (IMF) had agreed to provide an €80 billion bailout of Greece, the government needed to cut social programs and raise taxes to curb its very large budget deficit. Public sector pay would be frozen until 2014. VAT was increased from 19 to 23%. Taxes on fuel, alcohol, and tobacco were up 10%. The average retirement age was increased from 61 to 63.[375]

At midnight on May 5th all transportation in and out of the country ceased as workers at airports, train stations, and ferry terminals conducted a nation-wide strike. Most Greek schools, hospitals, and offices were shut down. The protests became violent during the day. Trash bins were set on fire. Windows were broken. Cars were burned. Petrol bombs were thrown. Shouts of "burn the parliament" were heard across the city. At the peak of the violence, protesters stormed a parliament building causing many of its ceremonial guards to flee the Tomb of the Unknown Soldier. Several buildings were set on fire including a department of the Greek Finance Ministry and a branch of Marfin Bank. Three people who unsuccessfully tried to escape via the roof of the bank were killed in the fire including one pregnant woman. Police were able to seize control of the crowds with pepper spray and tear gas. Over 70 people were detained for questioning.[376]

The Greek crisis continued to worsen in the following 18 months. It dominated newspaper headlines around the world for many months as more riots were held throughout 2011. In June of 2011, Standard & Poor's lowered Greece's sovereign debt rating to CCC, ranking it among the worst in the world.[377]

There is a lot of debate about the root causes of the Greek economic crisis and whether it could have been prevented. One of the more interesting theories surrounds the portion of the budget deficit created by the 2004 Summer Olympic Games, which was €2.4 billion over budget.[378] Athens hosted the first Olympic Games after the September 11th terrorist attacks. As a result security costs for the games in Athens were five times higher than Sydney incurred in 2000.[379] There was no way that the Greek government could have forecasted the need for heightened security when it bid on the games in 1997. However, in the end the security measures may have been necessary as a large amount of plastic explosives were discovered just a few days prior to the opening ceremony. In addition to unexpected security increases, the Greek government has failed to achieve the return on investment from many of its construction efforts. More than half of Athens' Olympic sites are barely used or empty including the baseball diamond and canoe course. Efforts to convert these venues into recreation sites have been stalled by bureaucracy and legal challenges.

Greece was not the only country to experience financial challenges. Numerous member states within the EU were shaken by concerns about government deficits and rising debt levels during 2010 and 2011. The greatest concerns were with the so-called PIIGS, which includes Portugal, Italy, Ireland, Greece, and Spain. Similar to Greece, the ratings agencies had downgraded many of these countries' credit ratings, which led to investors in the bond markets to demand a risk premium for financing. Also, similarly to Greece many of these other EU countries have elected to pursue painful fiscal austerity policies. Austerity measures vary by country, but generally include extensions of retirement ages for workers, increases in VAT and luxury taxes, and reductions in social benefit programs. Cuts and Limits are also placed on public sector wages, bonuses, and pension programs. Though unpopular, such measures will certainly provide immediate benefits. Unfortunately, many of the early cuts have an impact on wages or benefits to European citizens. Over the longer term, however, there are certainly opportunities to reduce costs without impacting public programs. One significant cost savings opportunity is to achieve radical improvements in public sector e-procurement practices.

EU Procurement Could Help Save the PIIGS

Efficiency in government procurement is particularly important as over 16% of the EU's GDP, or €1.5 trillion, is spent annually on goods and services procured by the public sector.[380] Unfortunately, these purchases are not always made in the most efficient way or procured for the lowest possible price. For example, Romania discovered that it was paying 10 times the European average for goods and services before implementing a new e-procurement program.[381]

Significant cost savings can be achieved through the use of technologies to better manage government procurement. In 2006, the EU member states agreed that all public administrations across Europe should be able to carry out 100% of procurement functions electronically.[382] Since then numerous national and local programs have leveraged e-procurement technology for cost savings. The Emilia Romagna region of Northern Italy has reported 16% in spending reductions through e-procurement.[383] Austria has saved 18% reductions from a total spend based of €830M.[384] Norway has achieved price savings of 2 to 10% and reduced transaction times of 20 to 40%.[385] Denmark has reported €100M in savings from the use of e-invoicing.[386] And several UK ministries have reported savings of 10 to 45% on certain merchandise categories through the use of electronic auctions.[387]

While many countries within the EU have deployed e-procurement, many of these platforms were implemented with a fragmented approach. Starting in the late 1990s each country developed its own system to source, tender, evaluate, order, and pay for goods. In some countries, multiple e-procurement initiatives operate on behalf of different agencies or at different tiers at government. For example, in the UK there are three primary procurement portals called Zanzibar, OPEN, and xchangewales. Why does the UK need three? The portals are used by different organizations. The Zanzibar platform is used by the National Health Service (NHS), Her Majesty's Treasury, the National Archives, and the Department for Work and Pensions. OPEN is used in the educational segment by the Department for Children, Schools and Families; Manchester's City Council; and the Royal Boroughs of Windsor and Kensington. xchangewales is used in the Welsh public sector by the local NHS and local universities in Cardiff.

The UK is not the only country with a fragmented e-procurement landscape. France has several public sector e-procurement platforms including Ixarm, Achats, Marches-publics, and e-Bourgogne. Germany has e-Vergabe and Kaufhaus des Bundes (KdB). Spain has Dirección General, Del Patrimonio, Del Estado, and PETM-BCS. Italy has Acquistinretepa, Belgium has .be-Procurement, and Denmark has DOIP and ETHICS. The current system provides advantages for buyers as they can use local portals designed for their specific needs. However, for suppliers, particularly those wishing to sell in multiple countries within the EU, the process is a nightmare. Suppliers must register separately on each of these different e-procurement portals. Once registered, they must monitor the websites for new RFPs that they could potentially bid on. If a supplier is successful in winning business within multiple jurisdictions they will have to interface with multiple different e-procurement platforms to accept purchase orders and submit invoices.

Looking back, one might question why the various countries within the EU would have allowed such a proliferation of e-procurement platforms to occur. However, such fragmentation is not unusual for new technologies. As many IT initiatives do, the e-procurement landscape in Europe evolved with a focus on gaining rapid return on investment. If the local governments had waited to form a pan-European committee to create standardized approaches and a shared platform, e-procurement initiatives may not have been launched until 2005.

PEPPOL

Recently the EU began an initiative to align public sector e-procurement initiatives on a Pan-European basis. The effort is part of a broader EU goal of transforming Europe into a single economic market. As mentioned in Chapter 16, the EU has also undertaken programs to harmonize the regulations, systems, processes for payments, invoicing, securities processing, and financial reporting.

The e-procurement initiative is called PEPPOL, which stands for Pan European Public Procurement Online. Eighteen different public sector buying organizations from twelve different countries participated in the pilot. PEPPOL seeks to unify the various local and national e-procurement exchanges into a single harmonized market across Europe. PEPPOL will provide new levels of efficiency for both buyers and suppliers. Furthermore, by simplifying the e-procurement processes, the EU hopes to gain greater adoption of these technologies.

What benefits can Europe expect to gain from the expanded use of e-procurement technologies? The first benefit is increased buying power. Spend management applications can aggregate the purchases made by different buyers within an organization. There are opportunities to consolidate spending with fewer vendors and to standardize the types of items purchased. In the long term the PEPPOL model could provide the ability to aggregate purchasing power across different countries or regions. For example, various regions within France could agree to standardize purchases of office supplies, rather than each purchasing independently. Such arrangements may be necessary to achieve the levels of budget reductions required across the EU.

A second benefit is increased participation and competition from the supplier community. Greater competition leads to more options and lower prices. For example, processes such as reverse auctions, in which suppliers compete to offer the lowest price, benefit significantly from increased participation. With PEPPOL the benefits will accelerate much faster than a country-level approach. In the past, suppliers were required to register with each regional or national government's e-procurement portal in order to gain access to tenders. However, with PEPPOL suppliers only need to register once to participate in any public sector e-procurement tender across the EU. Reducing the barriers to participation encourages more suppliers to participate in bids and auctions, creating a more competitive environment.

A third benefit is increased compliance. One of the key benefits of e-procurement applications is the ability to enforce the use of contractual arrangements in purchasing activities. For example, an e-procurement application can ensure that a public sector employee seeking to purchase desktop computers will receive the appropriate contracted discounts from the designated PC supplier. Furthermore, visibility is provided to employees purchasing computers off-contract, from unapproved vendors. Such maverick spending can be curtailed much more effectively with spend management applications bundled into e-procurement applications. Spend management can provide detailed category level-reporting on public sector purchases. The reports provide additional levels of transparency to government officials and citizens on the use of taxpayer funds.

A fourth benefit is reduced fraud and abuse. Government ministries have a natural monopoly on functions such as national defense or social services. In the absence of a competitive landscape, theft, fraud, and abuse are more easily obscured. E-procurement applications provide enhanced transparency to government purchasing activities. Electronic RFPs and RFQs are published to public websites with an open invitation to compete. Participation in the bidding process can be tracked electronically providing a better audit trail. Notification of awards is made public to the community of vendors. Such transparency serves to reduce the potential for kickbacks, bribes, and other forms of fraud that needlessly inflate government spending.

A fifth benefit is the reduction in transaction processing costs throughout the purchasing lifecycle. Through automation of supplier registration, order generation, and invoice processing, public sector organizations can reduce administrative costs by up to 25%. E-procurement applications now offer supplier information management modules that allow vendors to keep their own credentials up-to-date online. Orders can be electronically transmitted to suppliers reducing costs and the opportunity for errors. To reduce the exception processing, funds availability and budget compliance checks can be performed prior to creating a requisition. E-procurement suites accept electronic invoices from suppliers eliminating the costly and time-consuming process associated with paper bills. Furthermore, cost savings are achieved through automation of processes such as invoice capture, document matching and data field validation.

What Are the Benefits to Society?

A Pan-European e-procurement approach will not only benefit public sector organizations and their suppliers, but society in general. What if e-procurement could provide a 3% savings on the €1.5 trillion in annual public sector spend? The cost savings to tax payers would be €500 billion per year. The savings could be applied to reduce budget deficits in countries. Alternatively, the savings could be reinvested in local countries to improve the level of government programs and services available to citizens. Or, the savings could be utilized to fund new projects which lead to fiscal stimulus and job creation.

Perhaps most importantly, Pan-European e-procurement programs will accelerate the creation of a common market for goods and services within Europe. By reducing the barriers to participating in electronic procurement programs, cross-border trade will be enhanced. Suppliers based in any country within the EU will be able to bid and compete for government tenders in their home country or neighboring states. Over the long term, the unification of the commercial markets in Europe is believed to be a critical factor in sustained economic growth. Faster growth within the EU will generate greater tax receipts which can also be applied to deficit reductions.

Challenges with PEPPOL and E-Invoicing

While the benefits of PEPPOL are extremely compelling, a number of obstacles are slowing implementation. Fragmented standards and technologies for electronic catalogues, invoicing, and supplier registration are among the key concerns. For example, over 15 different e-invoicing standards are in use today within different vertical industries and country boundaries. A country-specific approach has dominated the development of many e-invoicing standards. Consider the different standards used in European nations—ebInterface (Austria), OIOUBL (Denmark), Finvoic (Finland), CBI (Italy), SAF-T (Portugal), e-facturae (Spain), ISDOC (Czech Republic), and Standaard Digitale Nota (Netherlands). Some countries have two different standards. For example, both e2bformat and NES UBL are used in Norway. Both SFTI and Svefaktura are used in Sweden. In some cases, there are standards for specific industries within specific countries. In Germany a specialized set of VDA standards are utilized in the automotive sector. The UK retail and consumer products industry utilizes a local standard called Tradacoms. There are also pan-European and global standards for e-invoices. The EDIFACT INVOIC standard has been popularly used throughout the world for several decades.

An effort was undertaken to create a new e-invoicing standard that could be used globally by all countries and all industry sectors. However, gaining general agreement on one standard proved more challenging than expected. An expert e-invoicing group was formed in Europe to provide recommendations on how to accelerate adoption of these technologies. The Expert Group originally recommended a standard called the Cross Industry Invoice Version 2 (CII2). However, shortly after issuing a recommendation several members of the group began to shift support towards a Financial Invoice created as part of the ISO 20022 XML standard explained in Chapter 16. Ironically, both of these e-invoicing standards, CII2 and ISO 20022, were created by different groups working for the same standards organization. Two different sub-committees within the United Nations Center for Trade Facilitation and Electronic Business (UN/CEFACT) organization developed the competing e-invoicing standards. Although both were created by members of the same organization during the same timeframe, the standards are noticeably different. For example, CII2 supports up to 80,000 line items on an invoice while ISO 20022 XML only supports 1,362 lines.[388]

While the EU PEPPOL initiative is fraught with challenges it remains far ahead of other multi-jurisdictional e-procurement platforms in other regions. For example, over 30 of the 50 American states have independent e-procurement platforms for which there is no harmonization plan. As a result, vendors seeking to sell to state governments across the US must independently register on each of these 30 portals and monitor for new opportunities on each of these 30 channels.

SECTION 7
Closing

Chapter 23
Carp EDI em

I often refer to the period between 2000 and 2010 as the Lost Decade of B2B. During these 10 years there were numerous attempts to revolutionize various industries with new B2B technologies. However, most of these initiatives met with only modest levels of success. We have discussed these new B2B e-commerce programs throughout the book, but let's quickly recap starting with the supply chain.

First, XML emerged in the late 1990s. Evangelists proclaimed it was going to eradicate EDI in a matter of years. Hundreds of XML standards have been created in industries such as chemicals, aerospace, high tech, consumer products and short sea shipping. Yet over 10 years later, EDI remains the dominant technology standard used in the retail, manufacturing and health care industries. While XML use has grown steadily, it only represents 20 to 30% of total transaction volumes.

Also in the late 1990s, the B2B e-marketplaces emerged, funded by venture capitalists and consortia of large Fortune 500 companies. With revolutionary capabilities such as reverse auctions, supplier discovery and electronic procurement these marketplaces were going to transform the supply chain forever. But most of the public and consortia marketplaces failed. Of the 1,300 that were launched, fewer than 50 exist today.

In 2002, Walmart announced its intention to switch from VANs to Internet EDI.[389] As a result, technologies such as AS2 gained massive adoption in a relatively short period following their launch. VANs were declared dead. In the following years, IT organizations leveraged the Internet to exchange EDI with their high-volume business partners. However, today approximately 50%

of all B2B transactions in the supply chain continue to be routed through EDI VANs. Furthermore AS2 was the only truly successful Internet communications protocol. AS3 and AS4 have failed miserably. FTP is extremely popular, but remains highly fragmented with over 30 different variants competing for domination.

The Global Data Synchronization Network (GDSN) emerged in 2004, led by the GS1 standards organizations. Data sync promised to accelerate new product introductions, reduce invoice discrepancies and eliminate various logistical inefficiencies in the supply chain. As B2C online and mobile shopping have become mainstream in the past few years, consumer demand for product information has reached an all-time high. However, adoption of GDSN services remains far short of expectations even eight years after its launch.

Also in 2004, RFID technology became commercially viable as price points for tags, printers and readers dropped dramatically. RFID promised to revolutionize the consumer products and pharmaceutical supply chains by offering a foursquare-like, self check-in approach to inventory management. Nearly eight years later, RFID has gained only modest adoption and primarily in the public sector. Meanwhile the barcode that RFID was intended to replace has grown even more pervasive in consumer and business processes.

A similar pattern of missed expectations can be found in the financial services industry. In the late 1990s, many of the world's largest brokers, custodial banks and investment managers invested in the Global Straight Through Processing Association (GSTPA). GSTPA promised to enable next-day settlement of securities trades. It would standardize the processes for the growing volumes of cross-border trade. However, by 2002 when the GSTPA launched, there was little actual adoption by its owners. A few months later the utility was shut down.[390]

Throughout most of the period between 2000 and 2010, the European Union worked aggressively to harmonize payment regulations, standards and processes across its member states. The vision for a Single European Payments Area (SEPA) would reduce barriers to cross-border commerce by enabling companies to perform payments in any EU state just as easily as they could in their home country. However, adoption of SEPA by corporate customers has fallen far below expectations with only minimal adoption of the new Pan-

European systems and standards.

In the past few years, the commercial banks around the world have launched electronic invoicing products. New regulations in the European Union and Latin America have provided a legal framework for businesses to replace paper invoices with electronic equivalents. E-invoicing is actually not a new idea. The first e-invoices were exchanged in the early 1980s. Nonetheless, an investment bubble has emerged with 500 vendors targeting the sector in Europe alone. Most vendors are focused only on a single country. Very few have more than $10 million in revenues.[391] And industry analysts state the market for the 30-year old e-invoicing technology has only reached $100 million per year.

The health care industry has been more successful than others, but nonetheless has experienced similar challenges with missed expectations.

In 1996, the US introduced its HIPAA regulations. By standardizing the approaches to claims submission, eligibility verification and payment processing, HIPAA attacked the 25% of US health care expenditures driven by administrative expenses. HIPAA presented a herculean challenge for many hospitals and insurers. As a result, the deadlines for compliance were extended several times. However, HIPAA was eventually successful in standardizing EDI transactions. But many smaller hospitals and physicians' offices still do not use EDI. Approximately 50% of claims and payment transactions are still processed using paper-based techniques.[392]

In 2001, the e-prescription networks RxHub and Surescripts were formed. E-prescription technology would provide physicians with real-time access to a patient's list of medications and formularies. It would reduce the administrative costs associated with the handling of paper prescriptions by patients and pharmacies. Surescripts has access to 65% of the US population's prescription benefit and history information. However, only 20% of the physicians in the US are issuing electronic prescriptions more than 10 years later.[393]

In the past few years, over 200 health information exchanges (HIEs) have emerged in the US for the purpose of exchanging electronic health records (EHRs). Many of these HIEs were created as a result of federal funding grants from the ARRA legislation, and many are dependent upon government subsidies for survival. As a result, financial viability is one of the top concerns for most HIEs.[394] Another challenge is the fact that most physicians continue to maintain health records on paper versus in electronic format. Without electronic records there will not be much to exchange. It is too early to declare any expectations have been missed, but it is hard to believe that many of these HIEs will achieve an independently profitable business model.

Adoption of new B2B initiatives in the health care sector has certainly been stronger than in the financial services, manufacturing or retail industries. However, it is important to note the influence of the government in adoption trends. For example, in the case of HIPAA, the need to use standardized EDI transactions was enacted into law. In other cases, hospitals and physicians' offices are at risk of non-payment by Medicare and Medicaid, which control more than 50% of claims reimbursement, if they do not comply. These factors certainly have an effect on the higher adoption rates.

There are Three Bs in Bubble

Most of the initiatives outlined previously follow a relatively predictable pattern of development. A new concept is introduced to the market. Shortly thereafter, a few large companies experiment with the technology and find significant business value. These early adopters become vocal public advocates sharing their future intentions to continue to invest in the technology. Industry analysts such as Aberdeen, IDC and Gartner fuel the hype cycle by publishing research that dramatically overstates the near-term market opportunity. Drawn by the buzz, hundreds of vendors swarm the market. Some are startups, while others are product divisions of larger companies. The bubble is growing. Customer adoption begins, but at a relatively slow and steady pace. Linear growth will occur over a 10 year period until customer adoption rates of 40% are achieved. Unfortunately, this growth curve is far less aggressive than the ones that the technology vendors used for their business plans. Instead, most vendors have forecasted an 80% market adoption over a three-year period.

Heavily over-capitalized, the market becomes over-saturated with supply at the end of year one. Too many vendors are chasing too few actual customers. By the end of year two, the big technology vendors begin to withdraw from the market writing off their investments. The startups attempt to hang on. By the end of year three, most of the smaller vendors will be acquired by a larger competitor. Others will file bankruptcy, and then attempt to auction their assets and customers to the remaining vendors. At year three or four the market begins to stabilize. The number of technology suppliers on the market becomes more closely balanced with the actual customer demand. Vendors can now achieve a profitable business model. The early majority of companies now begin to invest in the B2B technologies. Ironically, however, most of the larger vendors have withdrawn from the market.

There are certainly exceptions to these patterns. AS2 was a smashing success. Private e-marketplaces were adopted by many large companies in a relatively short period of time, as was e-procurement technology. Alibaba.com has enjoyed tremendous success in China with its online discovery business model that failed miserably in the US and Europe. However, most B2B e-commerce initiatives tend to follow a relatively predictable model of hype and over investment before stabilizing into a period of long-term growth.

Why do so many of these B2B e-commerce initiatives struggle for success? Throughout the book we have explored the radical improvements industries could gain by further adoption of B2B e-commerce technologies. With so much to be gained, why does adoption take such a long period of time?

First, most of the participants have unrealistic expectations about the definition of success. A longer time horizon is required for investment in B2B e-commerce initiatives than other technology segments. B2B e-commerce initiatives have very different adoption characteristics than technologies used by the consumer market or by an individual company. For example, suppose that the CIO of a Fortune Global 500 company decides that he or she wants the whole business to standardize on the Microsoft Office platform. The CIO only needs to gain the agreement of a handful of executives before issuing a mandate to the employee population about the initiative. Because everyone in the IT organization reports to the CIO they have no choice but to comply. There may be a few Google Docs users within the company that put up roadblocks to delay the switch. However, ultimately these end-users will have to convert to Microsoft as they all report up to the CEO, who is onboard with the plan.

While technology initiatives within a single company typically occur over a period of months or years, B2B e-commerce programs are rolled out over a period of decades. If you want to determine how long a B2B program will take to be adopted follow these steps. First, calculate what you expect a technology rollout to take within the four walls of a single company. Then, multiply it by 10.

As we have learned in this book the process for B2B technology rollouts is not nearly as simple. Only a handful of organizations with extremely large influence can successfully instruct their business partner community to adapt new B2B e-commerce technologies. For example, only the top few investment managers, such as UBS, Barclays and Fidelity with trillions of dollars in assets under management, have the ability to drive new technologies into the broker and custodial banking community. Fidelity was successful in the early 1990s driving FIX into the broker segment.[395] Merely a handful of the largest health insurers, public and private such as Medicare, Medicaid, United Healthcare and WellPoint have the ability to drive new initiatives into the community of hospital and physicians' offices. For example, the US government has been successful with HIPAA EDI and is now attempting a similar program with EHR. Only the retailers and manufacturers with the largest purchasing power such as Walmart, GE and Toyota have the ability to mandate e-commerce adoption by suppliers. Walmart was extremely successful with AS2, but has struggled more recently to convince its suppliers of the value of technologies such as data synchronization or RFID.

But most companies do not have the influence that Fidelity, Medicare or Walmart have over their business partners. What happens when a company that is not among the 50 largest in the world introduces a B2B e-commerce initiative? There is usually an early surge in adoption. Larger business partners who have the budget, resources and expertise to complete the initiative will comply rapidly. There will also be uptake by a subset of small- and medium-sized business partners that have deployed a similar technology initiative for another customer. The net of the initial surge is typically a yield of 20% participation. However, adoption then begins to slow. The remaining 80% of the business partner community is much more challenging to onboard.

In many cases there are good reasons for the business partner to delay participation in the B2B e-commerce initiative. First, the business partner may not have the appropriate budget, skills or resources to participate. Additional staff, software licenses and server hardware may need to be acquired. But even companies that overcome these hurdles and are eager to participate will confront challenges. As we learned in Chapter 7, over 100 different B2B e-commerce standards are in use today. These are just a few of the factors that serve to complicate and delay participation.

To B or Not to B

Another factor that has influenced the success of the B2B e-commerce programs is the investment model. Throughout the book I have cited examples of large, multi-billion dollar companies that have invested in B2B e-commerce technology vendors. Over 60% of the Fortune 50 have an ownership stake or have invested in a B2B e-commerce vendor in the past 15 years. The high levels of investment made by so many of the world's largest companies are evidence of the strategic nature of B2B e-commerce. However, it may also be part of the challenge. How many successful startups do you know that have been launched by consortia of Global 500 companies? Or to phrase the question differently, how many successful startups do you know that have been launched by joint ventures between competitors? There are very few.

We studied a handful in this book, companies such as Surescripts, E2open, Covisint, Exostar and Agentrics. These were the few that managed to survive a competitive shakeout that killed off several thousand of the other B2B e-marketplaces. However, of the handful of B2B e-marketplaces that did survive none have surpassed $50 million in revenues in their first 10 years. None have gone public. And none have achieved anywhere close to the billions in business benefits promised to their owners.

Another major community of investors and owners of B2B e-commerce initiatives has been the public sector and non-profit organizations. For example, most of the GDSN data pools discussed in Chapter 8 are owned and operated by non-profit GS1 organizations. How many startups do you know that have been launched by non-profits?

How many successful startups do you know that were launched by subsidies awarded from government regulations? We learned of a few in the book, such as Singapore's TradeNet and Hong Kong's TradeLink. However, there are very few examples from countries in Western Europe or North America. Most of the health information exchanges (HIEs) in the US are currently funded by federal grants from the US ARRA legislation.

Another major investor in B2B e-commerce technologies has been commercial banks. Many of the e-invoicing initiatives introduced in recent years have been led by banks. How many successful startups do you know that have been incubated or founded through investments from commercial banks? Although these institutions are trying hard to be innovative, the type of highly regulated, risk-averse culture that permeates most banks is in direct conflict with the factors that drive successful startups.

Why are most of the B2B e-commerce initiatives launched in the past 10 years driven by government entities, non-profits and financial institutions? Why aren't there more venture-capital backed startups as you would find in other parts of the technology sector? Silicon Valley has largely turned its back on B2B processes and technology in the past decade. The big problems being solved by today's Silicon Valley startups are in domains such as social networking, mobile applications and search engine marketing. You will not find many startups investing to automate the multi-trillion dollar bond trading, clearing and settlement process that remains largely paper-based today. Only a few are investing in the $75 billion of cost savings that can be achieved in the health care industry through EHR and HIEs.

One could certainly argue that Silicon Valley has good reason to avoid investments in B2B e-commerce technology vendors. Billions in funding were provided between 1996 and 2001 to launch 1,600 B2B vendors and fewer than 50 of them operate today. However, I'm not sure the dot-com failures are to blame for the lack of venture capital in B2B. Most investors seem to have a short memory. I suspect that the majority have forgotten about the failed marketplaces of the dot-com era.

Another plausible explanation for the lack of venture funding for B2B e-commerce startups is the long investment horizon. As mentioned previously, a ten-year period is required to achieve meaningful levels of adoption with most B2B e-commerce programs. Most venture firms would look for a faster payback period. However, I am not convinced that the investment horizon issue is the true root cause either. Most people in the B2B e-commerce industry are in a blissful state of denial about the length of time required for adoption, which is why the same pattern of unrealistic expectations continues to repeat every few years.

I think the primary reason for the lack of investment is simply that B2B isn't viewed as cool. The best and brightest graduating from universities in China, India, Western Europe or the United States do not have aspirations of solving B2B problems. They want to build a Facebook Killer or an iPad replacement. Part of the issue is that much of the technology that powers today's B2B e-commerce applications is considered "legacy." This is an industry in which Value Added Networks and Health Care Clearinghouses remain multi-billion dollar industries. Anachronisms, such as EDI, scare off top developers who would much rather build mobile phone-based, social media applications on open source platforms hosted in the cloud.

B2B Saves the World

The situation is unfortunate as B2B e-commerce is one of the technologies with the potential to help save the world. As we have discussed throughout the book, B2B e-commerce is a critical underpinning for the success of major initiatives in almost every industry. It helps law enforcement agencies identify the source of terrorist funding by monitoring international money laundering transactions. By providing homeland security officials with advanced access to forthcoming shipments, B2B helps prevent a dirty bomb from being imported to a California port. Similarly, advanced passenger manifests enable transportation security officials to identify potential terrorist threats to commercial airlines.

In the financial services industry, B2B could free up several trillions of dollars of investment capital that is locked up in unsettled securities trades by moving to a T+1 model.[396] In Europe, e-payment technologies are a critical foundation for the Single European Payments Area that have the potential to incrementally increase the $16 trillion EU economy by 1%.[397]

In the health care industry, B2B e-commerce plays a critical role in reducing the 25% of US health care costs associated with inefficient administrative overhead processes. Over $75 billion in savings is projected annually from better interoperability between hospitals, physicians, insurers and government entities in the US.[398] Perhaps, most importantly, real-time surveillance of trends in EHRs could help to identify emerging threats, such as a pandemic.

In the public sector, technologies such as e-procurement and e-invoicing could help governments to reduce their dangerous debt loads. Every dollar saved through more efficient government programs is one that could be applied to reduce a deficit. Furthermore, B2B can help contribute to revenue generation by reducing the frequency of VAT fraud. In countries like Brazil and Mexico that suffer from large gray market economies, B2B could help eliminate the tax evasion and illegal activities that limit growth.

The potential for B2B e-commerce is so compelling that in January 2009, shortly before President Obama's inauguration, I proposed that the US government appoint a cabinet-level official for B2B e-commerce. The "EDI Czar," as I called it, would be an advocate for B2B initiatives in both the private and public sector. Top policy items for the Obama administration included homeland security, health care reform, the credit crisis and US manufacturing sector competitiveness. Most Democrats and Republicans would probably agree that B2B e-commerce would be effective in monitoring terrorist threats; lowering health care costs; enabling supply chain finance; and promoting demand-driven manufacturing strategies.

The idea of the EDI Czar was not to increase regulation of B2B e-commerce in the US market, but to identify and champion catalysts that would aid in adoption. For example, many of the US federal government agencies do not fully embrace B2B e-commerce technologies such as e-invoicing. The EDI Czar would encourage federal agencies to mandate these technologies for government suppliers, effectively seeding the market. EU national governments embarked on similar initiatives years ago. The EDI Czar could also drive tax incentives that promote further adoption of B2B e-commerce. At the time of publication of this book, B2C e-commerce remains largely untaxed. Firms such as Amazon.com are not responsible for collecting sales taxes in many states. However, EDI VANs, data pools, HIEs and FIX networks enjoy no such advantages. Finally, an EDI Czar could lobby for federal subsidies to encourage adoption of B2B e-commerce. Small businesses are typically the most challenging to onboard to B2B programs due to budget, resource and skill limitations. Why not offer government programs to assist and catalyze adoption by small businesses?

There was a time when the American National Standards Institute (ANSI) was driving the formulation of EDI transactions for private sector. Today, the US government plays very little role in B2B e-commerce. By contrast, Asian governments are aggressively promoting and investing in B2B e-commerce technologies to increase the competitiveness of their local economies. In Chapter 19, we reviewed case studies of how Singapore and Hong Kong used EDI programs to increase foreign direct investment and grow their market share for international trade during the 1990s. Twenty years later, government ministries in Korea, China and various Southeast Asian countries remain strong advocates and investors in B2B.

As you may have guessed, there has yet to be anyone appointed to the US B2B e-commerce czar role despite the numerous potential benefits that could be achieved. Although the government could help to catalyze demand for B2B e-commerce, it is really the private sector that needs to lead investment.

Unfortunately, the altruistic goals outlined previously are unlikely to motivate most large corporations or venture capital firms to invest in B2B e-commerce technologies. So I should also point out that there is money to be made from B2B e-commerce. Emdeon generates over $1 billion per year from its health care clearinghouse and revenue cycle management applications.[399] SWIFT generates over €400 million from operating its electronic banking network.[400] Sterling Commerce generated over $600 million per year from its B2B e-commerce software and services prior to its acquisition by IBM.[401] GXS generates nearly $500 million per year from operating its Trading Grid and Supply Chain applications. Ariba generates over $400 million per year from its portfolio of e-procurement and supplier network services.[402]

Investments in B2B e-commerce ventures typically take one of three different models. Each of the models has a different payback period. First, let's discuss the short term approach. If you want to turn a quick profit the best model is to capitalize on investment bubbles. When a new bubble emerges the goal should be to sell as many software licenses and professional services hours as you can. It sounds obvious and easy, but only works with the right approach. The key is to avoid selling to the end-customers. There will only be a handful of early adopters buying in the first year which will limit your potential market. Instead focus on selling to the technology vendors "drinking the Kool-Aid." And be sure to collect payment upfront. Avoid any risky models that depend upon a future revenue stream from profit-sharing arrangements. Remember

50% of zero is zero.

With this approach you would not sell the e-invoicing solution to buyers and suppliers. The payoff period is too long and the odds of success are low. Instead you would sell the technology infrastructure required to set up the e-invoicing application to a bank or telco seeking to enter the market. Don't sell the HIE solution to individual hospitals or physicians' offices which need to share EHRs. Instead, sell the technology infrastructure required to set up the HIE and EHR platforms to a local county government with federal funding.

Companies, such as Ariba, Commerce One and i2, made a fortune selling software licenses to B2B e-marketplaces during the dot-com bubble. The large technology vendors, such as IBM, HP, Oracle, SAP and Microsoft, reaped a windfall in each one of these investment waves. When a bubble emerges, these tech giants avoid building the utilities, exchanges or networks to solve the actual problem. Instead, they sell server hardware, storage arrays, software licenses and consulting services to other technology vendors to enable them to solve the problem. In the technology sector this type of go-to-market model is referred to as the "arms dealer" approach.

I am actually not an advocate of these short-term investment strategies because such an approach does not provide long-term value towards solving the B2B process issues discussed in the book. I only point out these strategies so that investors in B2B initiatives are aware of the games being played by technology vendors.

Next let's discuss the long term approach. There is legitimate money to be made from operating a B2B network, data pool, exchange or industry utility. However, there is a greater risk and a different mindset required. A combination of persistence and patience is required that many investors do not have an appetite for. If you are going to build a GDSN data pool, HIE, FIX network or e-invoicing network, then you must be prepared to endure a six to ten year investment horizon. Furthermore, you will need to survive a post-bubble period of intense consolidation and pricing pressure. Network effects will drive only one to two dominant vendors to emerge around each initiative. But a lucrative business awaits those that can master this model. With a large captive community in place, you can begin to leverage network effects to up-sell and cross-sell new services. Alternatively, you could develop analytics based upon the massive amounts of data flowing through the community.

The approach that I think yields the greatest revenue opportunities is the medium-term approach. Instead of trying to solve the entire industry's problem, focus on solving the problems of an individual company, one at a time. Enter into a long-term relationship in which you share the risk for helping the company to achieve its B2B e-commerce goals—whatever those might be. Companies, particularly the largest ones, engage in a series of somewhat irrational behaviors when it comes to B2B e-commerce programs. Some customers will maintain an allegiance to legacy technologies, such as barcode labels and EDI, which are well-established within their business partner community and have been proven to work. Other customers will want to be the early adopter of leading edge technologies. Some customers will remain loyal to the standardized approaches developed for B2B e-commerce. These companies will use industry standards and to the extent possible, leverage shared utilities. Other customers will choose to ignore standards and shared utilities, instead pursuing what is best for their individual corporations.

At GXS we've grown this type of business model to $150 million in just six years. We host and operate the B2B e-commerce technology on behalf of our customers. We mediate all of the different standards that exist. And most importantly, we take responsibility for the onboarding of business partners. While we provide consultation, we do not try to steer our customers towards one B2B e-commerce approach or another. We enable our customers to utilize standards or to deviate from standards with a customized approach. We enable our customers to leverage legacy technologies or the newest Internet-based frameworks. We allow our customers to interoperate with industry utilities and networks or to circumvent them altogether.

Carp EDI em

Companies today view their information supply chains as providing a competitive advantage. Gordon Gekko stated in the movie Wall Street, "The most valuable commodity I know of is information."[403] It was a widely accepted truth in 1987 when the movie was filmed, but has become almost a universally agreed upon fact 25 years later. B2B e-commerce is about getting companies access to information. I am not proposing that companies pursue illegal insider trading schemes, but they should begin to think like hedge funds. What information can be obtained that would provide a competitive advantage in the marketplace?

If a bank knows before its competitors that a large retailer plans to pay a $20 million invoice to one of its suppliers, it can approach the vendor with an offer for supply chain finance that could generate substantial profits. If a high tech manufacturer detects that a shortage of the graphics chips used to make smartphones is expected in the next few weeks, it could secure contracts for remaining supplies in advance of its competitors.

Advantage is not only gained by obtaining earlier access to data from business partners. Sometimes the ability to push information faster into the information supply chain can provide competitive advantage as well. For example, if an electronics retailer is able to communicate price changes to consumers using mobile applications faster than its competitors, it will be better able to capture market share. If an investment manager can communicate clearing and settlement instructions to its brokers and custodians faster than competitors, then its trades will clear faster and with fewer exceptions. The ability to achieve higher straight through processing rates will not only reduce costs, but is attractive to new clientele seeking to free up funds from lengthy settlement processes.

Most companies understand the value of information, but still struggle to obtain the right quantity of data in the right timeframe. Obtaining information continues to grow more challenging every year because more and more of the data lies outside the four walls of the enterprise. Today's corporations are highly dependent upon outsourcing for success. The typical multinational corporation will identify a few "core competencies," then seek to outsource the remaining functions to business partners.

As we discussed in Chapter 1, manufacturing companies source not only parts and raw materials, but also entire business processes including product design, assembly, logistics, distribution and customer service from third parties. Many companies whose brand names are on mobile phones, digital cameras and video consoles perform none of the manufacturing activities associated with these devices. Doctors have always been specialized. The entire health care industry depends upon referrals. If you are diagnosed with a chronic condition, such as diabetes, cancer or heart disease, you will not only work with a primary care physician, but a series of specialists in different facilities. The financial services industry is extremely specialized as well. Consider the securities industry processes we discussed in Chapter 17. Investment managers are charged with making decisions about which stocks and bonds to buy and sell for a portfolio. However, the investment managers do not actually execute the trades nor do they safe-keep the records. Third parties, such as brokers and custodians, perform these functions.

It is hard to find any example of an industry today that has not become highly specialized and dependent upon business partners for success. For companies to operate their businesses they require access to real-time information about the activities of business partners. Companies that can gather information in greater quantities and faster speeds from business partners will have a competitive advantage in the market. This quest for competitive advantage is the reason we have 100 different EDI and XML standards in B2B e-commerce. It is the reason there are hundreds of different B2B e-commerce vendors in existence. It is the reason 60% of the Fortune 50 has made equity investments in B2B vendors over the past 15 years. Companies are seeking an information advantage. But, if everyone takes the same approach to B2B e-commerce, no one has an advantage. As a result, there continues to be a divergence rather than a convergence of B2B technologies, networks and standards.

Companies are going to pursue a myriad of different B2B e-commerce strategies—each hoping to outpace its competitors with an information advantage. As we close the chapter and the book I will leave you with final word—Carp EDI em. Note that I have changed it from its proper spelling of carpe diem to accentuate the fact that the letters EDI make up the center of the word.

Hopefully I have been able to educate you on the tremendous potential of B2B e-commerce technologies. And as we close this chapter, I hope you and your company will consider further investments in B2B technologies to help seize the day, no matter what your corporate ambitions are.

Epilogue

The original manuscript for this book was more than twice the length I actually decided to print. In addition to the examples I covered herein there are also numerous other stories about how B2B e-commerce is being used in the aerospace, computer, mobile phone, video game, music and movie sectors. For brevity's sake I omitted most of these stories along with additional explanations of how B2B is used in the health care supply chain and other aspects of securities trading (bonds, mutual funds, derivatives).

However, if you are interested in learning more about B2B e-commerce I have made much of this content available on several free online resources.

- EDInomics Blog—http://www.gxsblogs.com/keifers
- Squidoo Lens—http://www.squidoo.com/b2becommerce
- Scribd Documents—http://www.scribd.com/steve_keifer
- Slideshare Presentations—http://www.slideshare.net/stevekeifer

If you cannot find what you are looking for, feel free to contact me directly at steve.keifer@gxs.com or via twitter @EDInomics.

References

1 IHS iSuppli, "iPad 2 Carries Bill of Materials of $326.60, IHS iSuppli Teardown Analysis Shows," online article by Andrew Rassweiler, March 13, 2011, http://www.isuppli.com/teardowns/news/pages/ipad-2-carries-bill-of-materials-of-$326-60-ihs-isuppli-teardown-analysis-shows.aspx.

2 Shawn Tully, "Going, Going, Gone! The B2B Tool That Really Is Changing the World," Fortune, March 20, 2000, http://money.cnn.com/magazines/fortune/fortune_archive/2000/03/20/276391/index.htm.

3 Pierre Mitchell. "FreeMarkets Goes for the Sizzle in Strategic Sourcing." AMR Research, December 21, 1999.

4 Charles Phillips and Mary Meeker, "The B2B Internet Report," Morgan Stanley Dean Witter, April 2000.

5 "Agentrics History," accessed August 2011,http://www.agentrics.com/web/agentrics/company2.

6 Lynda M. Applegate. Ventro: Builder of B2B Businesses. Harvard Business School, July 24, 2001.

7 Ibid

8 Ibid

9 Ibid

10 Charles Phillips and Mary Meeker, "The B2B Internet Report," Morgan Stanley Dean Witter, April 2000.

11 Ibid

12 E2open, "E2open Recognizes Record Revenue and 30 Percent Growth in FY2010," news release, April 19, 2010, http://www.e2open.com/news/article/e2open-recognizes-record-revenue-and-30-percent-growth-in-fy2010/.

13 Charles Phillips and Mary Meeker, "The B2B Internet Report," Morgan Stanley Dean Witter, April 2000.

14 Thilo Koslowski. "B2B E-marketplaces: Fast Lane or Dead-End for the Automotive Industry," Gartner, December 2001.

15 W. Daniel Garretson. "The Build to Order Revolution," Forrester Research, January 2001.

16 Ibid

17 David Welch and Dan Beucke, "Why GM's plan won't work," Business Week, May 9, 2005, http://www.businessweek.com/magazine/content/05_19/b3932001_mz001.htm.

18 Nanette Byrnes and David Welch, "The Benefits Trap," Business Week, July 19, 2004, http://www.businessweek.com/magazine/content/04_29/b3892001_mz001.htm.

19 Lynda M. Applegate and Elizabeth L. Collins. "Covisint (A): The Evolution of a B2B Marketplace." Harvard Business School, June 29, 2005.

20 Ibid

21 Ibid

22 Ibid

23 Ibid

24 Ibid

25 Ibid

26 "SupplyOn Company Overview," accessed August 2011, http://www.supplyon.com/company.html.

27 Tom Henderson. "Covisint planning to go public." Automotive News, October 29, 2007.

28 "Kwame Kilpatrick," Wikipedia, accessed September 14, 2011, http://en.wikipedia.org/wiki/Kwame_Kilpatrick.

29 Covisint, "Covisint, a Compuware Company, Selected by HealthShare Montana to Provide Statewide Health Information Exchange," news release, February 21, 2011, http://www.covisint.com/web/guest/press/2011/covisint-selected-by-healthshare-montana-to-provide-statewide-hie.

30 Covisint, "Covisint, a Compuware Company, Wins New Business from Vermont Blueprint for Health," news release, January 24, 2011, http://www.covisint.com/web/guest/press/2011/covisint-wins-new-business-from-vermont-blueprint-for-health.

31 Covisint, "Covisint, a Compuware Company, Wins Northeastern Pennsylvania Health Information Exchange Business," news release, January 11, 2011, http://www.covisint.com/web/guest/press/2011/covisint-wins-northeastern-penn.

32 Compuware (CPWR) Q1 2012 Earnings Call, July 21, 2011, http://investor.compuware.com/events.cfm.

33 Nick Bunkley, "Retired GM Workers Struggle to Replace Health Care," New York Times, October 10, 2008, http://www.nytimes.com/2008/11/10/business/worldbusiness/10iht-gm.1.17681135.html.

34 General Motors Corporation, Form 8-K, Filed October 15, 2007.

35 "Automotive Crisis of 2008-2010," Wikipedia, last modified August 17, 2011, http://en.wikipedia.org/wiki/Automotive_crisis.

36 "About Us (Ariba)," accessed August 2011, http://www.ariba.com/about/.

37 "Ariba," Wikipedia, last modified September 14, 2011, http://en.wikipedia.org/wiki/Ariba.

38 Ibid

39 Pierre Mitchell, "Ariba and Commerce One blow out Q200," AMR Research, July 19, 2000.

40 Steve Hamm, "From Hot to Scorched at Commerce One," Business Week, February 3, 2003, http://www.businessweek.com/magazine/content/03_05/b3818110.htm.

41 Ibid

42 Ibid

43 Randy Covill, "SAP and Commerce One Partner to Jointly Develop End-to-End Buy-Side Business Process Automation." AMR Research, June 15, 2000.

44 Steve Hamm, "From Hot to Scorched at Commerce One," Business Week, February 3, 2003, http://www.businessweek.com/magazine/content/03_05/b3818110.htm.

45 Melanie Austria Farmer, "Covisint founders take $1.26 billion stake in Commerce One," CNET News, December 12, 2000, http://news.cnet.com/Covisint-founders-take-1.26-billion-stake-in-Commerce-One/2100-1017_3-249745.html.

46 Jennifer Friedlin, "Ariba buys Tradex in $1.86 Billion Stock Deal," New York Times, December 17, 1999, http://partners.nytimes.com/library/tech/99/12/biztech/articles/17ariba.html.

47 Stefanie Olsen, "Ariba to acquire SupplierMarket.com in stock deal," CNET News, June 26, 2000, http://news.cnet.com/Ariba-to-acquire-SupplierMarket.com-in-stock-deal/2100-1017_3-242425.html.

48 Commerce One, "Commerce One Acquires Veo Systems, Inc.," news release, January 19, 1999, http://www.allbusiness.com/technology/software-services-applications-electronic/6664928-1.html#ixzz1VDZtbwMA.

49 Alorie Gilbert, "Commerce One buys Web Integrator AppNet," Information Week, June 20, 2000, http://www.informationweek.com/news/6509088.

50 Steve Hamm, "From Hot to Scorched at Commerce One," Business Week, February 3, 2003, http://www.businessweek.com/magazine/content/03_05/b3818110.htm.

51 David Hope-Ross "Financial Results Signal Commerce One's Deepening Troubles," Gartner, April 19, 2002, FT-16-3034.

52 SAP Group, "(SAP) Consolidated Income Statements Six Months Ended June 30 (2001)," http://www.sap.com/corporate-en/investors/reports/quarterlyreport/2001/pdf/q2_2001_e.pdf.

53 David Hope-Ross, "Financial Results Signal Commerce One's Deepening Troubles." Gartner, April 19, 2002.

54 Alorie Gilbert, "Commerce One sells e-marketplace unit," CNET News, December 19, 2002, http://news.cnet.com/Commerce-One-sells-e-marketplace-unit/2100-1017_3-978457.html.

55 "Commerce One." Wikipedia, Last modified November 17, 2011, http://en.wikipedia.org/wiki/Commerce_One.

56 Rich Smith, "The Fall of Commerce One," Motley Fool, September 27, 2004, http://www.fool.com/investing/small-cap/2004/09/27/the-fall-of-commerce-one.aspx.

57 Bruce Richardson, "Of Commerce One and Public Trading Exchanges." AMR Research, November 6, 2003.

58 John Markoff, "Secretive buyer of some e-commerce patents turns out to be Novell," New York Times, May 2, 2005, http://www.nytimes.com/2005/05/02/technology/02novell.html.

59 Perfect Commerce, "Perfect Commerce acquires Commerce One," news release, February 7, 2006, http://www2.prnewswire.com/cgi-bin/stories.pl?ACCT=104&STORY=/www/story/02-07-2006/0004276505&EDATE.

60 "Reverse Auction," Wikipedia, accessed August 2011, http://en.wikipedia.org/wiki/Reverse_auction.

61 Ariba, "Ariba and FreeMarkets Announce Strategic Merger Agreement," news release, January 23, 2004, http://www.ariba.com/pdf/pr/aribaPR2419.pdf.

62 Ariba, "Ariba Announces Definitive Agreement to Acquire Procuri," news release, September 20, 2007. http://www.businesswire.com/news/home/20070920005595/en/Ariba-Announces-Definitive-Agreement-Acquire-Procuri.

63 Ariba, "Ariba Announces Definitive Agreement to Acquire Quadrem," news release, November 18, 2010, http://www.ariba.com/news/press_release.cfm?press_id=2927.

64 Ariba, "About Us," accessed August 2011, http://www.ariba.com/about/.

65 Alibaba.com, "About Us," accessed August 2011, http://www.alibaba.com/about/en/MediaRelations/cor_material.html.

66 Clay Chandler, "Open sesame for China's web king," Fortune Magazine, November 25, 2007, http://money.cnn.com/2007/11/23/magazines/fortune/China_WebKing.fortune/.

67 Ali Farhmoomand, "Alibaba.com." The Asia Case Research Centre, The University of Hong Kong, 2008.

68 Ibid

69 Clay Chandler, "Open sesame for China's web king," Fortune Magazine, November 25, 2007, http://money.cnn.com/2007/11/23/magazines/fortune/China_WebKing.fortune/.

70 Ibid

71 Ali Farhmoomand. "Alibaba.com." The Asia Case Research Centre, The University of Hong Kong, 2008.

72 Clay Chandler, "Open sesame for China's web king," Fortune Magazine, November 25, 2007, http://money.cnn.com/2007/11/23/magazines/fortune/China_WebKing.fortune/.

73 Ibid.

74 Ali Farhmoomand, "Alibaba.com." The Asia Case Research Centre, The University of Hong Kong, 2008.

75 Alibaba.com, "Alibaba.com acquires Vendio, continues to advance global e-commerce platform," news release, June 27, 2010, http://news.alibaba.com/article/detail/alibaba/100340213-1-alibaba.com-acquires-vendio%252C-continues-advance.html.

76 NY Times.com; "Alibaba acquires Auctiva, a California Tech Firm," online article by Dealbook, August 25, 2010, http://dealbook.nytimes.com/2010/08/25/alibaba-acquires-california-tech-firm-auctiva/.

77 Wordlab.com, "Where did Alibaba, the brand name, come from?" online article by abnu, October 15, 2007, http://www.wordlab.com/2007/10/where-did-alibaba-the-brand-name-come-from/.

78 Christopher A. Bartlett and Meg Glinska. "GE's Digital Revolution." Harvard Business School, May 3, 2005.

79 Ibid

80 Internet Week, "Internet Week Ranks Top 100 E-Businesses," news release, June 12, 2000, http://www.prnewswire.com/news-releases/internetweek-ranks-top-100-e-businesses-73523567.html.

81 Christopher A. Bartlett and Meg Glinska. "GE's Digital Revolution." Harvard Business School, May 3, 2005.

82 Walmart, "Walmart History," accessed August 2011, http://walmartstores.com/AboutUs/297.aspx.

83 Reference for Business," Wal-Mart Stores, Inc.—Company Profile," http://www.referenceforbusiness.com/history2/20/Wal-Mart-Stores-Inc.html.

84 Ibid

85 Anthony Bianco and Wendy Zellner, "Is Wal-Mart Too Powerful?" Business Week, October 6, 2003, http://www.businessweek.com/magazine/content/03_40/b3852001_mz001.htm.

86 Ibid

87 Ibid

88 Ibid

89 Ibid

90 Thomas, Wailgum, "45 Years of Wal-Mart History: A Technology Time Line," CIO.com, October 17, 2007, http://www.cio.com/article/147005/45_Years_of_Wal_Mart_History_A_Technology_Time_Line.

91 Ann Zimmerman, "To Sell Goods to Wal-Mart, Get on the Net." Wall Street Journal, November 21, 2003.

92 "Electronic Message Link Set Up by Sears," Chicago Tribune, February 05, 1989, http://articles.chicagotribune.com/1989-02-05/business/8903030046_1_electronic-data-interchange-electronic-post-office-sears-technology.

93 "Future of Newspapers," Wikipedia, last modified September 12, 2011, http://en.wikipedia.org/wiki/Future_of_newspapers.

94 Casestudyinc.com; "AOL-Time Warner Turnaround Strategy," online article, March 25, 2006, http://www.casestudyinc.com/aol-time-warner-turnaround-strategy.

95 nuBridges, "nuBridges acquires iSoft," news release, May 23, 2006, http://www.prnewswire.com/news-releases/nubridges-acquires-isoft-56523122.html.

96 Axway, "Cyclone Products," accessed August 2011, http://www.axway.com/products-solutions/ps-overview/axway-products-z/cyclone-products.

97 Hubbub Blog; "EDI Expert: Five Reasons to Get Off the VAN," blog entry by Jim Cantrell, June 13, 2011, http://www.hubspan.com/expert-blog-series/edi-expert-get-off-the-van/.

98 "Metcalfe's Law," Wikipedia, last modified September 14, 2011, http://en.wikipedia.org/wiki/Metcalfe's_law.

99 Bob Briscoe, Andrew Odlyzko and Benjamin Tilly, "Metcalfe's Law is Wrong," IEEE Spectrum, July 2006, http://spectrum.ieee.org/computing/networks/metcalfes-law-is-wrong/0.

100 "Robert Metcalfe," Wikipedia, last modified September 8, 2011, http://en.wikipedia.org/wiki/Robert_Metcalfe.

101 Andrew McAfee and Francois-Xavier Oliveau, "Confronting the Limits of Networks," MIT Sloan Management Review, Summer 2002.

102 Ibid

103 Ibid

104 "About Us (Ariba)," accessed August 2011, http://www.ariba.com/about/.

105 Sterling Commerce, "Software Magazine names Sterling Commerce among Top 100 Largest Software Companies in 27th Annual Software 500," news release, September 30, 2009.

106 "About the Petroleum Convenience Alliance for Technology Standards," accessed August 2011, http://www.pcats.org/.

107 "About Shortsea XML," accessed August 2011, http://www.shortseaxml.org/.

108 "Videotape format war," Wikipedia, last modified September 11, 2011, http://en.wikipedia.org/wiki/Videotape_format_war.

109 "Goodbye Beta: Sony will make VHS players," Time Magazine, January 25, 1988, http://www.time.com/time/magazine/article/0,9171,966523,00.html.

110 Ibid

111 "Video 2000," Wikipedia, last modified September 14, 2011, http://en.wikipedia.org/wiki/Video_2000.

112 "V-Cord," Wikipedia, last modified August 11, 2011, http://en.wikipedia.org/wiki/V-Cord.

113 "Quasar VX," accessed August 2011, http://www.videointerchange.com/quasar_vx_great_time_machine.htm.

114 Nathan Layne, "Toshiba to exit HD DVD, end format war-NHK," Reuters, February 16, 2008, http://www.reuters.com/article/2008/02/16/us-toshiba-hddvd-idUSL1627196120080216.

115 Dan Fost, "Divx's death pleases opponents," San Francisco Chronicle, June 18, 1999, http://www.sfgate.com/cgi-bin/article.cgi?file=/chronicle/archive/1999/06/18/BU89741.DTL.

116 "Metric Conversion Law," Title 15 U.S.C. Chapter 6 (204)205a-205l, enacted December 23, 1975, accessed August 2011, http://ts.nist.gov/WeightsAndMeasures/Metric/pub814.cfm#act.

117 "Metric Information and Conversions: A Capsule History," accessed August 2011, http://ts.nist.gov/WeightsAndMeasures/Metric/lc1136a.cfm.

118 "Omnibus Trade and Competitiveness Act of 1988 -Public Law 100-148", enacted August 23, 1988, accessed August 2011, http://gsi.nist.gov/global/docs/Omnibus.pdf.

119 CNN.com; "Metric mishap caused loss of NASA orbiter," September 30, 1999, accessed August 2011, http://articles.cnn.com/1999-09-30/tech/9909_30_mars.metric.02_1_climate-orbiter-spacecraft-team-metric-system?_s=PM:TECH.

120 Call for metric road sign switch," BBC News, February 23, 2006, http://news.bbc.co.uk/2/hi/uk_news/4741894.stm.

121 Coca-Cola Company, "The Real Story of New Coke," accessed August 2011, http://www.thecoca-colacompany.com/heritage/cokelore_newcoke.html.

122 Ibid

123 Ibid

124 Ibid

125 Ibid

126 "New Coke," Wikipedia, Last modified September 18, 2011, http://en.wikipedia.org/wiki/New_coke.

127 Ibid

128 Ibid

129 Ibid

130 Ilan Brat, Ellen Byron, and Ann Zimmerman, "Retailers Cut Back on Variety, Once the Spice of Marketing," Wall Street Journal, June 26, 2009, http://online.wsj.com/article/SB124597382334357329.html.

131 Ellen Byron, "Stores Stock So Many Types of Toothpaste, Consumers Are Annoyed; Some Wonder, Does Brand Matter?" Wall Street Journal, February 23, 2011, http://online.wsj.com/article/SB10001424052748703373404576148363319407354.html.

132 Ilan Brat, Ellen Byron and Ann Zimmerman, "Retailers Cut Back on Variety, Once the Spice of Marketing," Wall Street Journal, June 26, 2009, http://online.wsj.com/article/SB124597382334357329.html.

133 Alex Frangos and Laurie Burkitt, "The Incredible Shrinking Bottle," Wall Street Journal, May 20, 2011, http://online.wsj.com/article/SB10001424052748704083904576333141394904376.html.

134 Chris Baskind, "5 reasons not to drink bottled water," Mother Nature Network, March 15 2010, http://www.mnn.com/food/healthy-eating-recipes/stories/5-reasons-not-to-drink-bottled-water.

135 SymphonyIRI, "SymphonyIRI announces the most successful packaged goods brands of 2010," news release, March 29, 2011, http://symphonyiri.com/NewsEvents/PressReleases/tabid/97/ItemID/1248/View/Details/Default.aspx.

136 Ibid

137 1SYNC, Wegmans, Accenture, Grocery Manufacturers Association, and Food Marketing Institute, "Synchronization—Next Generation of Business Partnering," 2006, http://www.gs1.org/docs/gdsn/gdsn_SynchronizationNextGenofBizPartnering.pdf.

138 GS1; "GS1 Global Registry Statistics—Cumulative Results as of May 13, 2011," May 13, 2011, http://www.gs1.org/gdsn/statistics.

139 Ariba, "Ariba Supplier Network," accessed August 2011, http://www.ariba.com/pdf/Ariba_FactSheet_R8.pdf.

140 Kurt Peters, "UCCnet and Transora complete merger to form 1SYNC," Internet Retailer, August 26, 2005, http://www.internetretailer.com/2005/08/26/uccnet-and-transora-complete-merger-to-form-1sync.

141 SA2, "About SA2," accessed August 2011, http://gds.sa2worldsync.com/gds/about_SA2/index.html.en.

142 GS1, "GS1 Global Registry Statistics—Cumulative Results as of May 13, 2011," May 13, 2011, http://www.gs1.org/gdsn/statistics.

143 Ibid

144 Jeff Bezos, "2008 Amazon Frustration-Free Packaging Letter to Customers," accessed August 2011, http://www.amazon.com/gp/feature.html?ie=UTF8&docId=1000302261.

145 Sucharita Mulpuru and Peter Hult. "US Online Retail Forecast 2009 To 2014." Forrester Research, March 5, 2010.

146 Ibid

147 UDEX Limited. "Best Buy analysis reveals opportunities to improve PDQ." 2008.

148 David Lazarus, "Best Buy kiosks not connected to Internet," Los Angeles Times, December 23, 2007, http://www.latimes.com/business/la-fi-lazarus23dec23,1,5748783.column?track=rss.

149 FedEx, "FedEx Innovation," accessed August 2011, http://about.van.fedex.com/our_company/fedex_innovation.

150 Laura Rock Kopczak, Hau Lee, and Seungjin Whang, "Logistics in the Information Age." Stanford University: Graduate School of Business. May 2000.

151 Ibid

152 Fortune Magazine, "Fortune 500 List for 1998," accessed August 2011, http://money.cnn.com/magazines/fortune/fortune500_archive/full/1998/.

153 Fortune Magazine, "Fortune 500 List for 2002," accessed August 2011, http://money.cnn.com/magazines/fortune/fortune500_archive/full/2002/.

154 "Auto-ID Labs," Wikipedia. Last modified July 7, 2011http://en.wikipedia.org/wiki/Auto-ID_Labs.

155 Mary Hayes Weier, "RFID Makes Slow and Steady Progress," Information Week, November 13, 2009, http://www.informationweek.com/news/mobility/RFID/221601551.

156 World Health Organization, "Substandard and counterfeit medicines—Fact sheet N°275," November 2003, http://www.who.int/mediacentre/factsheets/2003/fs275/en/.

157 Ibid

158 Jonathan Collins, "School Studies RFID's Effect on Wal-Mart," RFID Journal, April 18, 2005, http://www.rfidjournal.com/article/view/1514.

159 Christine Spivey Overby Charles Homs, Sharyn Leaver, Noha Tohamy, Lars Godell, Navi Radjou, Laura Ramos, Simon Yates, and Josh Walker, "RFID: The Complete Guide." Forrester Research, Spring 2005.

160 Renee Boucher Ferguson, "IBM invests $250M in RFID," eWeek, September 27, 2004, http://mobile.eweek.com/c/a/Mobile-and-Wireless/IBM-Invests-250M-in-RFID/.

161 Wonders of Modern Technology, "Barcodes Sweep the World," Wonders of Modern Technology, online article by Tony Seideman, http://www.barcoding.com/information/barcode_history.shtml.

162 "Radio Frequency identification," Wikipedia, http://en.wikipedia.org/wiki/Radio-frequency_identification#History_and_technology_background.

163 Wonders of Modern Technology, "Barcodes Sweep the World," online article by Tony Seideman, http://www.barcoding.com/information/barcode_history.shtml.

164 Ibid

165 Ibid

166 Ibid

167 Tricia Bishop, "UPC bar code has been in use 30 years," San Francisco Chronicle, July 5, 2004, http://www.sfgate.com/cgi-bin/article.cgi?f=/c/a/2004/07/05/BUG6Q7G4AJ1.DTL&type=business&ao=2.

168 Bill Selmeier, Spreading the Barcode. 2008.

169 "Price Waterhouse Coopers Research," accessed August 2011, http://www.gs1us.org/about_us/history/pricewaterhouse_coopers_research.

170 Kate Linebaugh, "In a State of Sticker Shock, Stores Try to Sell Public on a Radical Idea." Wall Street Journal, February 11, 2011.

171 Mary Hayes Weier, "RFID Makes Slow and Steady Progress," Information Week, November 13, 2009, http://www.informationweek.com/news/mobility/RFID/221601551.

172 Ibid

173 Ibid

174 Justin Rohrlich, "The Bellagio Gest Robbed—But the House Doesn't Feel a Thing," Minyanville, December 15, 2010, http://www.minyanville.com/businessmarkets/articles/bellagio-wynn-casino-rfid-gambling-las/12/15/2010/id/31714.

175 P.C. Tang, D. Fafchamps, and E.H. Shortliffe, "Traditional medical records as a source of clinical data in the outpatient setting," Northwestern University School of Medicine, 1994, http://www.ncbi.nlm.nih.gov/pubmed/7949993.

176 R.A. Berenson and J. Horvath, "The clinical characteristics of Medicare beneficiaries and implications for Medicare reform." Partnership for Solutions, March 2002.

177 Eric Pan, Douglas Johnston, Janice Walker, Julia Adler-Milsten, David W Bates, and Blackford Middleton, "The Value of Healthcare Information Exchange and Interoperability." Center for Information Technology Leadership, 2004.

178 Ibid

179 Ibid

180 Ibid

181 Ibid

182 "Ledger's death caused by accidental overdose," CNN.com, February 6, 2008, http://articles.cnn.com/2008-02-06/entertainment/heath.ledger_1_accidental-overdose-anti-anxiety-prescription-drugs?_s=PM:SHOWBIZ.

183 US Food and Drug Administration, "Preventable Adverse Drug Reactions: A Focus on Drug Interactions," last updated April 30, 2009, http://www.fda.gov/drugs/developmentapprovalprocess/developmentresources/druginteractionslabeling/ucm110632.htm.

184 Pan, Eric, Douglas Johnston, Janice Walker, Julia Adler-Milsten, David W Bates, and Blackford Middleton. "The Value of Healthcare Information Exchange and Interoperability." Center for Information Technology Leadership, 2004.

185 Ibid

186 Ibid

187 Surescripts, "2009 National Progress Report on E-Prescribing," 2009, http://www.surescripts.com/media/515306/2009_national-progress-report.pdf.

188 Office of the National Coordinator for Health Information Technology, "State Health Information Exchange Cooperative Agreement Program,"accessed August 2011, http://healthit.hhs.gov/portal/server.pt?open=512&objID=1488&parentname=CommunityPage&parentid=58&mode=2&in_hi_userid=11113&cached=true.

189 eHealth Initiative, "State of Health Information Exchange in 2010—Connecting the Nation to Achieve Meaningful Use," 2010, http://www.ehealthinitiative.org.

190 Ibid

191 Nick A. LeCuyer and Shubham Singhal, “Overhauling the US health care payment system.” McKinsey Quarterly, June 2007.

192 Ibid

193 Ibid

194 Ibid

195 Ibid

196 Ibid

197 Associated Press, “California Hospital System Settles Celeb Records Cases,” Fox News, July 8, 2011, http://www.foxnews.com/health/2011/07/08/calif-hospital-system-settles-celeb-records-cases/.

198 “UB40,” Wikipedia, last modified September 10, 2011http://en.wikipedia.org/wiki/UB40.

199 Anne Wilde Mathews, “Walked into a Lamppost? Hurt while Crocheting? Help is on the Way,” Wall Street Journal, September 13, 2011, http://online.wsj.com/article/SB10001424053111904103404576560742746021106.html.

200 Ibid

201 Health Information and Management Systems Society (HIMSS. “HIPAA 5010: A Second Chance for the Industry to Implement Transaction Standards to Reduce Costs and Increase Efficiency.” February 2009.

202 “Health Insurance Reform: Modifications to the Health Insurance Portability and Accountability Act (HIPAA) Electronic Transaction Standards.” Federal Register. 73(164) August 22, 2008.

203 Emdeon Inc., US SEC Form S-1/A (Amended Registration Statement) filed August 7, 2009.

204 Emdeon Inc., Annual Report Form 10-K, filed on March 10th, 2011.

205 Michael Lewis, The New New Thing. (New York: Penguin Books, 2000), 89.

206 Ibid, 162.

207 “Healtheon,” Wikipedia, Last modified August 2, 2011 http://en.wikipedia.org/wiki/Healtheon.

208 Phil Wahba, “Emdeon increases IPO size, prices at top of range,” Reuters, August 11, 2009, http://www.reuters.com/article/2009/08/12/us-emdeon-ipo-idUSTRE57A6FF20090812.

209 Kurt Eichenwald, “U.S. Expands Search of Columbia/HCA in Texas,” New York Times, March 21, 1997, http://partners.nytimes.com/library/financial/032197columbia-hca-investigate.html.

210 Todd Wilkinson, “After eight years, an insider gets his reward,” Christian Science Monitor, July 24, 2001, http://www.csmonitor.com/2001/0724/p4s1.html.

211 Scott Hiaasen and John Dorschner, "Rick Scott touts CEO experience in run for Florida governor, to a degree," Miami Herald, June 27, 2010, http://www.tampabay.com/news/politics/rick-scott-touts-ceo-experience-in-run-for-florida-governor-to-a-degree/1105385.

212 Ibid

213 Ibid

214 Ibid

215 David Stires, "Bringing HCA Back to Life After years of scandal, the hospital chain is healthy again and might just be a buy", Fortune Magazine, February 9, 2004, http://money.cnn.com/magazines/fortune/fortune_archive/2004/02/09/360103/index.htm.

216 Scott Hiaasen and John Dorschner, "Rick Scott touts CEO experience in run for Florida governor, to a degree," Miami Herald, June 27, 2010, http://www.tampabay.com/news/politics/rick-scott-touts-ceo-experience-in-run-for-florida-governor-to-a-degree/1105385.

217 David Stires, "Bringing HCA Back to Life After years of scandal, the hospital chain is healthy again and might just be a buy," Fortune Magazine, February 9, 2004, http://money.cnn.com/magazines/fortune/fortune_archive/2004/02/09/360103/index.htm.

218 Andrew Ross Sorkin, "Hospital Giant HCA is close to a record buyout," New York Times, July 24, 2006, http://www.nytimes.com/2006/07/24/business/24hospital.html.

219 Debra Sherman, "HCA biggest-ever U.S. PE-backed IPO, shares gain 3 percent," Reuters, March 10, 2011, http://www.reuters.com/article/2011/03/10/us-hca-ipo-debut-idUSTRE72949H20110310.

220 "Medicare Fraud," Wikipedia, Last modified September 12, 2011, http://en.wikipedia.org/wiki/Medicare_fraud#South_Florida.

221 Ibid

222 Greg Allen, "Feds Fight Rampant Medicare Fraud in South Florida," NPR, November 6, 2007, http://www.npr.org/templates/story/story.php?storyId=16045685.

223 "Medicare Fraud," Wikipedia, http://en.wikipedia.org/wiki/Medicare_fraud#South_Florida.

224 Ibid

225 George Lazenby, Stop Paying the Crooks. (Washington D.C., CHT Press, 2009), 14.

226 "Payment Integrity: New perspectives on, and approaches to, mastering the challenge of healthcare fraud, abuse and waste." Emdeon, November 2009.

227 US Health & Human Services, "Medicare Fraud Strike Force Charges 111 Individuals for more than $225 Million in False Billing and Expands Operations to Two Additional Cities," news release, February 17, 2011, http://www.hhs.gov/news/press/2011pres/02/20110217a.html.

228 Lance Williams and Christina Jewett, "Hospital chain's high infection rate leads to fraudulent billing concerns," California Watch, October 11, 2010, http://californiawatch.org/health-and-welfare/hospital-chain-s-high-infection-rate-leads-fraudulent-billing-concerns-5647.

229 John Carreyrou and Tom McGinty, "Medicare Records Reveal Troubling Trail of Surgeries," Wall Street Journal, April 29, 2011.

230 "Audit of Selected States' Medicaid Payments for Services Claimed to Have Been Provided to Deceased Beneficiaries." Office of the Inspector General, U.S. Department of Health and Human Services, September 26, 2006.

231 Committee on Comparative Effectiveness Research Prioritization, Institute of Medicine, Initial National Priorities for Comparative Effectiveness Research, (Washington D.C., National Academies Press, 2009) 30.

232 Ibid, page 1.

233 Ingenix, "About Us," accessed August 2011, http://www.ingenix.com/about/.

234 Ingenix, "Helping reduce costs throughout health care," accessed August 2011, http://www.ingenix.com/reduce-costs/overview/.

235 Lewis Krauskopf, "UnitedHealth settles payment suits for $350 million," Reuters, January 15, 2009, http://www.reuters.com/article/2009/01/15/unitedhealth-idUSN1531133620090115.

236 Chris Ayres, "Mexico outbreak traced to manure lagoons at pig farm," The Times, April 2009, http://www.timesonline.co.uk/tol/life_and_style/health/article6182789.ece.

237 "Influenza A virus subtype H2N2," Wikipedia, Last modified July 13, 2011, http://en.wikipedia.org/wiki/Asian_Flu#Asian_flu.

238 "Hong Kong flu," Wikipedia, Last modified September 17, 2011, http://en.wikipedia.org/wiki/Hong_kong_flu.

239 Eric Pan, Douglas Johnston, Janice Walker, Julia Adler-Milsten, David W Bates, and Blackford Middleton, "The Value of Healthcare Information Exchange and Interoperability." Center for Information Technology Leadership, 2004.

240 Ibid

241 Ibid

242 Google. "How does this work (Google.org Flu Trends)," accessed August 2011, http://www.google.org/flutrends/about/how.html.

243 Center for Disease Control, "National Electronic Disease Surveillance System," accessed August 2011, http://www.cdc.gov/phin/tools/NEDSS/index.html.

244 Abla Mawudeku and Michael Blench, Global Public Health Intelligence Network (GPHIN), 2005, http://www.mt-archive.info/MTS-2005-Mawudeku.pdf.

245 Eric Lichtblau and James Risen, "Bank Data Is Sifted by U.S. in Secret to Block Terror," New York Times, June 23, 2006, http://www.nytimes.com/2006/06/23/washington/23intel.html?_r=1&scp=1&sq=SWIFT%20terrorist%20finance%20program%20June%202006&st=cse.

246 Ibid

247 Ibid

248 Ibid

249 European Parliament Hearing 04, "SWIFT Compliance with compulsory US subpoenas," October 2006, http://www.europarl.europa.eu/hearings/20061004/libe/background_swift_en.pdf.

250 Ibid

251 Eric Lichtblau and James Risen, "Bank Data Is Sifted by U.S. in Secret to Block Terror," New York Times, June 23, 2006, http://www.nytimes.com/2006/06/23/washington/23intel.html?_r=1&scp=1&sq=SWIFT%20terrorist%20finance%20program%20June%202006&st=cse.

252 Finextra, "EU reaches deal on transfer of SWIFT data to US," November 30, 2009, http://www.finextra.com/news/fullstory.aspx?newsitemid=20810.

253 Finextra, "Parliament votes to scrap EU-US SWIFT data transfer deal," February 11, 2010, http://www.finextra.com/news/fullstory.aspx?newsitemid=21071.

254 Finextra, "WikiLeaks: Merkel furious at MEPs over Swift data sharing deal rejection," December 6, 2010, http://www.finextra.com/news/fullstory.aspx?newsitemid=22073.

255 Campos, Lazaro, "Statement made at the LIBE-ECON hearing at the European Parliament on Thursday 3 September 2009," September 3, 2009.

256 Scott Shane and John F. Burns, "U.S. Subpoenas Twitter over WikiLeaks Supporters," New York Times, January 8, 2011, http://www.nytimes.com/2011/01/09/world/09wiki.html?pagewanted=all.

257 Finextra, "WikiLeaks: Merkel furious at MEPs over Swift data sharing deal rejection," December 6, 2010, http://www.finextra.com/news/fullstory.aspx?newsitemid=22073.

258 Anthony DiPaola, Hugo Miller, and Wael Mahdi, "RIM, Saudi Carriers in Talks to Avoid Blackberry Ban," Business Week, August 6 2010, http://www.businessweek.com/news/2010-08-06/rim-saudi-carriers-in-talks-to-avoid-blackberry-ban.html.

259 SWIFT, "SWIFT History," accessed August 2011, http://www.swift.com/about_swift/company_information/swift_history.page?lang=en.

260 SWIFT, "SWIFT Network Partners," accessed August 2011, http://www.swift.com/partners/network_partners.

261 SWIFT, "SWIFT Annual Review 2010," June 2011, accessed August 2011. http://www.swift.com/about_swift/publications/annual_reports/annual_review_2010/index.page.

262 "Frank Abagnale," Wikipedia, Last modified September 5, 2011, http://en.wikipedia.org/wiki/Frank_Abignale.

263 Ibid

264 NACHA, "NACHA Timeline," http://www.nacha.org/c/_content.cfm/AID/484.

265 Capgemini, ABN AMRO, and EFMA. "World Payments Report 2005." 2005.

266 Ibid

267 Ibid

268 European Central Bank, "SEPA Indicators—European Central Bank," accessed August 2011, http://www.ecb.europa.eu/paym/sepa/about/indicators/html/index.en.html.

269 Ibid

270 ISO20022.org; "About ISO 20022," accessed August 2011, http://www.iso20022.org/.

271 "2010 Flash Crash," Wikipedia, Last modified September 15, 2011, http://en.wikipedia.org/wiki/Flash_crash.

272 Washington's Blog, "What is High Frequency Trading and How Does it Distort the Markets?" blog entry, July 16, 2009, http://www.washingtonsblog.com/2009/07/what-is-high-frequency-trading-and-how.html.

273 Reuters, "Single U.S. trade helped spark May's flash crash," October 1, 2010, http://www.reuters.com/article/2010/10/01/financial-regulation-flashcrash-idUKN0114164220101001.

274 CFTC and SEC, "Findings Regarding the Market Events of May 6, 2010—Report of the staffs of the CFTC and SEC to the Joint Advisory Committee on emerging regulatory issues," September 30, 2010, http://www.sec.gov/news/studies/2010/marketevents-report.pdf.

275 Dr. Richard Olsen, "High frequency finance the hedge fund category of the future," August 2011, http://www.olsen.ch/fileadmin/Publications/Archive//hedgefuture.pdf.

276 "High Frequency Trading," Last modified September 12, 2011, http://en.wikipedia.org/wiki/High_frequency_trading.

277 Fix Protocol Limited, "What is FIX?"accessed August 2011, http://www.fixprotocol.org/what-is-fix.shtml.

278 Ibid

279 Ibid

280 Thomson Reuters, "Tradeweb Routing Network," accessed August 2011, http://www.thomsonreuters.com/products_services/financial/financial_products/products_az/tradeweb_routing_network.

281 Wyatt Wells, "Certificates and Computers—The Remaking of Wall Street, 1967 to 1971," Business History Review 74(2), http://www.jstor.org/pss/3116692.

282 Robert J.Cole, "Record stock volume a factor in brokerage crisis." New York Times, March 14, 1970.

283 Ibid

284 Ibid

285 Ibid

286 James McDonald, "Computers and Stocks." Computer Usage, Fall Issue 1968.

287 DTCC.com; "About DTCC," accessed August 2011, http://www.dtcc.com/about/business/.

288 Securities Industry Association. "T+1 Business case: Final Report." July 2000.

289 Ibid

290 "Remarks of Fed Chairman Alan Greenspan." Financial Markets Conference, Atlanta, GA. October 16, 2000.

291 Vinay Kumar and Gabriel David, "Global Straight Through Processing—The Evolution Continues." EDS, December 2000.

292 Dushyant Shahrawat, "Global Straight Through Processing: Emerging Trends and Update," Tower Group, February 2001.

293 Vinay Kumar and Gabriel David, "Global Straight Through Processing—The Evolution Continues." EDS, December 2000.

294 Dushyant Shahrawat, "Global Straight Through Processing: Emerging Trends and Update." Tower Group, February 2001.

295 Ibid

296 Ibid

297 Anthony Guerra, "GSTPA to Dissolve," Information Week, November 23, 2002, http://www.informationweek.com/news/6504027.

298 Ibid

299 Anthony Guerra, "Who Will Bid On the GSTPA's TFM?" Bank Systems & Technology, August 26, 2003. http://www.banktech.com/articles/14702321.

300 Changi Airport Group, "Enhancing the Changi Experience," news release, September 28, 2010.

301 "Milestones—Changi Airport Singapore," accessed August 2011, http://www.changiairport.com/our-business/about-changi-airport/milestones.

302 "Economy of Singapore," Wikipedia, September 21, 2011, http://en.wikipedia.org/wiki/Economy_of_Singapore.

303 John King and Professor Benn Konysnski, "Singapore TradeNet: A Tale of One City." Harvard Business School, September 30, 1995.

304 US Customs and Border Protection. Form 6059B. 2011

305 "2002 United States steel tariff," Wikipedia, Last modified June 30, 2011, http://en.wikipedia.org/wiki/2002_United_States_steel_tariff.

306 John King, and Professor Benn Konysnski, "Singapore TradeNet: A Tale of One City." Harvard Business School, September 30, 1995.

307 Ibid

308 Ibid

309 Ibid

310 Ibid

311 Ibid

312 Singapore Customs, "Latest release: TradeNet Version 4.0," accessed August 2011, http://www.customs.gov.sg/insync/issue02/features/features.html.

313 TradeXchange, "TradeXchange," accessed August 2011, https://www.tradexchange.gov.sg/tradexchange/default.portal.

314 Crimson Logic, "Corporate Overview," accessed August 2011, http://www.crimsonlogic.com/corpPortalWeb/Corporate.jsp?ln=en.

315 Doing Business.org; "Ranking of economies—Doing Business," accessed August 2011, http://www.doingbusiness.org/rankings.

316 DoingBusiness.org; "Trading Across Borders—Doing Business," accessed August 2011, http://www.doingbusiness.org/data/exploretopics/trading-across-borders.

317 Ibid

318 "Port of Hong Kong," Wikipedia, April 22, 2011, http://en.wikipedia.org/wiki/Port_of_Hong_Kong.

319 Ng, Pauline, Kwok-Keung Law, Dr. Jan Damsgaard, and Dr. Ali Farhoomand. "Tradelink Electronic Commerce Limited: Implementation Strategy." Centre for Asian Business Cases, School of Business: The University of Hong Kong, June 1, 1998.

320 Ibid

321 Tradelink.com; "About Tradelink," accessed August 2011, http://www.tradelink.com.hk/eng/company_profile.html.

322 "Northwest Airlines Flight 253," Wikipedia, last modified on September 6, 2011, http://en.wikipedia.org/wiki/Northwest_Airlines_Flight_253.

323 Ibid

324 TSA.gov; "US Transportation Security Administration—Secure Flight Program," accessed August 2011, http://www.tsa.gov/what_we_do/layers/secureflight/.

325 Ibid

326 Ibid

327 UN/EDIFACT—PAXLST, last updated January 27, 2000, accessed August 2011, http://live.unece.org/trade/untdid/d00a/trmd/paxlst_c.htm.

328 "Cargo planes bomb plot," Wikipedia, last modified August 7, 2011, http://en.wikipedia.org/wiki/Cargo_planes_bomb_plot.

329 Ibid

330 Ibid

331 TSA.gov; "US Transportation Security Administration—Certified Cargo Screening Program," accessed August 2011, http://www.tsa.gov/what_we_do/layers/aircargo/certified_screening.shtm.

332 Ibid

333 John F Fritelli, " Port and Maritime Security: Background and Issues for Congress," Congressional Research Service, May 27, 2005, http://www.fas.org/sgp/crs/homesec/RL31733.pdf.

334 Informed Trade, "The 5 Percent Myth vs. US Customs and Border Protection Reality," accessed August 2011, http://www.itintl.com/the-5-percent-myth-vs-us-customs-and-border-protection-reality.html.

335 Alex Roth, "Port Labor Talks Spur Optimism." Wall Street Journal, June 20, 2008.

336 PMANET.org; "Fast Facts—Pacific Maritime Association," accessed August 2011, http://www.pmanet.org/?cmd=main.category&id_category=126.

337 CBP.gov; "An Overall Picture of Port Security—US Customs and Border Patrol," July 12, 2006, accessed August 2011, http://www.cbp.gov/xp/cgov/newsroom/fact_sheets/port_security/securing_us_ports.xml.

338 CBP.gov; "Fact Sheet: C-TPAT, US Customs and Border Patrol," March 27, 2008, accessed August 2011, http://www.cbp.gov/xp/cgov/newsroom/fact_sheets/port_security/ctpat_sheet.xml.

339 CBP.gov; "Container Security Initiative—US Customs and Border Patrol," March 20, 2008, accessed August 2011, http://www.cbp.gov/xp/cgov/trade/cargo_security/csi/csi_in_brief.xml.

340 DHS.gov; "Secure Freight Initiative—US Department of Homeland Security," accessed August 2011, http://www.dhs.gov/files/programs/gc_1166037389664.shtm.

341 CBP.gov; "Importer Security Filing '10+2'—US Customs and Border Patrol," accessed August 2011, http://www.cbp.gov/xp/cgov/trade/cargo_security/carriers/security_filing/.

342 "Global Trade Exchange." Wikipedia, Last modified July 27, 2011, http://en.wikipedia.org/wiki/Global_Trade_Exchange.

343 Ibid

344 Phil Kemp, "Fraudster's 'pop star' lifestyle." BBC, October 4, 2008, http://news.bbc.co.uk/2/hi/uk_news/7650883.stm.

345 Dominic Kennedy, "Craig Johnson, the gang leader with a stately home, must repay £26m," The Times, November 22, 2008, http://www.timesonline.co.uk/tol/news/uk/crime/article5209131.ece.

346 Phil Kemp, "Fraudster's 'pop star' lifestyle," BBC, October 4, 2008, http://news.bbc.co.uk/2/hi/uk_news/7650883.stm.

347 Dominic Kennedy, "Craig Johnson, the gang leader with a stately home, must repay £26m," The Times, November 22, 2008, http://www.timesonline.co.uk/tol/news/uk/crime/article5209131.ece.

348 Phil Kemp, "Fraudster's 'pop star' lifestyle," BBC, October 4, 2008, http://news.bbc.co.uk/2/hi/uk_news/7650883.stm.

349 Ashley Seager and Ian Cobain, "VAT fraud costing Europe 50 billion a year," The Guardian, July 11, 2006, http://www.guardian.co.uk/business/2006/jul/11/crime.politics.

350 "MNEF Affair Mutuelle nationale des étudiants de France," Wikipedia, last modified June 5, 2011, http://en.wikipedia.org/wiki/The_MNEF_Affair.

351 Newton Oller De Melllo, Eduardo Mario Dias, Caio Fernando Fontana, and Marcelo Luiz Alves Fernandez, "Implementation of Electronic Tax Documents in Brazil as a tool to fight tax evasion," 2009, http://www.wseas.us/e-library/conferences/2009/rodos/SYSTEMS/SYSTEMS66.pdf.

352 Ibid

353 Joe Capp, Heinz-Peter Elestrodt, and William B Jones, Jr., "Reining in Brazil's informal economy." McKinsey Quarterly, January 2005.

354 Ibid

355 International Bank for Reconstruction and Development and World Bank, "Doing Business 2011—Brazil," http://www.doingbusiness.org/data/exploreeconomies/brazil/#paying-taxes.

356 Ibid

357 Joe Capp, Elestrodt Heinz-Peter, and William B Jones, Jr., "Reining in Brazil's informal economy." McKinsey Quarterly, January 2005.

358 "Uniform Invoice Lottery," Wikipedia, last modified February 27, 2011, http://en.wikipedia.org/wiki/Uniform_Invoice_lottery.

359 Ibid

360 Jianggan Li, "Taiwan Govt to make Uniform Tax Invoices Electronic," December 20, 2010, http://www.futuregov.asia/articles/2010/dec/20/taiwan-govt-make-uniform-tax-invoices-electronic/.

361 Johanna Morden, "Taiwan Government's E-Invoice Transactions Hit 50,000," March 8, 2011, http://www.futuregov.asia/articles/2011/mar/08/taiwan-govts-e-invoice-transactions-hit-50000/.

362 Innopay, "E-invoicing 2010 European Market Guide," May 2010, http://www.innopay.com/publications/e-invoicing-2010.

363 Bruno Koch, "E-Invoicing/E-Billing in Europe and abroad." Billentis, March 21, 2011.

364 Ibid

365 Ibid

366 SAP, "SAP facilitates business network transformation to help businesses compete and thrive in changing global economy," news release, November 14, 2008, http://www.crossgate.com/about-crossgate/press-item/article/sap-facilitates-business-network-transformation-to-help-businesses-compete-and-thrive-in-a-changing/.

367 Purchasing Insight, "Iron Mountain partners with Basware to deliver e-invoicing services," March 17, 2011, http://purchasinginsight.com/iron-mountain-partners-with-basware-to-deliver-e-invoicing-services/.

368 Finextra, "Mellon extends institutional BPO with SourceNet acquisition," November 16, 2004, http://www.finextra.com/news/fullstory.aspx?newsitemid=12856.

369 Schneider National, "US Bank to acquire Schneider Payment Services and with PowerTrack becomes world's largest freight payment provider," news release, June 21, 2006, http://www.schneider.com/news/News_Archive/PRD_001993.

370 Daniel Wolfe, "JPMorganChase acquires Xign," American Banker, May 18, 2007, http://www.americanbanker.com/issues/172_99/-312541-1.html.

371 BB&T, "BB&T unveils new supply chain management service," news release, March 4, 2008, http://bbt.mediaroom.com/index.php?s=43&item=676.

372 Finextra, "American Express buys Harbor Payments," December 5, 2006. http://www.finextra.com/news/fullstory.aspx?newsitemid=16236.

373 Syncada, "Visa and U.S. Bank Launch Syncada—a Global Financial Supply Chain Network," July 29, 2009, http://www.syncada.com/uploadedfiles/Content/News/SyncadaPressRelease_7_29_09_Syncada.pdf.

374 Finextra, "PayPal and OB10 team on e-invoicing," September 12, 2008, http://www.finextra.com/news/fullstory.aspx?newsitemid=18971.

375 Malcolm Brabant, "Three dead as Greece protests turn violent," BBC News, May 5 2010, http://news.bbc.co.uk/2/hi/8661385.stm.

376 Speigel Online International, May 5 2010, accessed August 2011, http://www.spiegel.de/international/europe/0,1518,693179,00.html.

377 Landon Thomas Jr. and Christine Hauser, "Agency cuts Greece's debt rating again," New York Times, June 13, 2011, http://www.nytimes.com/2011/06/14/business/14greece.html.

378 The Guardian Online, "Olympics E2.4 billion over budget," November 13, 2004, http://www.guardian.co.uk/world/2004/nov/13/athensolympics2004.sport.

379 BBC News, "Greek debt spirals after Olympics," September 12, 2004, http://news.bbc.co.uk/2/hi/business/3649268.stm.

380 PEPPOL.eu, "PEPPOL Fact Sheet," accessed August 2011, http://www.peppol.eu.

381 "General Inspectorate for Communications and Information (Case Study)," November 7, 2006, accessed August 2011, http://www.microsoft.com/casestudies/Case_Study_Detail.aspx?CaseStudyID=200135.

382 European Commission, Enterprise and Industry Directorate-General European e-Government Services (IDABC), "European eProcurement—An Overview," June 2006, http://ec.europa.eu/idabc/eprocurement.

383 Niall Bohan, "Gearing up for pan-European e-Procurement," European Commission Internal Market & Services DG, presentation at 5th International PEPPOL Conference, November 8 2010.

384 Ibid

385 Ibid

386 Ibid

387 Ibid

388 EEI Platform, "7 Major differences between the CII v2 and ISO 20022 new born standards," March 10, 2011, http://eeiplatform.com/4169/7-major-differences-between-the-ciiv2-and-iso20022-new-born-standards/.

389 Ann Zimmerman, "To Sell Goods to Wal-Mart, Get on the Net." Wall Street Journal, November 21, 2003.

390 Anthony Guerra, "GSTPA to Dissolve," Information Week, November 23, 2002, http://www.informationweek.com/news/6504027.

391 Bruno Koch, "E-Invoicing/E-Billing in Europe and abroad," Billentis, March 21, 2011.

392 Nick A LeCuyer and Shubham Singhal, "Overhauling the US health care payment system," McKinsey Quarterly, June 2007.

393 Surescripts, "2009 National Progress Report on E-Prescribing," 2009, accessed August 2011, http://www.surescripts.com/media/515306/2009_national-progress-report.pdf.

394 eHealth Initiative, "State of Health Information Exchange in 2010—Connecting the Nation to Achieve Meaningful Use," 2010, accessed August 2011, http://www.ehealthinitiative.org.

395 Fix Protocol Limited, "What is FIX?" accessed August 2011, http://www.fixprotocol.org/what-is-fix.shtml. Securities Industry Association, "T+1 Business case: Final Report," July 2000.

396 Securities Industry Association, "T+1 Business case: Final Report," July 2000.

397 Capgemini, ABN AMRO and EFMA, "World Payments Report 2005" 2005.

398 Eric Pan, Douglas Johnston, Janice Walker, Julia Adler-Milsten, David W Bates and Blackford Middleton, "The Value of Healthcare Information Exchange and Interoperability," Center for Information Technology Leadership, 2004.

399 Emdeon, "Emdeon Reports Fourth Quarter and Full Year 2010 Results," news release, March 8, 2011, http://investors.emdeon.com/phoenix.zhtml?c=230807&p=irol-newsArticle&ID=1537203&highlight=.

400 "SWIFT Annual Review 2010," last modified June 2011, accessed August 2011, http://www.swift.com/about_swift/publications/annual_reports/annual_review_2010/index.page.

401 Sterling Commerce, "Software Magazine names Sterling Commerce among Top 100 Largest Software Companies in 27th Annual Software 500," news release, September 30, 2009.

402 Ariba, "Ariba Reports Results for Third Quarter of Fiscal Year 2011," July 28, 2011, http://www.ariba.com/news/press_release.cfm?press_id=2980.

403 Quotation from Wall Street, 1987, http://www.imdb.com/title/tt0094291/quotes.

11565424R00194

Made in the USA
Charleston, SC
06 March 2012